DATA MINING WITH DECISION TREES

Theory and Applications

SERIES IN MACHINE PERCEPTION AND ARTIFICIAL INTELLIGENCE*

Editors: **H. Bunke** (Univ. Bern, Switzerland)
P. S. P. Wang (Northeastern Univ., USA)

*For the complete list of titles in this series, please write to the Publisher.

Series in Machine Perception and Artificial Intelligence – Vol. 69

DATA MINING WITH DECISION TREES

Theory and Applications

Lior Rokach
Ben-Gurion University, Israel

Oded Maimon
Tel-Aviv University, Israel

World Scientific

NEW JERSEY · LONDON · SINGAPORE · BEIJING · SHANGHAI · HONG KONG · TAIPEI · CHENNAI

Published by

World Scientific Publishing Co. Pte. Ltd.

5 Toh Tuck Link, Singapore 596224

USA office: 27 Warren Street, Suite 401-402, Hackensack, NJ 07601

UK office: 57 Shelton Street, Covent Garden, London WC2H 9HE

British Library Cataloguing-in-Publication Data
A catalogue record for this book is available from the British Library.

Series in Machine Perception and Artificial Intelligence — Vol. 69
DATA MINING WITH DECISION TREES
Theory and Applications

ISBN-13 978-981-277-171-1
ISBN-10 981-277-171-9

Printed in Singapore.

In memory of Moshe Flint
–L.R.
To my family
–O.M.

Preface

Data mining is the science, art and technology of exploring large and complex bodies of data in order to discover useful patterns. Theoreticians and practitioners are continually seeking improved techniques to make the process more efficient, cost-effective and accurate. One of the most promising and popular approaches is the use of decision trees. Decision trees are simple yet successful techniques for predicting and explaining the relationship between some measurements about an item and its target value. In addition to their use in data mining, decision trees, which originally derived from logic, management and statistics, are today highly effective tools in other areas such as text mining, information extraction, machine learning, and pattern recognition.

Decision trees offer many benefits:

- Versatility for a wide variety of data mining tasks, such as classification, regression, clustering and feature selection
- Self-explanatory and easy to follow (when compacted)
- Flexibility in handling a variety of input data: nominal, numeric and textual
- Adaptability in processing datasets that may have errors or missing values
- High predictive performance for a relatively small computational effort
- Available in many data mining packages over a variety of platforms
- Useful for large datasets (in an ensemble framework)

This is the first comprehensive book about decision trees. Devoted entirely to the field, it covers almost all aspects of this very important technique.

The book has twelve chapters, which are divided into three main parts:

- Part I (Chapters 1-3) presents the data mining and decision tree foundations (including basic rationale, theoretical formulation, and detailed evaluation).
- Part II (Chapters 4-8) introduces the basic and advanced algorithms for automatically growing decision trees (including splitting and pruning, decision forests, and incremental learning).
- Part III (Chapters 9-12) presents important extensions for improving decision tree performance and for accommodating it to certain circumstances. This part also discusses advanced topics such as feature selection, fuzzy decision trees, hybrid framework and methods, and sequence classification (also for text mining).

We have tried to make as complete a presentation of decision trees in data mining as possible. However new applications are always being introduced. For example, we are now researching the important issue of data mining privacy, where we use a hybrid method of genetic process with decision trees to generate the optimal privacy-protecting method. Using the fundamental techniques presented in this book, we are also extensively involved in researching language-independent text mining (including ontology generation and automatic taxonomy).

Although we discuss in this book the broad range of decision trees and their importance, we are certainly aware of related methods, some with overlapping capabilities. For this reason, we recently published a complementary book "Soft Computing for Knowledge Discovery and Data Mining", which addresses other approaches and methods in data mining, such as artificial neural networks, fuzzy logic, evolutionary algorithms, agent technology, swarm intelligence and diffusion methods.

An important principle that guided us while writing this book was the extensive use of illustrative examples. Accordingly, in addition to decision tree theory and algorithms, we provide the reader with many applications from the real-world as well as examples that we have formulated for explaining the theory and algorithms. The applications cover a variety of fields, such as marketing, manufacturing, and bio-medicine. The data referred to in this book, as well as most of the Java implementations of the pseudo-algorithms and programs that we present and discuss, may be obtained via the Web.

We believe that this book will serve as a vital source of decision tree techniques for researchers in information systems, engineering, computer science, statistics and management. In addition, this book is highly useful to researchers in the social sciences, psychology, medicine, genetics, business intelligence, and other fields characterized by complex data-processing problems of underlying models.

Since the material in this book formed the basis of undergraduate and graduates courses at Tel-Aviv University and Ben-Gurion University, it can also serve as a reference source for graduate/advanced undergraduate level courses in knowledge discovery, data mining and machine learning. Practitioners among the readers may be particularly interested in the descriptions of real-world data mining projects performed with decision trees methods.

We would like to acknowledge the contribution to our research and to the book to many students, but in particular to Dr. Barak Chizi, Dr. Shahar Cohen, Roni Romano and Reuven Arbel. Many thanks are owed to Arthur Kemelman. He has been a most helpful assistant in proofreading and improving the manuscript.

The authors would like to thank Mr. Ian Seldrup, Senior Editor, and staff members of World Scientific Publishing for their kind cooperation in connection with writing this book. Thanks also to Prof. H. Bunke and Prof P.S.P. Wang for including our book in their fascinating series in machine perception and artificial intelligence.

Last, but not least, we owe our special gratitude to our partners, families, and friends for their patience, time, support, and encouragement.

Beer-Sheva, Israel
Tel-Aviv, Israel

Lior Rokach
Oded Maimon

October 2007

Contents

Chapter 1

Introduction to Decision Trees

1.1 Data Mining and Knowledge Discovery

Data mining, the science and technology of exploring data in order to discover previously unknown patterns, is a part of the overall process of knowledge discovery in databases (KDD). In today's computer-driven world, these databases contain massive quantities of information. The accessibility and abundance of this information makes data mining a matter of considerable importance and necessity.

Most data mining techniques are based on inductive learning (see [Mitchell (1997)]), where a model is constructed explicitly or implicitly by generalizing from a sufficient number of training examples. The underlying assumption of the inductive approach is that the trained model is applicable to future, unseen examples. Strictly speaking, any form of inference in which the conclusions are not deductively implied by the premises can be thought of as induction.

Traditionally, data collection was regarded as one of the most important stages in data analysis. An analyst (e.g., a statistician) would use the available domain knowledge to select the variables that were to be collected. The number of variables selected was usually small and the collection of their values could be done manually (e.g., utilizing hand-written records or oral interviews). In the case of computer-aided analysis, the analyst had to enter the collected data into a statistical computer package or an electronic spreadsheet. Due to the high cost of data collection, people learned to make decisions based on limited information.

Since the dawn of the Information Age, accumulating data has become easier and storing it inexpensive. It has been estimated that the amount of stored information doubles every twenty months [Frawley *et al.* (1991)].

Unfortunately, as the amount of machine-readable information increases, the ability to understand and make use of it does not keep pace with its growth.

Data mining emerged as a means of coping with this exponential growth of information and data. The term describes the process of sifting through large databases in search of interesting patterns and relationships. In practise, data mining provides tools by which large quantities of data can be automatically analyzed. While some researchers consider the term "data mining" as misleading and prefer the term "knowledge mining" [Klosgen and Zytkow (2002)], the former term seems to be the most commonly used, with 59 million entries on the Internet as opposed to 52 million for knowledge mining.

Data mining can be considered as a central step in the overall KDD process. Indeed, due to the centrality of data mining in the KDD process, there are some researchers and practitioners that regard "data mining" and the complete KDD processas as synonymous.

There are various definintions of KDD. For instance [Fayyad *et al.* (1996)] define it as "the nontrivial process of identifying valid, novel, potentially useful, and ultimately understandable patterns in data". [Friedman (1997a)] considers the KDD process as an automatic exploratory data analysis of large databases. [Hand (1998)] views it as a secondary data analysis of large databases. The term "secondary" emphasizes the fact that the primary purpose of the database was not data analysis.

A key element characterizing the KDD process is the way it is divided into phases with leading researchers such as [Brachman and Anand (1994)], [Fayyad *et al.* (1996)], [Maimon and Last (2000)] and [Reinartz (2002)] proposing different methods. Each method has its advantages and disadvantages. In this book, we adopt a hybridization of these proposals and break the KDD process into eight phases. Note that the process is iterative and moving back to previous phases may be required.

(1) Developing an understanding of the application domain, the relevant prior knowledge and the goals of the end-user.
(2) Selecting a dataset on which discovery is to be performed.
(3) Data Preprocessing: This stage includes operations for dimension reduction (such as feature selection and sampling); data cleansing (such as handling missing values, removal of noise or outliers); and data transformation (such as discretization of numerical attributes and attribute extraction).

(4) Choosing the appropriate data mining task such as classification, regression, clustering and summarization.
(5) Choosing the data mining algorithm. This stage includes selecting the specific method to be used for searching patterns.
(6) Employing the data mining algorithm.
(7) Evaluating and interpreting the mined patterns.
(8) The last stage, deployment, may involve using the knowledge directly; incorporating the knowledge into another system for further action; or simply documenting the discovered knowledge.

1.2 Taxonomy of Data Mining Methods

It is useful to distinguish between two main types of data mining: verification-oriented (the system verifies the user's hypothesis) and discovery-oriented (the system finds new rules and patterns autonomously) [Fayyad *et al.* (1996)]. Figure 1.1 illustrates this taxonomy. Each type has its own methodology.

Discovery methods, which automatically identify patterns in the data, involve both prediction and description methods. Description methods focus on understanding the way the underlying data operates while prediction-oriented methods aim to build a behavioral model for obtaining new and unseen samples and for predicting values of one or more variables related to the sample. Some prediction-oriented methods, however, can also help provide an understanding of the data.

Most of the discovery-oriented techniques are based on inductive learning [Mitchell (1997)], where a model is constructed explicitly or implicitly by generalizing from a sufficient number of training examples . The underlying assumption of the inductive approach is that the trained model is applicable to future unseen examples. Strictly speaking, any form of inference in which the conclusions are not deductively implied by the premises can be thought of as induction.

Verification methods, on the other hand, evaluate a hypothesis proposed by an external source (like an expert etc.). These methods include the most common methods of traditional statistics, like the goodness-of-fit test, the t-test of means, and analysis of variance. These methods are less associated with data mining than their discovery-oriented counterparts because most data mining problems are concerned with selecting a hypothesis (out of a set of hypotheses) rather than testing a known one. The focus of tra-

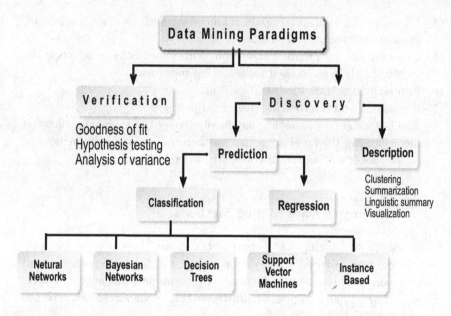

Fig. 1.1   Taxonomy of data mining Methods.

ditional statistical methods is usually on model estimation as opposed to one of the main objectives of data mining: model identification [Elder and Pregibon (1996)].

1.3   Supervised Methods

1.3.1   Overview

In the machine learning community, prediction methods are commonly referred to as supervised learning. Supervised learning stands opposed to unsupervised learning which refers to modeling the distribution of instances in a typical, high-dimensional input space.

According to [Kohavi and Provost (1998)], the term "unsupervised learning" refers to "learning techniques that group instances without a prespecified dependent attribute". Thus the term "unsupervised learning" covers only a portion of the description methods presented in Figure 1.1. For instance the term covers clustering methods but not visualization methods.

Supervised methods are methods that attempt to discover the relationship between input attributes (sometimes called independent variables) and a target attribute (sometimes referred to as a dependent variable). The relationship that is discovered is represented in a structure referred to as a *Model*. Usually models describe and explain phenomena, which are hidden in the dataset, and which can be used for predicting the value of the target attribute when the values of the input attributes are known. The supervised methods can be implemented in a variety of domains such as marketing, finance and manufacturing.

It is useful to distinguish between two main supervised models: *Classification Models (Classifiers)* and *Regression Models.*Regression models map the input space into a real-valued domain. For instance, a regressor can predict the demand for a certain product given its characteristics. On the other hand, classifiers map the input space into predefined classes. For instance, classifiers can be used to classify mortgage consumers as good (full mortgage pay back the on time) and bad (delayed pay back). Among the many alternatives for representing classifiers, there are, for example, support vector machines, decision trees, probabilistic summaries, algebraic function, etc.

This book deals mainly in classification problems. Along with regression and probability estimation, classification is one of the most studied approaches, possibly one with the greatest practical relevance. The potential benefits of progress in classification are immense since the technique has great impact on other areas, both within data mining and in its applications.

1.4 Classification Trees

In data mining, a decision tree is a predictive model which can be used to represent both classifiers and regression models. In operations research, on the other hand, decision trees refer to a hierarchical model of decisions and their consequences. The decision maker employs decision trees to identify the strategy most likely to reach her goal.

When a decision tree is used for classification tasks, it is more appropriately referred to as a classification tree. When it is used for regression tasks, it is called regression tree.

In this book we concentrate mainly on classification trees. Classification trees are used to classify an object or an instance (such as insurant) to a predefined set of classes (such as risky/non-risky) based on their attributes values (such as age or gender). Classification trees are frequently used in applied fields such as finance, marketing, engineering and medicine. The classification tree is useful as an exploratory technique. However it does not attempt to replace existing traditional statistical methods and there are many other techniques that can be used classify or predict the membership of instances to a predefined set of classes, such as artificial neural networks or support vector machines.

Figure 1.2 presents a typical decision tree classifier. This decision tree is used to facilitate the underwriting process of mortgage applications of a certain bank. As part of this process the applicant fills in an application form that include the following data: number of dependents (DEPEND), loan-to-value ratio (LTV), marital status (MARST), payment-to-income ratio (PAYINC), interest rate (RATE), years at current address (YRSADD), and years at current job (YRSJOB).

Based on the above information, the underwriter will decide if the application should be approved for a mortgage. More specifically, this decision tree classifies mortgage applications into one of the following two classes:

- Approved (denoted as "A") The application should be approved.
- Denied (denoted as "D") The application should be denied.
- Manual underwriting (denoted as "M") An underwriter should manually examine the application and decide if it should be approved (in some cases after requesting additional information from the applicant). The decision tree is based on the fields that appear in the mortgage applications forms.

The above example illustrates how a decision tree can be used to represent a classification model. In fact it can be seen as an expert system, which partially automates the underwriting process and which was built manually by a knowledge engineer after interrogating an experienced underwriter in the company. This sort of expert interrogation is called knowledge elicitation namely obtaining knowledge from a human expert (or human experts) for use by an intelligent system. Knowledge elicitation is usually difficult because it is not easy to find an available expert who is able, has the time and is willing to provide the knowledge engineer with the information he needs to create a reliable expert system. In fact, the difficulty inherent in the process is one of the main reasons why companies avoid intelligent systems. This phenomenon is known as the knowledge elicitation bottleneck.

A decision tree can be also used to analyze the payment ethics of customers who received a mortgage. In this case there are two classes:

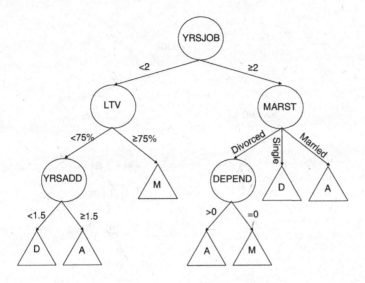

Fig. 1.2   Underwriting Decision Tree.

- Paid (denoted as "P") - the recipient has fully paid off his or her mortgage.
- Not Paid (denoted as "N") - the recipient has not fully paid off his or her mortgage.

This new decision tree can be used to improve the underwriting decision model presented in Figure 9.1. It shows that there are relatively many customers pass the underwriting process but that they have not yet fully paid back the loan. Note that as opposed to the decision tree presented in Figure 9.1, this decision tree is constructed according to data that was accumulated in the database. Thus, there is no need to manually elicit knowledge. In fact the tree can be grown automatically. Such a kind of knowledge acquisition is referred to as knowledge discovery from databases.

The use of a decision tree is a very popular technique in data mining. In the opinion of many researchers, decision trees are popular due to their simplicity and transparency. Decision trees are self-explanatory; there is no need to be a data mining expert in order to follow a certain decision tree. Classification trees are usually represented graphically as hierarchical structures, making them easier to interpret than other techniques. If the classification tree becomes complicated (i.e. has many nodes) then its straightforward, graphical representation become useless. For complex

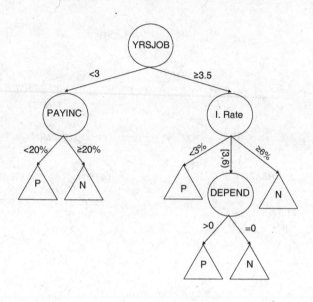

Fig. 1.3   Actual behavior of customer.

trees, other graphical procedures should be developed to simplify interpretation.

1.5   Characteristics of Classification Trees

A decision tree is a classifier expressed as a recursive partition of the instance space. The decision tree consists of nodes that form a rooted tree, meaning it is a directed tree with a node called a "root" that has no incoming edges. All other nodes have exactly one incoming edge. A node with outgoing edges is referred to as an "internal" or "test" node. All other nodes are called "leaves" (also known as "terminal" or "decision" nodes). In the decision tree, each internal node splits the instance space into two or more sub-spaces according to a certain discrete function of the input attribute values. In the simplest and most frequent case, each test considers a single attribute, such that the instance space is partitioned according to the attributes value. In the case of numeric attributes, the condition refers to a range.

Each leaf is assigned to one class representing the most appropriate target value. Alternatively, the leaf may hold a probability vector (affinity vector) indicating the probability of the target attribute having a certain value. Figure 1.4 describes another example of a decision tree that reasons whether or not a potential customer will respond to a direct mailing. Internal nodes are represented as circles, whereas leaves are denoted as triangles. Two or more branches may grow from each internal node (i.e. not a leaf). Each node corresponds with a certain characteristic and the branches correspond with a range of values. These ranges of values must give a partition of the set of values of the given characteristic.

Instances are classified by navigating them from the root of the tree down to a leaf, according to the outcome of the tests along the path. Specifically, we start with a root of a tree; we consider the characteristic that corresponds to a root; and we define to which branch the observed value of the given characteristic corresponds. Then we consider the node in which the given branch appears. We repeat the same operations for this node etc., until we reach a leaf.

Note that this decision tree incorporates both nominal and numeric attributes. Given this classifier, the analyst can predict the response of a potential customer (by sorting it down the tree), and understand the behavioral characteristics of the entire potential customer population regarding direct mailing. Each node is labeled with the attribute it tests, and its branches are labeled with its corresponding values.

In case of numeric attributes, decision trees can be geometrically interpreted as a collection of hyperplanes, each orthogonal to one of the axes.

1.5.1 *Tree Size*

Naturally, decision makers prefer a decision tree that is not complex since it is apt to be more comprehensible. Furthermore, according to [Breiman *et al.* (1984)], tree complexity has a crucial effect on its accuracy. Usually the tree complexity is measured by one of the following metrics: the total number of nodes, total number of leaves, tree depth and number of attributes used. Tree complexity is explicitly controlled by the stopping criteria and the pruning method that are employed.

1.5.2 *The hierarchical nature of decision trees*

Another characterstic of decision trees is their hierarchical nature. Imagine that you want to develop a medical system for diagnosing patients according

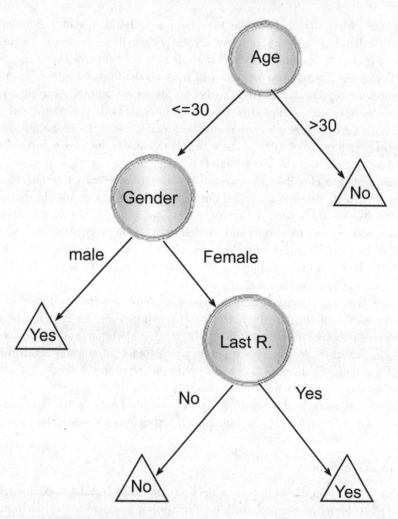

Fig. 1.4   Decision Tree Presenting Response to Direct Mailing.

to the results of several medical tests. Based on the result of one test, the physician can perform or order additional laboratory tests. Specifically, Figure 1.5 illustrates the diagnosis process, using decision trees, of patients that suffer from a certain respiratory problem. The decision tree employs the following attributes: CT finding (CTF); X-ray finding (XRF); chest pain type (CPT); and blood test finding (BTF). The physician will order an X-ray, if chest pain type is "1". However, if chest pain type is "2", then the phsician will not oder a X-ray but will order a blood test. Thus medical tests are perfomed just when needed and the total cost of medical tests is reduced.

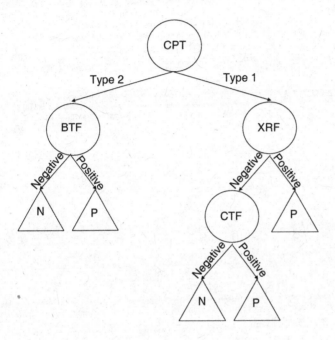

Fig. 1.5   Decision Tree For Medical Applications.

1.6   Relation to Rule Induction

Decision tree induction is closely related to rule induction. Each path from the root of a decision tree to one of its leaves can be transformed into a rule simply by conjoining the tests along the path to form the antecedent part, and taking the leaf's class prediction as the class value. For example, one of the paths in Figure 1.4 can be transformed into the rule: "If customer age is less than or equal to 30, and the gender of the customer is male — then the customer will respond to the mail". The resulting rule set can then be simplified to improve its comprehensibility to a human user, and possibly its accuracy [Quinlan (1987)].

Chapter 2

Growing Decision Trees

2.0.1 *Training Set*

In a typical supervised learning scenario, a training set is given and the goal is to form a description that can be used to predict previously unseen examples.

The training set can be described in a variety of ways. Most frequently, it is described as a bag instance of a certain bag schema. A bag instance is a collection of tuples (also known as records, rows or instances) that may contain duplicates. Each tuple is described by a vector of attribute values. The bag schema provides the description of the attributes and their domains. In this book, a bag schema is denoted as $B(A \cup y)$ where A denotes the set of input attributes containing n attributes: $A = \{a_1, \ldots, a_i, \ldots, a_n\}$ and y represents the class variable or the target attribute.

Attributes (sometimes called field, variable or feature) are typically one of two types: nominal (values are members of an unordered set), or numeric (values are real numbers). When the attribute a_i, it is useful to denote its domain values by $dom(a_i) = \{v_{i,1}, v_{i,2}, \ldots, v_{i,|dom(a_i)|}\}$, where $|dom(a_i)|$ stands for its finite cardinality. In a similar way, $dom(y) = \{c_1, \ldots, c_{|dom(y)|}\}$ represents the domain of the target attribute. Numeric attributes have infinite cardinalities.

The instance space (the set of all possible examples) is defined as a Cartesian product of all the input attributes domains: $X = dom(a_1) \times dom(a_2) \times \ldots \times dom(a_n)$. The universal instance space (or the *labeled instance space*) U is defined as a Cartesian product of all input attribute domains and the target attribute domain, i.e.: $U = X \times dom(y)$.

The training set is a bag instance consisting of a set of m tuples. Formally the training set is denoted as $S(B) = (\langle x_1, y_1 \rangle, \ldots, \langle x_m, y_m \rangle)$ where $x_q \in X$ and $y_q \in dom(y)$.

Usually, it is assumed that the training set tuples are generated randomly and independently according to some fixed and unknown joint probability distribution D over U. Note that this is a generalization of the deterministic case when a supervisor classifies a tuple using a function $y = f(x)$.

This book uses the common notation of bag algebra to present projection (π) and selection (σ) of tuples ([Grumbach and Milo (1996)]. For example given the dataset S presented in Table 2.1, the expression $\pi_{a_2,a_3}\sigma_{a_1="Yes" \ AND\ a_4>6}S$ corresponds with the dataset presented in Table 2.2.

Table 2.1   Illustration of a dataset S with five attributes.

a_1	a_2	a_3	a_4	y
Yes	17	4	7	0
No	81	1	9	1
Yes	17	4	9	0
No	671	5	2	0
Yes	1	123	2	0
Yes	1	5	22	1
No	6	62	1	1
No	6	58	54	0
No	16	6	3	0

Table 2.2   The result of the expression $\pi_{a_2,a_3}\sigma_{a_1="Yes"AND_{a_4>6}}S$ based on Table 2.1.

a_2	a_3
17	4
17	4
1	5

2.0.2   *Definition of the Classification Problem*

The machine learning community was among the first to introduce the problem of *concept learning*. Concepts are mental categories for objects, events, or ideas that have a common set of features. According to [Mitchell (1997)]: "each concept can be viewed as describing some subset of objects or events defined over a larger set" (e.g., the subset of a vehicle that constitues trucks). To learn a concept is to infer its general definition from a set of examples. This definition may be either explicitly formulated or left implicit, but either way it assigns each possible example to the concept or not. Thus, a concept can be regarded as a function from the instance space to the Boolean set, namely: $c : X \to \{-1, 1\}$. Alternatively one can refer a concept c as a subset of X, namely: $\{x \in X : c(x) = 1\}$. A *concept class* C is a set of concepts.

To learn a concept is to infer its general definition from a set of examples. This definition may be either explicitly formulated or left implicit, but either way it assigns each possible example to the concept or not. Thus, a concept can be formally regarded as a function from the set of all possible examples to the Boolean set {True, False}.

Other communities, such as the KDD community prefer to deal with a straightforward extension of *concept learning*, known as the *classification problem*. In this case we search for a function that maps the set of all possible examples into a predefined set of class labels which are not limited to the Boolean set. Most frequently the goal of the classifiers inducers is formally defined as:

Given a training set S with input attributes set $A = \{a_1, a_2, \ldots, a_n\}$ and a nominal target attribute y from an unknown fixed distribution D over the labeled instance space, the goal is to induce an optimal classifier with minimum generalization error.

The generalization error is defined as the misclassification rate over the distribution D. In case of the nominal attributes it can be expressed as:

$$\varepsilon(DT(S), D) = \sum_{\langle x, y \rangle \in U} D(x, y) \cdot L(y, DT(S)(x)) \qquad (2.1)$$

where $L(y, DT(S)(x)$ is the zero one loss function defined as:

$$L(y, DT(S)(x)) = \begin{cases} 0 \ if \ y = DT(S)(x) \\ 1 \ if \ y \neq DT(S)(x) \end{cases} \qquad (2.2)$$

In case of numeric attributes the sum operator is replaced with the integration operator.

Consider the training set in Table 2.3 containing data about ten customers. Each customer is characterized by three attributes: Age, Gender and Last Reaction (an indication whether the customer has positively responded to the last previous direct mailing campaign). The last attribute ("Buy") describes whether that customer was willing to purchase a product in the current campaign. The goal is to induce a classifier that most accurately classifies a potential customer to "Buyers" and "Non-Buyers" in the current campaign, given the attributes: Age, Gender, Last Reaction.

Table 2.3　An Illustration of Direct Mailing Dataset.

Age	Gender	Last Reaction	Buy
35	Male	Yes	No
26	Female	No	No
22	Male	Yes	Yes
63	Male	No	Yes
47	Female	No	No
54	Male	No	No
27	Female	Yes	Yes
38	Female	No	Yes
42	Female	Yes	Yes
19	Male	No	No

2.0.3　*Induction Algorithms*

An *induction algorithm*, or more concisely an *inducer* (also known as learner), is an entity that obtains a training set and forms a model that generalizes the relationship between the input attributes and the target attribute. For example, an inducer may take as an input specific training tuples with the corresponding class label, and produce a *classifier*.

The notation DT represents a decision tree inducer and $DT(S)$ represents a classification tree which was induced by performing DT on a training set S. Using $DT(S)$ it is possible to predict the target value of a tuple x_q. This prediction is denoted as $DT(S)(x_q)$.

Given the long history and recent growth of the machine learning field, it is not surprising that several mature approaches to induction are now available to the practitioner.

2.0.4　*Probability Estimation in Decision Trees*

The classifier generated by the inducer can be used to classify an unseen tuple either by explicitly assigning it to a certain class (crisp classifier) or by providing a vector of probabilities representing the conditional probability of the given instance to belong to each class (probabilistic classifier). Inducers that can construct probabilistic classifiers are known as probabilistic inducers. In decision trees, it is possible to estimate the conditional probability $\hat{P}_{DT(S)}(y = c_j \,|a_i = x_{q,i} \;; i = 1, \ldots, n)$ of an observation x_q. Note the addition of the "hat" — ^ — to the conditional probability estimation is used for distinguishing it from the actual conditional probability.

In classification trees, the probability is estimated for each leaf separately by calculating the frequency of the class among the training instances that belong to the leaf.

Using the frequency vector as is, will typically over-estimate the probability. This can be problematic especially when a given class never occurs in a certain leaf. In such cases we are left with a zero probability. There are two known corrections for the simple probability estimation which avoid this phenomenon. The following sections describe these corrections.

2.0.4.1 *Laplace Correction*

According to Laplace's law of succession [Niblett (1987)], the probability of the event $y = c_i$ where y is a random variable and c_i is a possible outcome of y which has been observed m_i times out of m observations is:

$$\frac{m_i + k p_a}{m + k} \tag{2.3}$$

where p_a is an *a-priori* probability estimation of the event and k is the equivalent sample size that determines the weight of the *a-priori* estimation relative to the observed data. According to [Mitchell (1997)] k is called "equivalent sample size" because it represents an augmentation of the m actual observations by additional k virtual samples distributed according to p_a. The above ratio can be rewritten as the weighted average of the *a-priori* probability and the posteriori probability (denoted as p_p):

$$
\begin{aligned}
\frac{m_i + k \cdot p_a}{m + k} \\
= \frac{m_i}{m} \cdot \frac{m}{m+k} + p_a \cdot \frac{k}{m+k} \\
= p_p \cdot \frac{m}{m+k} + p_a \cdot \frac{k}{m+k} = \\
= p_p \cdot w_1 + p_a \cdot w_2
\end{aligned}
\tag{2.4}
$$

In the case discussed here the following correction is used:

$$\hat{P}_{Laplace}(a_i = x_{q,i} \mid y = c_j) = \frac{\left| \sigma_{y=c_j \ AND \ a_i = x_{q,i}} S \right| + k \cdot p}{\left| \sigma_{y=c_j} S \right| + k} \tag{2.5}$$

In order to use the above correction, the values of p and k should be selected. It is possible to use $p = 1/|dom(y)|$ and $k = |dom(y)|$. [Ali and Pazzani (1996)] suggest using $k = 2$ and $p = 1/2$ in any case even if

$|dom(y)| > 2$ in order to emphasize the fact that the estimated event is always compared to the opposite event. [Kohavi *et al.* (1997)] suggest using $k = |dom(y)| / |S|$ and $p = 1/ |dom(y)|$.

2.0.4.2 *No Match*

According to [Clark and Niblett (1989)] only zero probabilities are corrected and replaced by the following value: $p_a/|S|$. [Kohavi *et al.* (1997)] suggest using $p_a = 0.5$. They also empirically compared the Laplace correction and the no-match correction and indicate that there is no significant difference between them. However, both of them are significantly better than not performing any correction at all.

2.1 Algorithmic Framework for Decision Trees

Decision tree inducers are algorithms that automatically construct a decision tree from a given dataset. Typically the goal is to find the optimal decision tree by minimizing the generalization error. However, other target functions can be also defined, for instance, minimizing the number of nodes or minimizing the average depth of the tree.

Induction of an optimal decision tree from a given data is considered to be a difficult task. [Hancock *et al.* (1996)] have shown that finding a minimal decision tree consistent with the training set is NP-hard while [Hyafil and Rivest (1976)] have demonstrated that constructing a minimal binary tree with respect to the expected number of tests required for classifying an unseen instance is NP-complete. Even finding the minimal equivalent decision tree for a given decision tree [Zantema and Bodlaender (2000)] or building the optimal decision tree from decision tables is known to be NP-hard [Naumov (1991)].

These results indicate that using optimal decision tree algorithms is feasible only in small problems. Consequently, heuristics methods are required for solving the problem. Roughly speaking, these methods can be divided into two groups: top-down and bottom-up with clear preference in the literature to the first group.

There are various top-down decision trees inducers such as ID3 [Quinlan (1986)], C4.5 [Quinlan (1993)], CART [Breiman *et al.* (1984)]. Some inducers consist of two conceptual phases: Growing and Pruning (C4.5 and CART). Other inducers perform only the growing phase.

Figure 2.1 presents a typical pseudo code for a top-down inducing algo-

rithm of a decision tree using growing and pruning. Note that these algorithms are greedy by nature and construct the decision tree in a top-down,
recursive manner (also known as divide and conquer). In each iteration, the
algorithm considers the partition of the training set using the outcome of
discrete input attributes. The selection of the most appropriate attribute
is made according to some splitting measures. After the selection of an
appropriate split, each node further subdivides the training set into smaller
subsets, until a stopping criterion is satisfied.

2.2 Stopping Criteria

The growing phase continues until a stopping criterion is triggered. The
following conditions are common stopping rules:

(1) All instances in the training set belong to a single value of y.
(2) The maximum tree depth has been reached.
(3) The number of cases in the terminal node is less than the minimum
    number of cases for parent nodes.
(4) If the node were split, the number of cases in one or more child nodes
    would be less than the minimum number of cases for child nodes.
(5) The best splitting criterion is not greater than a certain threshold.

TreeGrowing $(S,A,y,SplitCriterion,StoppingCriterion)$

Where:

S - Training Set

A - Input Feature Set

y - Target Feature

$SplitCriterion$ - the method for evaluating a certain split

$StoppingCriterion$ - the criteria to stop the growing process

Create a new tree T with a single root node.

IF $StoppingCriterion(S)$ THEN

    Mark T as a leaf with the most

    common value of y in S as a label.

ELSE

    $\forall a_i \in A$ find a that obtain the best $SplitCriterion(a_i, S)$.

    Label t with a

    FOR each outcome v_i of a:

        Set $Subtree_i$= TreeGrowing $(\sigma_{a=v_i}S, A, y)$.

        Connect the root node of t_T to $Subtree_i$ with

            an edge that is labelled as v_i

    END FOR

END IF

RETURN TreePruning (S,T,y)

TreePruning (S,T,y)

Where:

S - Training Set

y - Target Feature

T - The tree to be pruned

DO

    Select a node t in T such that pruning it

        maximally improve some evaluation criteria

    IF $t \neq \emptyset$ THEN $T = pruned(T,t)$

UNTIL $t = \emptyset$

RETURN T

Fig. 2.1   Top-Down Algorithmic Framework for Decision Trees Induction.

Chapter 3

Evaluation of Classification Trees

3.1 Overview

An important problem in the KDD process is the development of efficient indicators for assessing the quality of the analysis results. In this chapter we introduce the main concepts and quality criteria in decision trees evaluation.

Evaluating the performance of a classification tree is a fundamental aspect of machine learning. As stated above, the decision tree inducer receives a training set as input and constructs a classification tree that can classify an unseen instance. Both the classification tree and the inducer can be evaluated using evaluation criteria. The evaluation is important for understanding the quality of the classification tree and for refining parameters in the KDD iterative process

While there are several criteria for evaluating the predictive performance of classification trees, other criteria such as the computational complexity or the comprehensibility of the generated classifier can be important as well.

3.2 Generalization Error

Let $DT(S)$ represent a classification tree trained on dataset S. The generalization error of $DT(S)$ is its probability to misclassify an instance selected according to the distribution D of the labeled instance space. The *classification accuracy* of a classification tree is one minus the generalization error. The *training error* is defined as the percentage of examples in the training set correctly classified by the classification tree, formally:

$$\hat{\varepsilon}(DT(S), S) = \sum_{\langle x,y \rangle \in S} L\left(y, DT(S)(x)\right) \tag{3.1}$$

where $L(y, DT(S)(x))$ is the zero-one loss function defined in Equation 2.2.

In this book, classification accuracy is the primary evaluation criterion for experiments.

Although generalization error is a natural criterion, its actual value is known only in rare cases (mainly synthetic cases). The reason for that is that the distribution D of the labeled instance space is not known.

One can take the training error as an estimation of the generalization error. However, using the training error as is will typically provide an optimistically biased estimate, especially if the inducer *over-fits* the training data. There are two main approaches for estimating the generalization error: Theoretical and Empirical. In this book we utilize both approaches.

3.2.1 *Theoretical Estimation of Generalization Error*

A low training error does not guarantee low generalization error. There is often a trade-off between the training error and the confidence assigned to the training error as a predictor for the generalization error, measured by the difference between the generalization and training errors. The capacity of the inducer is a major factor in determining the degree of confidence in the training error. In general, the capacity of an inducer indicates the variety of classifiers it can induce. The VC-dimension presented below can be used as a measure of the inducers capacity.

Decision trees with many nodes, relative to the size of the training set, are likely to obtain a low training error. On the other hand, they might just be memorizing or overfitting the patterns and hence exhibit a poor generalization ability. In such cases, the low error is likely to be a poor predictor of the higher generalization error. When the opposite occurs, that is to say, when capacity is too small for the given number of examples, inducers may underfit the data, and exhibit both poor training and generalization error.

In "Mathematics of Generalization", [Wolpert (1995)] discuss four theoretical frameworks for estimating the generalization error: PAC, VC and Bayesian, and statistical physics. All these frameworks combine the training error (which can be easily calculated) with some penalty function expressing the capacity of the inducers.

3.2.2 *Empirical Estimation of Generalization Error*

Another approach for estimating the generalization error is the holdout method in which the given dataset is randomly partitioned into two sets: training and test sets. Usually, two-thirds of the data is considered for the training set and the remaining data are allocated to the test set. First, the training set is used by the inducer to construct a suitable classifier and then we measure the misclassification rate of this classifier on the test set. This test set error usually provides a better estimation of the generalization error than the training error. The reason for this is the fact that the training error usually under-estimates the generalization error (due to the overfitting phenomena). Nevertheless since only a proportion of the data is used to derive the model, the estimate of accuracy tends to be pessimistic.

A variation of the holdout method can be used when data is limited. It is common practice to resample the data, that is, partition the data into training and test sets in different ways. An inducer is trained and tested for each partition and the accuracies averaged. By doing this, a more reliable estimate of the true generalization error of the inducer is provided.

Random subsampling and n-fold cross-validation are two common methods of resampling. In random subsampling, the data is randomly partitioned several times into disjoint training and test sets. Errors obtained from each partition are averaged. In n-fold cross-validation, the data is randomly split into n mutually exclusive subsets of approximately equal size. An inducer is trained and tested n times; each time it is tested on one of the k folds and trained using the remaining $n - 1$ folds.

The cross-validation estimate of the generalization error is the overall number of misclassifications divided by the number of examples in the data. The random subsampling method has the advantage that it can be repeated an indefinite number of times. However, a disadvantage is that the test sets are not independently drawn with respect to the underlying distribution of examples. Because of this, using a t-test for paired differences with random subsampling can lead to an increased chance of type I error, i.e., identifying a significant difference when one does not actually exist. Using a t-test on the generalization error produced on each fold lowers the chances of type I error but may not give a stable estimate of the generalization error. It is common practice to repeat n-fold cross-validation n times in order to provide a stable estimate. However, this, of course, renders the test sets non-independent and increases the chance of type I error. Unfortunately, there is no satisfactory solution to this problem. Alternative tests suggested by [Dietterich (1998)] have a low probability of type I error but a higher chance of type II error that is, failing to identify a significant difference when one does actually exist.

Stratification is a process often applied during random subsampling and n-fold cross-validation. Stratification ensures that the class distribution from the whole dataset is preserved in the training and test sets. Stratification has been shown to help reduce the variance of the estimated error especially for datasets with many classes.

Another cross-validation variation is the bootstraping method which is a n-fold cross validation, with n set to the number of initial samples. It samples the training instances uniformly with replacement and leave-one-out. In each iteration, the classifier is trained on the set of $n - 1$ samples that is randomly selected from the set of initial samples, S. The testing is performed using the remaining subset.

3.2.3   *Alternatives to the Accuracy Measure*

Accuracy is not a sufficient measure for evaluating a model with an imbalanced distribution of the class. There are cases where the estimation of an accuracy rate may mislead one about the quality of a derived classifier. In such circumstances, where the dataset contains significantly more majority class than minority class instances, one can always select the majority class and obtain good accuracy performance. Therefore, in these cases, the sensitivity and specificity measures can be used as an alternative to the accuracy measures [Han and Kamber (2001)].

Sensitivity (also known as recall) assesses how well the classifier can recognize positive samples and is defined as

$$Sensitivity = \frac{true\_positive}{positive} \tag{3.2}$$

where *true_positive* corresponds to the number of the true positive samples and positive is the number of positive samples.

Specificity measures how well the classifier can recognize negative samples. It is defined as

$$Specificity = \frac{true\_negative}{negative} \tag{3.3}$$

where *true_negative* corresponds to the number of the true negative examples and negative the number of samples that is negative.

Another well-known performance measure is precision. Precision measures how many examples classified as "positive" class are indeed "positive". This measure is useful for evaluating crisp classifiers that are used to classify an entire dataset. Formally:

$$Precision = \frac{true\_positive}{true\_positive + false\_positive} \qquad (3.4)$$

Based on the above definitions the *accuracy* can be defined as a function of *sensitivity* and *specificity*:

$$Accuracy = Sensitivity \cdot \frac{positive}{positive+negative} + \\ Specificity \cdot \frac{negative}{positive+negative} \qquad (3.5)$$

3.2.4 The F-Measure

Usually there is a tradeoff between the precision and recall measures. Trying to improve one measure often results in a deterioration of the second measure. Figure 3.1 illustrates a typical precision-recall graph. This two-dimensional graph is closely related to the well-known receiver operating characteristics (ROC) graphs in which the true positive rate (recall) is plotted on the Y-axis and the false positive rate is plotted on the X-axis [Ferri *et al.* (2002)]. However unlike the precision-recall graph, the ROC diagram is always convex.

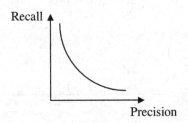

Fig. 3.1   A Typical precision-recall diagram.

Given a probabilistic classifier, this trade-off graph may be obtained by setting different threshold values. In a binary classification problem, the

classifier prefers the class "not pass" over the class "pass" if the probability
for "not pass" is at least 0.5. However, by setting a different threshold
value other than 0.5, the trade-off graph can be obtained.

The problem here is described as multi-criteria decision-making
(MCDM). The simplest and the most commonly used method to solve
MCDM is the weighted sum model. This technique combines the criteria into a single value by using appropriate weighting. The basic principle behind this technique is the additive utility assumption. The criteria
measures must be numerical, comparable and expressed in the same unit.
Nevertheless, in the case discussed here, the arithmetic mean can mislead.
Instead, the harmonic mean provides a better notion of "average". More
specifically, this measure is defined as [Van Rijsbergen (1979)]:

$$F = \frac{2 \cdot P \cdot R}{P + R} \tag{3.6}$$

The intuition behind the F-measure can be explained using Figure 3.2.
Figure 3.2 presents a diagram of a common situation in which the right
ellipsoid represents the set of all defective batches and the left ellipsoid
represents the set of all batches that were classified as defective by a certain
classifier. The intersection of these sets represents the true positive (TP),
while the remaining parts represent false negative (FN) and false positive
(FP). An intuitive way of measuring the adequacy of a certain classifier
is to measure to what extent the two sets match, namely to measure the
size of the unshaded area. Since the absolute size is not meaningful, it
should be normalized by calculating the proportional area. This value is
the F-measure:

$$\text{Proportion of unshaded area} = \frac{2 \cdot (True\ Positive)}{False\ Positive + False\ Negative + 2 \cdot (True\ Positve)} = F \tag{3.7}$$

The F-measure can have values between 0 to 1. It obtains its highest
value when the two sets presented in Figure 3.2 are identical and it obtains
its lowest value when the two sets are mutually exclusive. Note that each
point on the precision-recall curve may have a different F-measure. Furthermore, different classifiers have different precision-recall graphs.

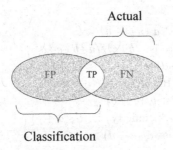

Fig. 3.2 A graphic explanation of the F-measure.

3.2.5 *Confusion Matrix*

The confusion matrix is used as an indication of the properties of a classification (discriminant) rule. It contains the number of elements that have been correctly or incorrectly classified for each class. We can see on its main diagonal the number of observations that have been correctly classified for each class; the off-diagonal elements indicate the number of observations that have been incorrectly classified. One benefit of a confusion matrix is that it is easy to see if the system is confusing two classes (i.e. commonly mislabelling one as an other).

For every instance in the test set, we compare the actual class to the class that was assigned by the trained classifier. A positive (negative) example that is correctly classified by the classifier is called a true positive (true negative); a positive (negative) example that is incorrectly classified is called a false negative (false positive). These numbers can be organized in a confusion matrix shown in Table 3.1.

Table 3.1 A confusion matrix

	Predicted negative	Predicted positive
Negative Examples	A	B
Positive Examples	C	D

Based on the values in Table 3.1, one can calculate all the measures defined above:

- Accuracy is: $(a+d)/(a+b+c+d)$
- Misclassification rate is: $(b+c)/(a+b+c+d)$
- Precision is: $d/(b+d)$
- True positive rate (Recall) is: $d/(c+d)$
- False positive rate is: $b/(a+b)$
- True negative rate (Specificity) is: $a/(a+b)$
- False negative rate is: $c/(c+d)$

3.2.6 *Classifier Evaluation under Limited Resources*

The above mentioned evaluation measures are insufficient when probabilistic classifiers are used for choosing objects to be included in a limited quota. This is a common situation that arises in real-life applications due to resource limitations that require cost-benefit considerations. Resource limitations prevent the organization from choosing all the instances. For example, in direct marketing applications, instead of mailing everybody on the list, the marketing efforts must implement a limited quota, i.e., target the mailing audience with the highest probability of positively responding to the marketing offer without exceeding the marketing budget.

Another example deals with a security officer in an air terminal. Following September 11, the security officer needs to search all passengers who may be carrying dangerous instruments (such as scissors, penknives and shaving blades). For this purpose the officer is using a classifier that is capable of classifying each passenger either as class A, which means, "Carry dangerous instruments" or as class B, "Safe".

Suppose that searching a passenger is a time-consuming task and that the security officer is capable of checking only 20 passengers prior to each flight. If the classifier has labeled exactly 20 passengers as class A, then the officer will check all these passengers. However if the classifier has labeled more than 20 passengers as class A, then the officer is required to decide which class A passenger should be ignored. On the other hand, if less than 20 people were classified as A, the officer, who must work constantly, has to decide who to check from those classified as B after he has finished with the class A passengers.

There also cases in which a quota limitation is known to exist but its size is not known in advance. Nevertheless, the decision maker would like to evaluate the expected performance of the classifier. Such cases occur, for example, in some countries regarding the number of undergraduate students that can be accepted to a certain department in a state university. The actual quota for a given year is set according to different parameters including governmental budget. In this case, the decision maker would like to evaluate several classifiers for selecting the applicants while not knowing the actual quota size. Finding the most appropriate classifier in advance is important because the chosen classifier can dictate what the important attributes are, i.e. the information that the applicant should provide the registration and admission unit.

In probabilistic classifiers, the above mentioned definitions of precision and recall can be extended and defined as a function of a probability threshold τ . If we evaluate a classifier based on a given a test set which consists of n instances denoted as $(< x_1, y_1 >, ..., < x_n, y_n >)$ such that x_i represents the input features vector of instance i and y_i represents its true class ("positive" or "negative"), then:

$$\text{Precision } (\tau) = \frac{\left| \{< x_i, y_i >: \hat{P}_{DT}(pos\,|x_i) > \tau, y_i = pos\} \right|}{\left| \{< x_i, y_i >: \hat{P}_{DT}(pos\,|x_i) > \tau \right|} \tag{3.8}$$

$$\text{Recall } (\tau) = \frac{\left| \{< x_i, y_i >: \hat{P}_{DT}(pos\,|x_i) > \tau, y_i = pos\} \right|}{\left| \{< x_i, y_i >: y_i = pos\} \right|} \tag{3.9}$$

where DT represents a probabilistic classifier that is used to estimate the conditional likelihood of an observation x_i to "positive" which is denoted as $\hat{P}_{DT}(pos\,|x_i)$. The typical threshold value of 0.5 means that the predicted probability of "positive" must be higher than 0.5 for the instance to be predicted as "positive". By changing the value of τ, one can control the number of instances that are classified as "positive". Thus, the τ value can be tuned to the required quota size. Nevertheless because there might be several instances with the same conditional probability, the quota size is not necessarily incremented by one.

The above discussion is based on the assumption that the classification problem is binary. In cases where there are more than two classes, adaptation could be easily made by comparing one class to all the others.

3.2.6.1   *ROC Curves*

Another measure is the receiver operating characteristic (ROC) curves which illustrate the tradeoff between true positive to false positive rates [Provost and Fawcett (1998)]. Figure 3.3 illustrates a ROC curve in which the X-axis represents a false positive rate and the Y-axis represents a true positive rate. The ideal point on the ROC curve would be (0,100), that is, all positive examples are classified correctly and no negative examples are misclassified as positive.

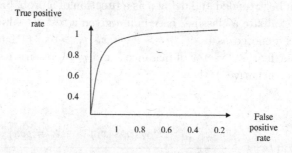

Fig. 3.3   A Typical ROC curve.

The ROC convex hull can also be used as a robust method of identifying potentially optimal classifiers [Provost and Fawcett (2001)]. Given a family of ROC curves, the ROC convex hull can include points that are more towards the north-west frontier of the ROC space. If a line passes through a point on the convex hull, then there is no other line with the same slope passing through another point with a larger true positive (TP) intercept. Thus, the classifier at that point is optimal under any distribution assumptions in tandem with that slope.

3.2.6.2   *Hit Rate Curve*

The hit rate curve presents the hit ratio as a function of the quota size[An and Wang (2001)]. *Hit rate* is calculated by counting the actual positive labeled instances inside a determined quota. More precisely for a quota of size j and a ranked set of instances, *hit rate* is defined as:

$$\text{HitRate}(j) = \frac{\sum\limits_{k=1}^{j} t^{[k]}}{j} \qquad (3.10)$$

where $t^{[k]}$ represents the truly expected outcome of the instance located in the k'th position when the instances are sorted according to their conditional probability for "positive" by descending order. Note that if the k'th position can be uniquely defined (i.e. there is exactly one instance that can be located in this position) then $t^{[k]}$ is either 0 or 1 depending on the actual outcome of this specific instance. Nevertheless if the k'th position is not uniquely defined and there are $m_{k,1}$ instances that can be located in this position, and $m_{k,2}$ of which are truly positive, then:

$$t^{[k]} = {m_{k,2}}\big/{m_{k,1}} \qquad (3.11)$$

The sum of $t^{[k]}$ over the entire test set is equal to the number of instances that are labeled "positive". Moreover $Hit - Rate(j) \approx Precision(p^{[j]})$ where $p^{[j]}$ denotes the j'th order of $\hat{P}_I(pos\,|x_1), ..., \hat{P}_I(pos\,|x_m)$. The values are strictly equal when the value of j'th is uniquely defined.

It should be noted that the hit rate measure was originally defined without any reference to the uniqueness of a certain position. However, there are some classifiers that tend to provide the same conditional probability to several different instances. For instance, in a decision tree, any instances in the test set that belongs to the same leaf get the same conditional probability. Thus, the proposed correction is required in those cases. Figure 3.4 illustrates a hit-curve.

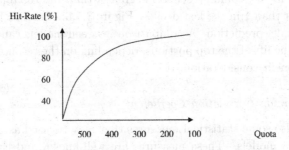

Fig. 3.4   A typical hit curve.

3.2.6.3   *Qrecall (Quota Recall)*

The hit-rate measure, presented above, is the "precision" equivalent for quota-limited problems. Similarly, we suggest the Qrecall (for quota recall) to be the "recall" equivalent for quota-limited problems. The Qrecall for a certain position in a ranked list is calculated by dividing the number of positive instances, from the head of the list until that position, by the total positive instances in the entire dataset. Thus, the Qrecall for a quota of j is defined as:

$$\text{Qrecall}(j) = \frac{\sum_{k=1}^{j} t^{[k]}}{n^+} \tag{3.12}$$

The denominator stands for the total number of instances that are classified as positive in the entire dataset. Formally it can be calculated as:

$$n^+ = |\{<x_i, y_i>: y_i = pos\}| \tag{3.13}$$

3.2.6.4   *Lift Curve*

A popular method of evaluating probabilistic models is *lift* [Coppock (2002)]. After a ranked test set is divided into several portions (usually deciles), lift is calculated as follows: the ratio of really positive instances in a specific decile is divided by the average ratio of really positive instances in the population. Regardless of how the test set is divided, a good model is achieved if the lift decreases when proceeding to the bottom of the scoring list. A good model would present a lift greater than 1 in the top deciles and a lift smaller than 1 in the last deciles. Figure 3.5 illustrates a lift chart for a typical model prediction. A comparison between models can be done by comparing the lift of the top portions, depending on the resources available and cost/benefit considerations.

3.2.6.5   *Pearson Correlation Coefficient*

There are also some statistical measures that may be used as performance evaluators of models. These measures are well-known and can be found in many statistical books. In this section we examine the Pearson correlation coefficient. This measure can be used to find the correlation between the ordered estimated conditional probability ($p^{[k]}$) and the ordered actual

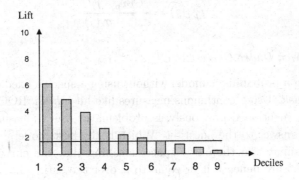

Fig. 3.5 A typical lift chart.

expected outcome $(t^{[k]})$. A Pearson correlation coefficient can have any value between -1 and 1 where the value 1 represents the strongest positive correlation. It should be noticed that this measure take into account not only the ordinal place of an instance but also its value (i.e. the estimated probability attached to it). The *Pearson* correlation coefficient for two random variables is calculated by dividing the co-variance by the product of both standard deviations. In this case, the standard deviations of the two variables assuming a quota size of j are:

$$\sigma_p(j) = \sqrt{\frac{1}{j} \sum_{i=1}^{j'} \left(p^{[i]} - \bar{p}(j)\right)} \; ; \; \sigma_t(j) = \sqrt{\frac{1}{j} \sum_{i=1}^{j} \left(t^{[i]} - \bar{t}(j)\right)} \qquad (3.14)$$

where $\bar{p}(j), \bar{t}(j)$ represent the average of $p^{[i]}$'s and $t^{[i]}$'s respectively:

$$\bar{p}(j) = \frac{\sum_{i=1}^{j} p^{[i]}}{j} \quad ; \quad \bar{t}(j) = \frac{\sum_{i=1}^{j} t^{[i]}}{j} = HitRate(j) \qquad (3.15)$$

The co-variance is calculated as follows:

$$Cov_{p,t}(j) = \frac{1}{j} \sum_{i-1}^{j} \left(p^{[i]} - \bar{p}(j)\right) \left(t^{[i]} - \bar{t}(j)\right) \qquad (3.16)$$

Thus, the Pearson correlation coefficient for a quota j, is:

$$\rho_{p,t}(j) = \frac{Cov_{p,t}(j)}{\sigma_p(j) \cdot \sigma_t(j)} \tag{3.17}$$

3.2.6.6   *Area Under Curve (AUC)*

Evaluating a probabilistic model without using a specific fixed quota is not a trivial task. Using continuous measures like hit curves, ROC curves and lift charts, mentioned previously, is problematic. Such measures can give a definite answer to the question "Which is the best model?" only if one model dominates in the curve space, meaning that the curves of all the other model are beneath it or equal to it over the entire chart space. If a dominating model does not exist, then there is no answer to that question, using only the continuous measures mentioned above.. Complete order demands no intersections of the curves. Of course, in practice there is almost never one dominating model. The best answer that can be obtained is in regard to which areas one model outperforms the others. As shown in Figure 3.6, every model gets different values in different areas. If a complete order of model performance is needed, another measure should be used.

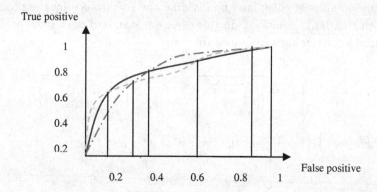

Fig. 3.6   Areas of dominancy. A ROC curve is an example of a measure that gives areas of dominancy and not a complete order of the models. In this example the equally dashed line model is the best for f.p (false positive) < 0.2. The full line model is the best for 0.2 < f.p <0.4. The dotted line model is best for 0.4 < f.p < 0.9 and from 0.9 to 1 again the dashed line model is the best.

Area under the ROC curve (AUC) is a useful metric for classifier performance since it is independent of the decision criterion selected and prior probabilities. The AUC comparison can establish a dominance relationship between classifiers. If the ROC curves are intersecting, the total AUC is an average comparison between models [Lee (2000)]. The bigger it is, the better the model is. As opposed to other measures, the area under the ROC curve (AUC) does not depend on the imbalance of the training set [Kolcz (2003)]. Thus, the comparison of the AUC of two classifiers is fairer and more informative than comparing their misclassification rates.

3.2.6.7 *Average Hit Rate*

The average hit rate is a weighted average of all hit-rate values. If the model is optimal, then all the really positive instances are located in the head of the ranked list, and the value of the average hit rate is 1. The use of this measure fits an organization that needs to minimize type II statistical error (namely, to include a certain object in the quota although in fact this object will be labeled as "negative"). Formally the Average Hit Rate for binary classification problems is defined as:

$$AverageHitRate = \frac{\sum_{j=1}^{n} t^{[j]} \cdot HitRate(j)}{n^+} \qquad (3.18)$$

where $t^{[j]}$ is defined as in Equation 4 and is used as a weighting factor. Note that the average hit rate ignores all hit rate values on unique positions that are actually labeled as "negative" class (because $t^{[j]}=0$ in these cases).

3.2.6.8 *Average Qrecall*

Average Qrecall is the average of all the Qrecalls which extends from the position that is equal to the number of positive instances in the test set to the bottom of the list. Average Qrecall fits an organization that needs to minimize type I statistical error (namely, not including a certain object in the quota although in fact this object will be labeled as "positive"). Formally, average Qrecall is defined as:

$$\frac{\sum_{j=n^+}^{n} Qrecall(j)}{n - (n^+ - 1)} \qquad (3.19)$$

where n is the total number of instances and n^+ is defined in Equation (3.13).

Table 3.2 illustrates the calculation of average Qrecall and average hit-rate for a dataset of ten instances. The table presents a list of instances in descending order according to their predicted conditional probability to be classified as "positive". Because all probabilities are unique, the third column ($t^{[k]}$) indicates the actual class ("1" represent "positive" and "0" represents "negative"). The average values are simple algebraic averages of the highlighted cells.

Table 3.2   An example for calculating Average Qrecall and Average Hit-rate

Place in list (j)	Positive probability	$t^{[k]}$	Qrecall	Hit rate
1	0.45	1	0.25	1
2	0.34	0	0.25	0.5
3	0.32	1	0.5	0.667
4	0.26	1	0.75	0.75
5	0.15	0	0.75	0.6
6	0.14	0	0.75	0.5
7	0.09	1	1	0.571
8	0.07	0	1	0.5
9	0.06	0	1	0.444
10	0.03	0	1	0.4
		Average:	0.893	0.747

Note that both *average Qrecall* and *average hit rate* get the value 1 in an optimum classification, where all the positive instances are located at the head of the list. This case is illustrated in Table 3.3. A summary of the key differences are provided in Table 3.4.

3.2.6.9 *Potential Extract Measure (PEM)*

To better understand the behavior of Qrecall curves, consider the cases of random prediction and optimum prediction.

Suppose no learning process was applied on the data and the list produced as a prediction would be the test set in its original (random) order. On the assumption that positive instances are distributed uniformly in the population, then a quota of random size contains a number of positive instances that are proportional to the a-priori proportion of positive instances in the population. Thus, a Qrecall curve that describes a uniform distribu-

Table 3.3 Qrecall and Hit-rate in an optimum prediction

Place in list (j)	Positive probability	$t^{[k]}$	Qrecall	Hit rate
1	0.45	1	0.25	1
2	0.34	1	0. 5	1
3	0.32	1	0.75	1
4	0.26	1	1	1
5	0.15	0	1	0.8
6	0.14	0	1	0.667
7	0.09	0	1	0.571
8	0.07	0	1	0.5
9	0.06	0	1	0.444
10	0.03	0	1	0.4
		Average:	1	1

Table 3.4 Characteristics of Qrecall and Hit-rate

Parameter	Hit-rate	Qrecall
Function increasing/decreasing	Non monotonic	Monotonically increasing
End point	Proportion of positive samples in the set	1
Sensitivity of the measures value to positive instances	Very sensitive to positive instances at the top of the list. Less sensitive on going down to the bottom of the list.	Same sensitivity to positive instances in all places in the list.
Effect of negative class on the measure	A negative instance affects the measure and cause its value to decrease.	A negative instance does not affect the measure.
Range	$0 \leq$ Hit-rate ≤ 1	$0 \leq$ Qrecall ≤ 1

tion (which can be considered as a model that predicts as well as a random guess, without any learning) is a linear line (or semi-linear because values are discrete) which starts at 0 (for zero quota size) and ends in 1.

Suppose now that a model gave an optimum prediction, meaning that all positive instances are located at the head of the list and below them, all the negative instances. In this case, the Qrecall curve climbs linearly until a value of 1 is achieved at point n^+ (n^+ = number of positive samples). From that point any quota that has a size bigger than n^+, fully extracts test set potential and the value 1 is kept until the end of the list.

Note that a "good model", which outperforms random classification, though not an optimum one, will fall "on average" between these two curves. It may drop sometimes below the random curve but generally, more area is delineated between the "good model" curve and the random curve, above the latter than below it. If the opposite is true then the model is a "bad model" that does worse than a random guess.

The last observation leads us to consider a measure that evaluates the performance of a model by summing the areas delineated between the Qrecall curve of the examined model and the Qrecall curve of a random model (which is linear). Areas above the linear curve are added and areas below the linear curve are subtracted. The areas themselves are calculated by subtracting the Qrecall of a random classification from the Qrecall of the model's classification in every point as shown in Figure 3.7. The areas where the model performed better than a random guess increase the measure's value while the areas where the model performed worse than a random guess decrease it. If the last total computed area is divided in the area delineated between the optimum model Qrecall curve and the random model (linear) Qrecall curve, then it reaches the extent to which the potential is extracted, independently of the number of instances in the dataset.

Formally, the PEM measure is calculated as:

$$PEM = \frac{S_1 - S_2}{S_3} \tag{3.20}$$

where S_1 is the area delimited by the Qrecall curve of the examined model above the Qrecall curve of a random model; S_2 is the area delimited by the Qrecall curve of the examined model under the Qrecall curve of a random model; and S_3 is the area delimited by the optimal Qrecall curve and the curve of the random model. The division in S_3 is required in order to normalize the measure, thus datasets of different size can be compared. In this way, if the model is optimal, then PEM gets the value 1. If the model is as good as a random choice, then the PEM gets the value 0. If it gives the worst possible result (that is to say, it puts the positive samples at the bottom of the list), then its PEM is -1. Based on the notations defined above, the PEM can be formulated as:

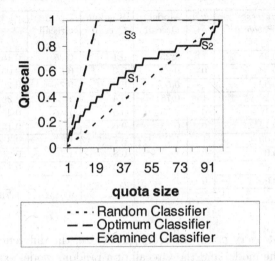

Fig. 3.7   A qualitative representation of PEM.

$$PEM = \frac{S_1 - S_2}{S_3} = \frac{\sum\limits_{j=1}^{n} \left(qrecall(j) - \frac{j}{n}\right)}{\sum\limits_{j=1}^{n^+} \left(\frac{j}{n^+}\right) + n^- - \sum\limits_{j=1}^{n} \left(\frac{j}{n}\right)} \qquad (3.21)$$

$$= \frac{\sum\limits_{j=1}^{n} \left(qrecall(j)\right) - \frac{(n+1)}{2}}{\frac{(n^+ + 1)}{2} + n^- - \frac{(n+1)}{2}} = \frac{\sum\limits_{j=1}^{n} \left(qrecall(j)\right) - \frac{(n+1)}{2}}{\frac{n^-}{2}} \qquad (3.22)$$

where n^- denotes the number of instances that are actually classified as "negative". Table 3.5 illustrates the calculation of PEM for the instances in Table 3.2. Note that the random Qrecall does not represent a certain realization but the expected values. The optimal qrecall is calculated as if the "positive" instances have been located in the top of the list.

Note that the PEM somewhat resembles the Gini index produced from Lorentz curves which appear in economics when dealing with the distribution of income. Indeed, this measure indicates the difference between the distribution of positive samples in a prediction and the uniform distribution. Note also that this measure gives an indication of the total lift of

Table 3.5	An example for calculating PEM for instances of Table 3.2.

Place in list	Success probability	$t^{[k]}$	Model Qrecall	Random Qrecall	Optimal Qrecall	S1	S2	S3
1	0.45	1	0.25	0.1	0.25	0.15	0	0.15
2	0.34	0	0.25	0.2	0.5	0.05	0	0.3
3	0.32	1	0.5	0.3	0.75	0.2	0	0.45
4	0.26	1	0.75	0.4	1	0.35	0	0.6
5	0.15	0	0.75	0.5	1	0.25	0	0.5
6	0.14	0	0.75	0.6	1	0.15	0	0.4
7	0.09	1	1	0.7	1	0.3	0	0.3
8	0.07	0	1	0.8	1	0.2	0	0.2
9	0.06	0	1	0.9	1	0.1	0	0.1
10	0.03	0	1	1	1	0	0	0
					Total	1.75	0	3

the model at every point. In every quota size, the difference between the Qrecall of the model and the Qrecall of a random model expresses the lift in extracting the potential of the test set due to the use in the model (for good or for bad).

### 3.2.7	*Which Decision Tree Classifier is Better?*

Below we discuss some of the most common statistical methods proposed [Dieterich (1998)] for answering the following question: *Given two inducers A and B and a dataset S, which inducer will produce more accurate classifiers when trained on datasets of the same size?*

#### 3.2.7.1	*McNemar's Test*

Let S be the available set of data, which is divided into a training set R and a test set T. Then we consider two inducers A and B trained on the training set and the result is two classifiers. These classifiers are tested on T and for each example $x \in T$ we record how it was classified. Thus, the contingency table presented in Table 3.6 is constructed.

Table 3.6	McNemar's test: contingency table

Number of examples misclassified by both classifiers (n_{00})	Number of examples misclassified by $\hat{f}_A$ but not by $\hat{f}_B$(n_{01})
Number of examples misclassified by $\hat{f}_B$ but not by $\hat{f}_A$(n_{10})	Number of examples misclassified neither by $\hat{f}_A$ nor by $\hat{f}_B$(n_{11})

The two inducers should have the same error rate under the null hypothesis H_0. McNemar's test is based on a χ^2 test for goodness-of-fit that compares the distribution of counts expected under null hypothesis to the observed counts. The expected counts under Ho are presented in Table 3.7.

Table 3.7　Expected counts under Ho

n_{00}	$(n_{01} + n_{10})/2$
$(n_{01} + n_{10})/2$	$n_{11})$

The following statistic, s, is distributed as χ^2 with 1 degree of freedom. It incorporates a "continuity correction" term (of -1 in the numerator) to account for the fact that the statistic is discrete while the χ^2 distribution is continuous:

$$s = \frac{(|n_{10} - n_{01}| - 1)^2}{n_{10} + n_{01}} \tag{3.23}$$

According to the probabilistic theory [Athanasopoulos, 1991], if the null hypothesis is correct, the probability that the value of the statistic, s, is greater than $\chi^2_{1,0.95}$ is less than 0.05, i.e. $P(|s| > \chi^2_{1,0.95}) < 0.05$. Then, to compare the inducers A and B, the induced classifiers $\hat{f}_A$ and $\hat{f}_B$ are tested on T and the value of s is estimated as described above. Then if $|s| > \chi^2_{1,0.95}$, the null hypothesis could be rejected in favor of the hypothesis that the two inducers have different performance when trained on the particular training set R.

The shortcomings of this test are:

(1) It does not directly measure variability due to the choice of the training set or the internal randomness of the inducer. The inducers are compared using a single training set R. Thus McNemar's test should be only applied if we consider that the sources of variability are small.

(2) It compares the performance of the inducers on training sets, which are substantially smaller than the size of the whole dataset. Hence we must assume that the relative difference observed on training sets will still hold for training sets of size equal to the whole dataset.

3.2.7.2　*A Test for the Difference of Two Proportions*

This statistical test is based on measuring the difference between the error rates of algorithms A and B [Snedecor and Cochran (1989)]. More specifically, let $p_A = (n_{00} + n_{01})/n$ be the proportion of test examples incorrectly classified by algorithm A and let $p_B = (n_{00} + n_{10})/n$ be the proportion of test examples incorrectly classified by algorithm B. The assumption underlying this statistical test is that when algorithm A classifies an example x from the test set T, the probability of misclassification is p_A. Then the number of misclassifications of n test examples is a binomial random variable with mean np_A and variance $p_A(1 - p_A)n$.

The binomial distribution can be well approximated by a normal distribution for reasonable values of n. The difference between two independent normally distributed random variables is itself normally distributed. Thus, the quantity $p_A - p_B$ can be viewed as normally distributed if we assume that the measured error rates p_A and p_B are independent. Under the null hypothesis, Ho, the quantity $p_A - p_B$ has a mean of zero and a standard deviation error of

$$se = \sqrt{2p \cdot \left(1 - \frac{p_A + p_B}{2}\right)/n} \qquad (3.24)$$

where n is the number of test examples.

Based on the above analysis, we obtain the statistic:

$$z = \frac{p_A - p_B}{\sqrt{2p(1 - p)/n}} \qquad (3.25)$$

which has a standard normal distribution. According to the probabilistic theory, if the z value is greater than $Z_{0.975}$, the probability of incorrectly rejecting the null hypothesis is less than 0.05. Thus, if $|z| > Z_{0.975} = 1.96$, the null hypothesis could be rejected in favor of the hypothesis that the two algorithms have different performances. Two of the most important problems with this statistic are:

(1) The probabilities p_A and p_B are measured on the same test set and thus they are not independent.
(2) The test does not measure variation due to the choice of the training set or the internal variation of the learning algorithm. Also it measures the performance of the algorithms on training sets of a size significantly smaller than the whole dataset.

3.2.7.3   *The Resampled Paired t Test*

The resampled paired t test is the most popular in machine learning. Usually, there are a series of 30 trials in the test. In each trial, the available sample S is randomly divided into a training set R (it is typically two thirds of the data) and a test set T. The algorithms A and B are both trained on R and the resulting classifiers are tested on T. Let $p_A^{(i)}$ and $p_B^{(i)}$ be the observed proportions of test examples misclassified by algorithm A and B respectively during the i-th trial. If we assume that the 30 differences $p^{(i)} = p_A^{(i)} - p_B^{(i)}$ were drawn independently from a normal distribution, then we can apply Student's t test by computing the statistic:

$$t = \frac{\bar{p} \cdot \sqrt{n}}{\sqrt{\frac{\sum_{i=1}^{n}(p^{(i)} - \bar{p})^2}{n-1}}} \qquad (3.26)$$

where $\bar{p} = \frac{1}{n} \cdot \sum_{i=1}^{n} p^{(i)}$. Under the null hypothesis, this statistic has a t distribution with $n - 1$ degrees of freedom. Then for 30 trials, the null hypothesis could be rejected if $|t| > t_{29,0.975} = 2.045$. The main drawbacks of this approach are:

(1) Since $p_A^{(i)}$ and $p_B^{(i)}$ are not independent, the difference $p^{(i)}$ will not have a normal distribution.
(2) The $p^{(i)}$'s are not independent, because the test and training sets in the trials overlap.

3.2.7.4   *The k-fold Cross-validated Paired t Test*

This approach is similar to the resampled paired t test except that instead of constructing each pair of training and test sets by randomly dividing S, the dataset is randomly divided into k disjoint sets of equal size, $T_1, T_2, \ldots, T_k$. Then k trials are conducted. In each trial, the test set is T_i and the training set is the union of all of the others T_j, $j \neq i$. The t statistic is computed as described in Section 3.2.7.3. The advantage of this approach is that each test set is independent of the others. However, there is the problem that the training sets overlap. This overlap may prevent this statistical test from obtaining a good estimation of the amount of variation that would be observed if each training set were completely independent of the others training sets.

3.3   Computational Complexity

Another useful criterion for comparing inducers and classifiers is their computational complexity. Strictly speaking computational complexity is the amount of CPU consumed by each inducer. It is convenient to differentiate between three metrics of computational complexity:

- Computational complexity for generating a new classifier: This is the most important metric, especially when there is a need to scale the data mining algorithm to massive datasets. Because most of the algorithms have computational complexity, which is worse than linear in the numbers of tuples, mining massive datasets might be prohibitively expensive.
- Computational complexity for updating a classifier: Given new data, what is the computational complexity required for updating the current classifier such that the new classifier reflects the new data?
- Computational complexity for classifying a new instance: Generally this type of metric is neglected because it is relatively small. However, in certain methods (like k-nearest neighborhood) or in certain real-time applications (like anti-missiles applications), this type can be critical.

3.4   Comprehensibility

Comprehensibility criterion (also known as interpretability) refers to how well humans grasp the induced classifier. While the generalization error measures how the classifier fits the data, comprehensibility measures the "mental fit" of that classifier.

Many techniques, like neural networks or support vector machines (SVM), are designed solely to achieve accuracy. However, as their classifiers are represented using large assemblages of real valued parameters, they are also difficult to understand and are referred to as black-box models.

However it is often important for the researcher to be able to inspect an induced classifier. For such domains as medical diagnosis, users must understand how the system makes its decisions in order to be confident of the outcome. Since data mining can also play an important role in the process of scientific discovery, a system may discover salient features in the input data whose importance was not previously recognized. If the representations formed by the inducer are comprehensible, then these discoveries can be made accessible to human review [Hunter and Klein (1993)].

Comprehensibility can vary between different classifiers created by the same inducer. For instance, in the case of decision trees, the size (number of nodes) of the induced trees is also important. Smaller trees are preferred because they are easier to interpret. There also other reasons for preferring smaller decision trees. According to a fundamental principle in science, known as the Occam's razor, when searching for the explanation of any phenomenon, one should make as few assumptions as possible, and eliminating those that make no difference in the observable predictions of the explanatory hypothesis. The implication in regard to decision trees is that the tree which can be defined as the smallest decision tree that is consistent with the training set is the one that is most likely to classify unseen instances correctly. However, this is only a rule of thumb; in some pathologic cases a large and unbalanced tree can still be easily interpreted [Buja and Lee (2001)]. Moreover the problem of finding the smallest consistent tree is known to be NP-complete [Murphy and McCraw (1991)].

As the reader can see, the accuracy and complexity factors can be quantitatively estimated; the comprehensibility is more subjective.

3.5 Scalability to Large Datasets

Scalability refers to the ability of the method to construct the classification model efficiently given large amounts of data. Classical induction algorithms have been applied with practical success in many relatively simple and small-scale problems. However, trying to discover knowledge in real life and large databases introduces time and memory problems.

As large databases have become the norm in many fields (including astronomy, molecular biology, finance, marketing, health care, and many others), the use of data mining to discover patterns in them has become a potentially very productive enterprise. Many companies are staking a large part of their future on these "data mining" applications, and looking to the research community for solutions to the fundamental problems they encounter.

While a very large amount of available data used to be a dream of any data analyst, nowadays the synonym for "very large" has become "terabyte", a hardly imaginable volume of information. Information-intensive organizations (like telecom companies and banks) are supposed to accumulate several terabytes of raw data every one to two years.

However, the availability of an electronic data repository (in its enhanced form known as a "data warehouse") has caused a number of previously unknown problems, which, if ignored, may turn the task of efficient data mining into mission impossible. Managing and analyzing huge data warehouses requires special and very expensive hardware and software, which often causes a company to exploit only a small part of the stored data.

According to [Fayyad et al. (1996)] the explicit challenges for the data mining research community is to develop methods that facilitate the use of data mining algorithms for real-world databases. One of the characteristics of a real-world databases is high volume data.

Huge databases pose several challenges:

- Computing complexity: Since most induction algorithms have a computational complexity that is greater than linear in the number of attributes or tuples, the execution time needed to process such databases might become an important issue.
- Poor classification accuracy due to difficulties in finding the correct classifier. Large databases increase the size of the search space, and thus it increases the chance that the inducer will select an over fitted classifier that is not valid in general.
- Storage problems: In most machine learning algorithms, the entire training set should be read from the secondary storage (such as magnetic storage) into the computer's primary storage (main memory) before the induction process begins. This causes problems since the main memory's capability is much smaller than the capability of magnetic disks.

The difficulties in implementing classification algorithms as-is on high volume databases derives from the increase in the number of records/instances in the database and from the increase in the number of attributes/features in each instance (high dimensionality).

Approaches for dealing with a high number of records include:

- Sampling methods — statisticians are selecting records from a population by different sampling techniques.
- Aggregation — reduces the number of records either by treating a group of records as one, or by ignoring subsets of "unimportant" records.
- Massively parallel processing — exploiting parallel technology — to simultaneously solve various aspects of the problem.

- Efficient storage methods — enabling the algorithm to handle many records. For instance [Shafer *et al.* (1996)] presented the SPRINT which constructs an attribute list data structure.
- Reducing the algorithm's search space — For instance the PUBLIC algorithm [Rastogi and Shim (2000)] integrates the growing and pruning of decision trees by using MDL (Minimum Description Length) approach in order to reduce the computational complexity.

3.6 Robustness

The ability of the model to handle noise or data with missing values and make correct predictions is called robustness. Different decision trees algorithms have different robustness levels. In order to estimate the robustness of a classification tree, it is common to train the tree on a clean training set and then train a different tree on a noisy training set. The noisy training set is usually the clean training set to which some artificial noisy instances have been added. The robustness level is measured as the difference in the accuracy of these two situations.

3.7 Stability

Formally, stability of a classification algorithm is defined as the degree to which an algorithm generates repeatable results, given different batches of data from the same process. In mathematical terms, stability is the expected agreement between two models on a random sample of the original data, where agreement on a specific example means that both models assign it to the same class. The instability problem raises questions about the validity of a particular tree provided as an output of a decision-tree algorithm. The users view the learning algorithm as an oracle. Obviously, it is difficult to trust an oracle that says something radically different each time you make a slight change in the data.

Existing methods of constructing decision trees from data suffer from a major problem of instability. The symptoms of instability include variations in the predictive accuracy of the model and in the model's topology. Instability can be revealed not only by using disjoint sets of data, but even by replacing a small portion of training cases, like in the cross-validation procedure. If an algorithm is unstable, the cross-validation results become estimators with high variance which means that an algorithm fails to make a clear distinction between persistent and random patterns in the data. As we will see below, certain type of decision trees can be used to solve the instability problem [Last *et al.* (2002)].

3.8   Interestingness Measures

The number of classification patterns generated could be very large and it is possible that different approaches result in different sets of patterns. The patterns extracted during the classification process could be represented in the form of rules, known as classification rules. It is important to evaluate the discovered patterns identifying the ones that are valid and provide new knowledge. Techniques that aim at this goal are broadly referred to as interestingness measures and the interestingness of the patterns that are discovered by a classification approach may also be considered as another quality criterion. Some representative measures [Hilderman and Hamilton, 1999] for ranking the usefulness and utility of discovered classification patterns (each path from the root to the leaf represents a different pattern) are:

- *Rule-Interest Function.* Piatetsky-Shapiro introduced the rule-interest [Piatetsky-Shapiro, (1991)] that is used to quantify the correlation between attributes in a classification rule. It is suitable only for single classification rules, i.e. rules where both the left- and right-hand sides correspond to a single attribute.
- *Smyth and Goodman's J-Measure.* The J-measure [Smyth and Goodman (1991)] is a measure for probabilistic classification rules and is used to find the best rules relating discrete-valued attributes. A probabilistic classification rule is a logical implication, $X \rightarrow Y$, satisfied with some probability p. The left- and right-hand sides of this implication correspond to a single attribute. The right-hand side is restricted to simple single-valued assignment expressions while the left-hand-side may be a conjunction of simple expressions.
- *General Impressions.* In [Liu et al., 1997] general impression is proposed as an approach for evaluating the importance of classification rules. It compares discovered rules to an approximate or vague description of what is considered to be interesting. Thus a general impression can be considered as a kind of specification language.
- *Gago and Bento's Distance Metric.* The distance metric [Gago and Bentos, 1998] measures the distance between classification rules and is

used to determine the rules that provide the highest coverage for the given data. The rules with the highest average distance to the other rules are considered to be most interesting.

3.9 Overfitting and Underfitting

The concept of overfitting is very important in data mining. It refers to the situation in which the induction algorithm generates a classifier which perfectly fits the training data but has lost the capability of generalizing to instances not presented during training. In other words, instead of learning, the classifier just memorizes the training instances. Overfitting is generally recognized to be a violation of the principle of Occams razor presented in Section 3.4.

In decision trees overfitting usually occurs when the tree has too many nodes relative to the amount of training data available. By increasing the number of nodes, the training error usually decreases while at some point the generalization error becomes worse.

Figure 3.8 illustrates the overfitting process. The figure presents the training error and the generalization error of a decision tree as a function of the number of nodes for a fixed training set. The training error continues to decline as the tree become bigger. On the other hand, the generalization error declines at first then at some point starts to increase due to overfitting. The optimal point for the generalization error is obtained for a tree with 130 nodes. In bigger trees the classifier is overfitted. In smaller trees the classifier is underfitted.

Another aspect of overfitting is presented in Figure 3.9. This graph presents the generalization error for increasing training set sizes. The generalization error decreases with the training set size. This can be explained by the fact that for a small training set, it is relatively hard to generalize, and the classifier memorizes all instances.

It was found that overfitting decreases prediction accuracy in decision trees either in the presence of significant noise or when the input attributes are irrelevant to the classification problem [Schaffer (1991)].

In order to avoid overfitting, it is necessary to estimate when further training will not result in a better generalization. In decision trees there are two mechanisms that help to avoid overfitting. The first is to avoid splitting the tree if the split is not useful (for instance by approving only statistically significant splits). The second approach is to use pruning; after

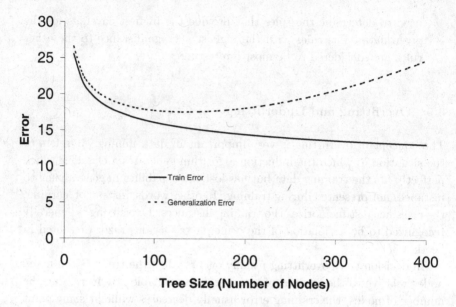

Fig. 3.8   Overfitting in Decision Trees.

growing the tree, we prune unnecessary nodes.

3.10   "No Free Lunch" Theorem

Empirical comparison of the performance of different approaches and their variants in a wide range of application domains has shown that each performs best in some, but not all, domains. This has been termed the selective superiority problem [Brodley (1995)].

It is well known that no induction algorithm can be the best in all possible domains; each algorithm contains an explicit or implicit bias [Mitchell (1980)] that leads it to prefer certain generalizations over others. The algorithm will be successful only insofar as this bias matches the characteristics of the application domain [Brazdil *et al.* (1994)]. Furthermore, other results have demonstrated the existence and correctness of the "conservation law" [Schaffer (1994)] or "no free lunch theorem" [Wolpert (1996)]: if one inducer is better than another in some domains, then there are necessarily other domains in which this relationship is reversed.

The "no free lunch theorem" implies that for a given problem, a cer-

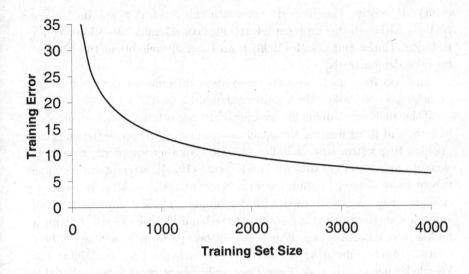

Fig. 3.9 Overfitting in Decision Trees.

tain approach can yield more information from the same data than other approaches.

A distinction should be made between all the mathematically possible domains, which are simply a product of the representation languages used, and the domains that occur in the real world, and are therefore the ones of primary interest [Rao *et al.* (1995)]. Without doubt there are many domains in the former set that are not in the latter, and average accuracy in the realworld domains can be increased at the expense of accuracy in the domains that never occur in practice. Indeed, achieving this is the goal of inductive learning research. It is still true that some algorithms will match certain classes of naturallyoccurring domains better than other algorithms, and so achieve higher accuracy than these algorithms. While this may be reversed in other realworld domains, it does not preclude an improved algorithm from being as accurate as the best in each of the domain classes.

Indeed, in many application domains, the generalization error of even the best methods is far above 0%, and the question of whether it can be improved, and if so how, is an open and important one. One aspect in answering this question is determining the minimum error achievable by any classifier in the application domain (known as the optimal Bayes error). If existing classifiers do not reach this level, new approaches are needed. Although this problem has received considerable attention (see for instance [Tumer and Ghosh (1996)]), no generally reliable method has so far been demonstrated.

The "no free lunch" concept presents a dilemma to the analyst approaching a new task: Which inducer should be used?

If the analyst is looking for accuracy only, one solution is to try each one in turn, and by estimating the generalization error, to choose the one that appears to perform best [Schaffer (1994)]. Another approach, known as *multistrategy learning* [Michalski and Tecuci (1994)], attempts to combine two or more different paradigms in a single algorithm. Most research in this area has been concerned with combining empirical approaches with analytical methods (see for instance [Towell and Shavlik (1994)]. Ideally, a multistrategy learning algorithm would always perform as well as the best of its "parents" obviating the need to try each one and simplifying the knowledge acquisition task. Even more ambitiously, there is hope that this combination of paradigms might produce synergistic effects (for instance by allowing different types of frontiers between classes in different regions of the example space), leading to levels of accuracy that neither atomic approach by itself would be able to achieve.

Unfortunately, this approach has often been used with only moderate success. Although it is true that in some industrial applications (like in the case of demand planning) this strategy proved to boost the error performance, in many other cases the resulting algorithms are prone to be cumbersome, and often achieve an error that lies between those of their parents, instead of matching the lowest.

The dilemma of what method to choose becomes even greater, if other factors such as comprehensibility are taken into consideration. For instance, for a specific domain, a neural network may outperform decision trees in accuracy. However, from the comprehensibility aspect, decision trees are considered better. In other words, even if the researcher knows that neural network is more accurate, he still has a dilemma what method to use.

Chapter 4

Splitting Criteria

4.1 Univariate Splitting Criteria

4.1.1 *Overview*

In most decision trees inducers discrete splitting functions are univariate, i.e., an internal node is split according to the value of a single attribute. Consequently, the inducer searches for the best attribute upon which to perform the split. There are various univariate criteria which can be characterized in different ways, such as:

- according to the origin of the measure: Information Theory, Dependence, and Distance.
- according to the measure structure: Impurity Based criteria, Normalized Impurity Based criteria and Binary criteria.

The following section describes the most common criteria appearing in the literature.

4.1.2 *Impurity based Criteria*

Given a random variable x with k discrete values, distributed according to $P = (p_1, p_2, \ldots, p_k)$, an impurity measure is a function $\phi:[0, 1]^k \to R$ that satisfies the following conditions:

- $\phi(P) \geq 0$
- $\phi(P)$ is minimum if $\exists i$ such that component $p_i = 1$.
- $\phi(P)$ is maximum if $\forall i, 1 \leq i \leq k, p_i = 1/k$.
- $\phi(P)$ is symmetric with respect to components of P.
- $\phi(P)$ is smooth (differentiable everywhere) in its range.

It should be noted that if the probability vector has a component of 1 (the variable x gets only one value), then the variable is defined as pure. On the other hand, if all components are equal the level of impurity reaches maximum.

Given a training set S the probability vector of the target attribute y is defined as:

$$P_y(S) = \left(\frac{|\sigma_{y=c_1} S|}{|S|}, \ldots, \frac{|\sigma_{y=c_{|dom(y)|}} S|}{|S|} \right) \tag{4.1}$$

The goodness-of-split due to discrete attribute a_i is defined as reduction in impurity of the target attribute after partitioning S according to the values $v_{i,j} \in dom(a_i)$:

$$\Delta\Phi(a_i, S) = \phi(P_y(S)) - \sum_{j=1}^{|dom(a_i)|} \frac{|\sigma_{a_i=v_{i,j}} S|}{|S|} \cdot \phi(P_y(\sigma_{a_i=v_{i,j}} S)) \tag{4.2}$$

4.1.3   *Information Gain*

Information Gain is an impurity-based criteria that uses the entropy measure (originating from information theory) as the impurity measure [Quinlan (1987)].

$$\text{InformationGain}(a_i, S) =$$
$$Entropy(y, S) - \sum_{v_{i,j} \in dom(a_i)} \frac{|\sigma_{a_i=v_{i,j}} S|}{|S|} \cdot Entropy(y, \sigma_{a_i=v_{i,j}} S) \tag{4.3}$$

where:

$$Entropy(y, S) = \sum_{c_j \in dom(y)} -\frac{|\sigma_{y=c_j} S|}{|S|} \cdot \log_2 \frac{|\sigma_{y=c_j} S|}{|S|} \tag{4.4}$$

Information gain is closely related to the Maximum likelihood estimation (MLE), which is a popular statistical method used to make inferences about parameters of the underlying probability distribution from a given data set.

4.1.4   *Gini Index*

The Gini index is an impurity-based criteria that measures the divergences between the probability distributions of the target attributes values. The Gini index has been used in various works such as [Breiman *et al.* (1984)] and [Gelfand *et al.* (1991)] and it is defined as:

$$Gini(y, S) = 1 - \sum_{c_j \in dom(y)} \left(\frac{|\sigma_{y=c_j} S|}{|S|} \right)^2 \tag{4.5}$$

Consequently the evaluation criterion for selecting the attribute a_i is defined as:

$$GiniGain(a_i, S) = Gini(y, S) -$$
$$\sum_{v_{i,j} \in dom(a_i)} \frac{|\sigma_{a_i=v_{i,j}} S|}{|S|} \cdot Gini(y, \sigma_{a_i=v_{i,j}} S) \tag{4.6}$$

4.1.5   *Likelihood Ratio Chi-squared Statistics*

The likelihood-ratio is defined as [Attneave (1959)]

$$G^2(a_i, S) = 2 \cdot \ln(2) \cdot |S| \cdot \text{InformationGain}(a_i, S) \tag{4.7}$$

This ratio is useful for measuring the statistical significance of the information gain criterion. The zero hypothesis (H_0) is that both the input and target attributes are conditionally independent. If H_0 holds, the test statistic is distributed as χ^2 with degrees of freedom equal to: $(dom(a_i) - 1) \cdot (dom(y) - 1)$.

4.1.6   *DKM Criterion*

The DKM criterion is an impurity-based splitting criteria designed for binary class attributes [Dietterich *et al.* (1996)] and [Kearns and Mansour (1999)]. The impurity-based function is defined as:

$$DKM(y, S) = 2 \cdot \sqrt{ \left(\frac{|\sigma_{y=c_1} S|}{|S|} \right) \cdot \left(\frac{|\sigma_{y=c_2} S|}{|S|} \right) } \tag{4.8}$$

It has been theoretically proved that this criterion requires smaller trees for obtaining a certain error than other impurity-based criteria (information gain and Gini index).

4.1.7   Normalized Impurity-based Criteria

The impurity-based criterion described above is biased towards attributes with larger domain values. Namely, it prefers input attributes with many values over those with less values [Quinlan (1986)]. For instance, an input attribute that represents the national security number will probably get the highest information gain. However, adding this attribute to a decision tree will result in a poor generalized accuracy. For that reason, it is useful to "normalize" the impurity-based measures, as described in the following sections.

4.1.8   Gain Ratio

The gain ratio normalizes the information gain as follows [Quinlan (1993)]:

$$GainRatio(a_i, S) = \frac{\text{InformationGain}(a_i, S)}{Entropy(a_i, S)} \tag{4.9}$$

Note that this ratio is not defined when the denominator is zero. Furthermore, the ratio may tend to favor attributes for which the denominator is very small. Accordingly it is suggested that the ratio be carried out in two stages. First the information gain is calculated for all attributes. As a consequence of considering only attributes that have performed at least as well as the average information gain, the attribute that has obtained the best ratio gain is selected. [Quinlan (1988)] has shown that the gain ratio tends to outperform simple information gain criteria, both in accuracy and in terms of classifier complexity. A penalty is assessed for the information gain of a continuous attribute with many potential splits.

4.1.9   Distance Measure

The Distance Measure, like the Gain Ratio, normalizes the impurity measure. However, it suggests normalizing it in a different way [Lopez de Mantras (1991)]:

$$\frac{\Delta\Phi(a_i, S)}{-\sum\limits_{v_{i,j}\in dom(a_i)}\sum\limits_{c_k\in dom(y)}\frac{\left|\sigma_{a_i=v_{i,j}\ AND\ y=c_k}S\right|}{|S|}\cdot \log_2\frac{\left|\sigma_{a_i=v_{i,j}\ AND\ y=c_k}S\right|}{|S|}} \tag{4.10}$$

4.1.10 Binary Criteria

The binary criteria are used for creating binary decision trees. These measures are based on division of the input attribute domain into two subdomains.

Let $\beta(a_i, dom_1(a_i), dom_2(a_i), S)$ denote the binary criterion value for attribute a_i over sample S when $dom_1(a_i)$ and $dom_2(a_i)$ are its corresponding subdomains. The value obtained for the optimal division of the attribute domain into two mutually exclusive and exhaustive subdomains is used for comparing attributes, namely:

$$\beta^*(a_i, S) = \max_{\forall dom_1(a_i);\ dom_2(a_i)} \beta(a_i, dom_1(a_i), dom_2(a_i), S) \tag{4.11}$$

4.1.11 Twoing Criterion

The Gini index may encounter problems when the domain of the target attribute is relatively wide [Breiman *et al.* (1984)]. In such cases it is possible to employ binary criterion called twoing criterion. This criterion is defined as:

$$twoing(a_i, dom_1(a_i), dom_2(a_i), S) =$$
$$0.25 \cdot \frac{\left|\sigma_{a_i\in dom_1(a_i)}S\right|}{|S|} \cdot \frac{\left|\sigma_{a_i\in dom_2(a_i)}S\right|}{|S|} \cdot$$
$$\left(\sum_{c_i\in dom(y)}\left|\frac{\left|\sigma_{a_i\in dom_1(a_i)\ AND\ y=c_i}S\right|}{\left|\sigma_{a_i\in dom_1(a_i)}S\right|} - \frac{\left|\sigma_{a_i\in dom_2(a_i)\ AND\ y=c_i}S\right|}{\left|\sigma_{a_i\in dom_2(a_i)}S\right|}\right|\right)^2 \tag{4.12}$$

When the target attribute is binary the Gini and twoing criteria are equivalent. For multi-class problems the twoing criteria prefers attributes with evenly divided splits.

4.1.12   Orthogonal Criterion

The ORT criterion was presented by [Fayyad and Irani (1992)]. This binary criterion is defined as:

$$ORT(a_i, dom_1(a_i), dom_2(a_i), S) = 1 - cos\theta(P_{y,1}, P_{y,2}) \tag{4.13}$$

where $\theta(P_{y,1}, P_{y,2})$ is the angle between two vectors $P_{y,1}$ and $P_{y,2}$. These vectors represent the probability distribution of the target attribute in the partitions $\sigma_{a_i \in dom_1(a_i)}S$ and $\sigma_{a_i \in dom_2(a_i)}S$ respectively.

It has been shown that this criterion performs better than the information gain and the Gini index for specific constellations of problems.

4.1.13   Kolmogorov–Smirnov Criterion

A binary criterion that uses Kolmogorov–Smirnov distance has been proposed by [Friedman (1977)] and [Rounds (1980)]. Assuming a binary target attribute, namely $dom(y) = \{c_1, c_2\}$, the criterion is defined as:

$$KS(a_i, dom_1(a_i), dom_2(a_i), S) =$$
$$\left| \frac{\left| \sigma_{a_i \in dom_1(a_i) \ AND \ y=c_1} S \right|}{\left| \sigma_{y=c_1} S \right|} - \frac{\left| \sigma_{a_i \in dom_1(a_i) \ AND \ y=c_2} S \right|}{\left| \sigma_{y=c_2} S \right|} \right| \tag{4.14}$$

This measure was extended by [Utgoff and Clouse (1996)] to handle target attribute with multiple classes and missing data values. Their results indicate that the suggested method outperforms the gain ratio criteria.

4.1.14   AUC Splitting Criteria

The idea of using the AUC metric as a splitting criterion was recently proposed by [Ferri *et al.* (2002)]. The attribute that obtains the maximal area under the convex hull of the ROC curve is selected. It has been shown that the AUC-based splitting criterion outperforms other splitting criteria both with respect to classification accuracy and area under the ROC curve. It is important to note that unlike impurity criteria, this criterion does not perform a comparison between the impurity of the parent node with the weighted impurity of the children after splitting.

4.1.15 *Other Univariate Splitting Criteria*

Additional univariate splitting criteria can be found in the literature, such as permutation statistic [Li and Dubes (1986)]; mean posterior improvement [Taylor and Silverman (1993)]; and hypergeometric distribution measure [Martin (1997)].

4.1.16 *Comparison of Univariate Splitting Criteria*

Over the past 30 years, several researchers have conducted comparative studies of splitting criteria both those described above and others. Among these researchers are: [Breiman (1996)]; [Baker and Jain (1976)]; [Ben-Bassat (1978)]; [Mingers (1989)]; [Fayyad and Irani (1992)]; [Buntine and Niblett (1992)]; [Loh and Shih (1997)]; [Loh and Shih (1999)]; and [Lim *et al.* (2000)]. The majority of the comparisons are based on empirical results, although there are some theoretical conclusions.

Most of the researchers point out that in nearly all of the cases the choice of splitting criteria will not make much difference on the tree performance. As the no-free lunch theorem suggests, each criterion is superior in some cases and inferior in others.

4.2 Handling Missing Values

Missing values are a common experience in real-world datasets. This situation can complicate both induction (a training set where some of its values are missing) as well as classification of a new instance that is missing certain values.

The problem of missing values has been addressed by several researchers such as [Friedman (1977)], [Breiman *et al.* (1984)] and [Quinlan (1989)]. [Friedman (1977)] suggests handling missing values in the training set in the following way. Let $\sigma_{a_i=?}S$ indicate the subset of instances in S whose a_i values are missing. When calculating the splitting criteria using attribute a_i, simply ignore all instances whose values in attribute a_i are unknown. Instead of using the splitting criteria $\Delta\Phi(a_i, S)$ we use $\Delta\Phi(a_i, S - \sigma_{a_i=?}S)$.

On the other hand, [Quinlan (1989)] argues that in case of missing values, the splitting criteria should be reduced proportionally as nothing has been learned from these instances. In other words, instead of using the splitting criteria $\Delta\Phi(a_i, S)$, we use the following correction:

$$\frac{|S - \sigma_{a_i=?}S|}{|S|}\Delta\Phi(a_i, S - \sigma_{a_i=?}S). \tag{4.15}$$

In cases where the criterion value is normalized (as in the case of gain ratio), the denominator should be calculated as if the missing values represent an additional value in the attribute domain. For instance, the gain ratio with missing values should be calculated as follows:

$$GainRatio(a_i, S) = \frac{\frac{|S - \sigma_{a_i=?}S|}{|S|}InformationGain(a_i, S - \sigma_{a_i=?}S)}{-\frac{|\sigma_{a_i=?}S|}{|S|}\log(\frac{|\sigma_{a_i=?}S|}{|S|}) - \sum\limits_{v_{i,j}\in dom(a_i)}\frac{|\sigma_{a_i=v_{i,j}}S|}{|S|}\log(\frac{|\sigma_{a_i=v_{i,j}}S|}{|S|})} \tag{4.16}$$

Once a node is split, [Quinlan (1989)] suggests adding $\sigma_{a_i=?}S$ to each one of the outgoing edges with the following corresponding weight: $|\sigma_{a_i=v_{i,j}}S|/|S - \sigma_{a_i=?}S|$.

The same idea is used for classifying a new instance with missing attribute values. When an instance encounters a node where its splitting criteria can be evaluated due to a missing value, it is passed through to all outgoing edges. The predicted class will be the class with the highest probability in the weighted union of all the leaf nodes at which this instance ends up.

Another approach known as *surrogate splits* was presented by [Breiman *et al.* (1984)] and is implemented in the CART algorithm. The idea is to find for each split in the tree a surrogate split which uses a different input attribute and which most resembles the original split. If the value of the input attribute used in the original split is missing, then it is possible to use the surrogate split. The resemblance between two binary splits over sample S is formally defined as:

$$res(a_i, dom_1(a_i), dom_2(a_i), a_j, dom_1(a_j), dom_2(a_j), S) =$$
$$\frac{|\sigma_{a_i\in dom_1(a_i)\ AND\ a_j\in dom_1(a_j)}S|}{|S|} + \frac{|\sigma_{a_i\in dom_2(a_i)\ AND\ a_j\in dom_2(a_j)}S|}{|S|} \tag{4.17}$$

where the first split refers to attribute a_i and it splits $dom(a_i)$ into $dom_1(a_i)$ and $dom_2(a_i)$. The alternative split refers to attribute a_j and splits its domain to $dom_1(a_j)$ and $dom_2(a_j)$.

The missing value can be estimated based on other instances [Loh and Shih (1997)]. On the learning phase, if the value of a nominal attribute

a_i in tuple q is missing, then it is estimated by its mode over all instances having the same target attribute value. Formally,

$$estimate(a_i, y_q, S) = \underset{v_{i,j} \in dom(a_i)}{\operatorname{argmax}} \left| \sigma_{a_i = v_{i,j} \ AND \ y = y_q} S \right| \qquad (4.18)$$

where y_q denotes the value of the target attribute in the tuple q. If the missing attribute a_i is numeric, then, instead of using mode of a_i, it is more appropriate to use its mean.

Chapter 5

Pruning Trees

5.1 Stopping Criteria

The growing phase continues until a stopping criterion is triggered. The following conditions are common stopping rules:

(1) All instances in the training set belong to a single value of y.
(2) The maximum tree depth has been reached.
(3) The number of cases in the terminal node is less than the minimum number of cases for parent nodes.
(4) If the node were split, the number of cases in one or more child nodes would be less than the minimum number of cases for child nodes.
(5) The best splitting criteria is not greater than a certain threshold.

5.2 Heuristic Pruning

5.2.1 *Overview*

Employing tight stopping criteria tends to create small and underfitted decision trees. On the other hand, using loose stopping criteria tends to generate large decision trees that are overfitted to the training set. To solve this dilemma, [Breiman *et al.* (1984)] developed a pruning methodology based on a loose stopping criterion and allowing the decision tree to overfit the training set. Then the overfitted tree is cut back into a smaller tree by removing sub-branches that are not contributing to the generalization accuracy. It has been shown in various studies that pruning methods can improve the generalization performance of a decision tree, especially in noisy domains.

Another key motivation of pruning is "trading accuracy for simplicity" as presented by [Bratko and Bohanec (1994)]. When the goal is to produce a sufficiently accurate, compact concept description, pruning is highly useful. Since within this process the initial decision tree is seen as a completely accurate one, the accuracy of a pruned decision tree indicates how close it is to the initial tree.

There are various techniques for pruning decision trees. Most perform top down or bottom up traversal of the nodes. A node is pruned if this operation improves a certain criteria. The following subsections describe the most popular techniques.

5.2.2   *Cost Complexity Pruning*

Cost complexity pruning (also known as weakest link pruning or error complexity pruning) proceeds in two stages [Breiman *et al.* (1984)]. In the first stage, a sequence of trees $T_0, T_1, \ldots, T_k$ is built on the training data where T_0 is the original tree before pruning and T_k is the root tree.

In the second stage, one of these trees is chosen as the pruned tree, based on its generalization error estimation.

The tree T_{i+1} is obtained by replacing one or more of the sub-trees in the predecessor tree T_i with suitable leaves. The sub-trees that are pruned are those that obtain the lowest increase in apparent error rate per pruned leaf:

$$\alpha = \frac{\varepsilon(pruned(T,t),S) - \varepsilon(T,S)}{|leaves(T)| - |leaves(pruned(T,t))|} \tag{5.1}$$

where $\varepsilon(T,S)$ indicates the error rate of the tree T over the sample S and $|leaves(T)|$ denotes the number of leaves in T. $pruned(T,t)$ denotes the tree obtained by replacing the node t in T with a suitable leaf.

In the second phase, the generalization error of each pruned tree $T_0, T_1, \ldots, T_k$ is estimated. The best pruned tree is then selected. If the given dataset is large enough, the authors suggest breaking it into a training set and a pruning set. The trees are constructed using the training set and evaluated on the pruning set. On the other hand, if the given dataset is not large enough, they propose using cross-validation methodology, despite the computational complexity implications.

5.2.3 Reduced Error Pruning

A simple procedure for pruning decision trees, known as Reduced Error Pruning, has been suggested by [Quinlan (1987)]. While traversing over the internal nodes from the bottom to the top, the procedure checks each internal node to determine whether replacing it with the most frequent class does not reduce the trees accuracy. The node is pruned if accuracy is not reduced. The procedure continues until any further pruning would decrease the accuracy.

In order to estimate the accuracy [Quinlan (1987)] proposes using a pruning set. It can be shown that this procedure ends with the smallest accurate sub-tree with respect to a given pruning set.

5.2.4 Minimum Error Pruning (MEP)

Minimum error pruning, proposed by [Niblett and Bratko (1986)], involves bottom-up traversal of the internal nodes. This technique compares, in each node, the l-probability error rate estimation with and without pruning.

The l-probability error rate estimation is a correction to the simple probability estimation using frequencies. If S_t denotes the instances that have reached a leaf t, then the expected error rate in this leaf is:

$$\varepsilon'(t) = 1 - \max_{c_i \in dom(y)} \frac{|\sigma_{y=c_i} S_t| + l \cdot p_{apr}(y = c_i)}{|S_t| + l} \tag{5.2}$$

where $p_{apr}(y = c_i)$ is the *a-priori* probability of y getting the value c_i, and l denotes the weight given to the *a-priori* probability.

The error rate of an internal node is the weighted average of the error rate of its branches. The weight is determined according to the proportion of instances along each branch. The calculation is performed recursively up to the leaves.

If an internal node is pruned, then it becomes a leaf and its error rate is calculated directly using the last equation. Consequently, we can compare the error rate before and after pruning a certain internal node. If pruning this node does not increase the error rate, the pruning should be accepted.

5.2.5 Pessimistic Pruning

Pessimistic pruning avoids the need of a pruning set or cross validation and uses the pessimistic statistical correlation test instead [Quinlan (1993)].

The basic idea is that the error ratio that was estimated using the training set is not reliable enough. Instead, a more realistic measure, known as the continuity correction for binomial distribution, should be used:

$$\varepsilon'(T,S) = \varepsilon(T,S) + \frac{|leaves(T)|}{2 \cdot |S|} \tag{5.3}$$

However, this correction still produces an optimistic error rate. Consequently, [Quinlan (1993)] suggests pruning an internal node t if its error rate is within one standard error from a reference tree, namely:

$$\varepsilon'(pruned(T,t),S) \leq \varepsilon'(T,S) + \sqrt{\frac{\varepsilon'(T,S) \cdot (1 - \varepsilon'(T,S))}{|S|}} \tag{5.4}$$

The last condition is based on the statistical confidence interval for proportions. Usually the last condition is used such that T refers to a subtree whose root is the internal node t and S denotes the portion of the training set that refers to the node t.

The pessimistic pruning procedure performs top-down traversal over the internal nodes. If an internal node is pruned, then all its descendants are removed from the pruning process, resulting in a relatively fast pruning.

5.2.6   *Error-Based Pruning (EBP)*

Error-based pruning is an evolution of the pessimistic pruning. It is implemented in the well-known C4.5 algorithm.

As in pessimistic pruning, the error rate is estimated using the upper bound of the statistical confidence interval for proportions.

$$\varepsilon_{UB}(T,S) = \varepsilon(T,S) + Z_\alpha \cdot \sqrt{\frac{\varepsilon(T,S) \cdot (1 - \varepsilon(T,S))}{|S|}} \tag{5.5}$$

where $\varepsilon(T,S)$ denotes the misclassification rate of the tree T on the training set S; Z is the inverse of the standard normal cumulative distribution; and α is the desired significance level.

Let $subtree(T,t)$ denote the subtree rooted by the node t. Let $maxchild(T,t)$ denote the most frequent child node of t (namely most of the instances in S reach this particular child) and let S_t denote all instances

in S that reach the node t. The procedure traverses bottom-up all nodes
and compares the following values:

(1) $\varepsilon_{UB}(subtree(T,t), S_t)$
(2) $\varepsilon_{UB}(pruned(subtree(T,t), t), S_t)$
(3) $\varepsilon_{UB}(subtree(T, maxchild(T,t)), S_{maxchild(T,t)})$

According to the lowest value, the procedure either leaves the tree as
is; prune the node t; or replaces the node t with the subtree rooted by
$maxchild(T,t)$.

5.2.7 *Minimum Description Length (MDL) Pruning*

The Minimum Description Length can be used for evaluating the generalized accuracy of a node [Rissanen (1989)], [Quinlan and Rivest (1989)]
and [Mehta *et al.* (1995)]. This method measures the size of a decision tree
by means of the number of bits required to encode the tree. The MDL
method prefers decision trees that can be encoded with fewer bits. [Mehta
et al. (1995)] indicate that the cost of a split at a leaf t can be estimated
as:

$$\text{Cost}(t) = \sum_{c_i \in dom(y)} |\sigma_{y=c_i} S_t| \cdot \ln \frac{|S_t|}{|\sigma_{y=c_i} S_t|} + \frac{|dom(y)|-1}{2} \ln \frac{|S_t|}{2} + \\ \ln \frac{\pi^{\frac{|dom(y)|}{2}}}{\Gamma(\frac{|dom(y)|}{2})} \tag{5.6}$$

where S_t denotes the instances that have reached node t. The splitting
cost of an internal node is calculated based on the cost aggregation of its
children.

5.2.8 *Other Pruning Methods*

There are other pruning methods reported in the literature. [Wallace
and Patrick (1993)] proposed a Minimum Message Length (MML) pruning
method while [Kearns and Mansour (1998)] provide a theoretically-justified
pruning algorithm. [Mingers (1989)] proposed the Critical Value Pruning
(CVP). This method, which prunes an internal node if its splitting criterion
is not greater than a certain threshold, is similar to a stopping criterion.
However, contrary to a stopping criterion, a node is not pruned if at least
one of its children does not fulfill the pruning criterion.

5.2.9 *Comparison of Pruning Methods*

Several studies compare the performance of different pruning techniques: ([Quinlan (1987)], [Mingers (1989)] and [Esposito *et al.* (1997)]). The results indicate that some methods (such as Cost-Complexity Pruning, Reduced Error Pruning) tend to over-pruning, i.e. creating smaller but less accurate decision trees. Other methods (like error-based pruning, pessimistic error pruning and minimum error pruning) bias toward under-pruning. Most of the comparisons concluded that the no free lunch theorem also applies to pruning, namely, there is no pruning method that outperforms other pruning methods.

5.3 Optimal Pruning

The issue of finding the optimal pruning method has been studied by [Bratko and Bohanec (1994)] and [Almuallim (1996)]. [Bratko and Bohanec (1994)] introduce an algorithm which guarantees optimality, knows as OPT. This algorithm finds the optimal pruning technique based on dynamic programming, with the complexity of $\Theta(|leaves(T)|^2)$, where T is the initial decision tree. [Almuallim (1996)] introduced an improvement of OPT called OPT-2, which also performs optimal pruning using dynamic programming. However, the time and space complexities of OPT-2 are both $\Theta(|leaves(T^*)| \cdot |internal(T)|)$, where T^* is the target (pruned) decision tree and T is the initial decision tree.

Since the pruned tree is habitually much smaller than the initial tree and the number of internal nodes is smaller than the number of leaves, OPT-2 is usually more efficient than OPT in terms of computational complexity.

According to Almuallim, when pruning a given decision tree (DT) with s leaves, it is common to progressively replace various sub-trees of DT by leaves, thus leading to a sequence of pruned decision trees, DT_{s-1}, $DT_{s-2}, \ldots, DT_i, \ldots, DT_1$, such that each DT_i has at most i leaves. When seeing the error as the difference from the original tree *(DT)*, the trees in the sequence are of increasing error. The goal in choosing the best tree from the above sequence of pruned trees, according to some appropriate criteria, is to achieve a good balance between the trees size and accuracy.

In their paper, [Bratko and Bohanec (1994)] address the following problem: "Given a completely accurate but complex definition of a concept, simplify the definition, possibly at the expanse of accuracy, so that the simplified definition still corresponds to the concept 'sufficiently' well". In this context "concepts" are represented by decision trees and the method of simplification is tree pruning. Therefore, the problem can be stated as: "Given a decision tree that accurately specifies a concept, the problem is to find the smallest pruned tree that still represents the concept within some specified accuracy".

In (Almuallim, 1996) a new algorithm, OPT-2, which also performs optimal pruning, is introduced. The problem of optimal pruning is formally presented in this paper as follows: "Given a decision tree DT and a positive integer C, find a pruned decision tree DT' from DT such that $s(DT') \leq C$ and error(DT') is minimized." where $s(DT')$ is the size of DT' (number of leaves in DT') and error(DT') is the proportion of cases that are incorrectly handled by DT'.

The OPT-2 algorithm is based on dynamic programming. In its most basic form, the time and space complexities of OPT-2 are both $\Theta(nC)$, where n is the number of internal nodes in the initial decision tree and C is the number of leaves in the target (pruned) decision tree. This is an improvement of the OPT algorithm presented by Bohanec and Bratko (1994). One important characteristic of the OPT-2 algorithm is its significant flexibility. The OPT-2 works sequentially, generating the trees of the sequence one after the other in increasing order of the number of leaves (that is in the order $DT_1, DT_2, DT_3, \ldots$). This differs from OPT which simultaneously generates the whole sequence of pruned trees. Sequence generation in OPT-2 can be terminated once a tree with adequate predetermined criteria is found.

Given that trees $DT_1, DT_2, \ldots, DT_{i-1}$ have already been generated, OPT-2 finds DT_i in time $\Theta(n)$, where n is the number of the internal nodes of the initial decision tree. Thus if the number of leaves of the target tree is C, the total running time of OPT-2 will be $\Theta(nC)$. Since the goal is to prune the tree, C is habitually much smaller then s. Additionally, n is smaller than s, specifically in the case of attributes with many values. Hence, OPT-2 is usually more efficient than OPT in terms of execution time.

Although both OPT and OPT-2 are based on dynamic programming the two algorithms differ substantially in the way the problem is divided into sub-problems. The approach adopted in OPT is usually viewed as a "bottom-up" approach, where the idea is to compute solutions for the sub-trees rooted at the lowest level of the tree. These solutions are then used to compute the nodes of the next upper level. This process is repeated until the root of the initial tree is reached. A basic characteristic of this "bottom-up" approach is that the trees DT_i of the pruning sequence are simultaneously computed as we advance towards the root. These pruned trees are not final unless we reach the root. However, once it is reached, the whole sequence becomes available at once.

The OPT-2 produces the pruned trees one after the other using an algorithm derivative of a dynamic programming method given by Johnson & Niemi (1983). Unlike the bottom-up approach of OPT, processing in OPT-2 is done in a left to right fashion: Given that we have already computed trees $DT_1, DT_2, \ldots, DT_{i-1}$ and that necessary intermediate results for these computations are kept in memory the OPT-2 algorithm finds DT_i from these through a linear 'left to right' pass over the tree.

In optimal pruning the error of each DT_i in the sequence should be a minimum over all pruned trees of i (or less) leaves. To date, the only two works that address optimal pruning are Bohanec and Bratko's paper (1994) and Almuallim's paper (1996).

Chapter 6

Advanced Decision Trees

6.1 Survey of Common Algorithms for Decision Tree Induction

6.1.1 *ID3*

The ID3 algorithm is considered to be a very simple decision tree algorithm [Quinlan (1986)]. Using information gain as splitting criteria, the ID3 ceases to grow when all instances belong to a single value of a target feature or when best information gain is not greater than zero. ID3 does not apply any pruning procedure nordoes it handle numeric attributes or missing values.

6.1.2 *C4.5*

C4.5, an evolution of ID3, presented by the same author [Quinlan (1993)], uses gain ratio as splitting criteria. The splitting ceases when the number of instances to be split is below a certain threshold. Error-based pruning is performed after the growing phase. C4.5 can handle numeric attributes. It can also induce from a training set that incorporates missing values by using corrected gain ratio criteria as presented above.

6.1.3 *CART*

CART stands for Classification and Regression Trees. It was developed by [Breiman *et al.* (1984)] and is characterized by the fact that it constructs binary trees, namely each internal node has exactly two outgoing edges. The splits are selected using the Twoing Criteria and the obtained tree is pruned by Cost-Complexity Pruning. When provided, CART can consider misclassification costs in the tree induction. It also enables users to provide prior probability distribution.

An important feature of CART is its ability to generate regression trees. In regression trees, the leafs predict a real number and not a class. In case of regression, CART looks for splits that minimize the prediction squared error (the least-squared deviation). The prediction in each leaf is based on the weighted mean for node.

6.1.4   *CHAID*

Starting from the early Seventies, researchers in applied statistics developed procedures for generating decision trees, such as: AID [Sonquist *et al.* (1971)]; MAID [Gillo (1972)]; THAID [Morgan and Messenger (1973)]; and CHAID [Kass (1980)]. CHIAD (Chi-squared-Automatic-Interaction-Detection) was originally designed to handle nominal attributes only. For each input attribute a_i, CHAID finds the pair of values in V_i that is least significantly different with respect to the target attribute. The significant difference is measured by the p value obtained from a statistical test. The statistical test used depends on the type of target attribute. An F test is used if the target attribute is continuous; a Pearson chi-squared test if it is nominal; and a likelihood ratio test if it is ordinal.

For each selected pair of values, CHAID checks if the p value obtained is greater than a certain merge threshold. If the answer is positive, it merges the values and searches for an additional potential pair to be merged. The process is repeated until no significant pairs are found.

The best input attribute to be used for splitting the current node is then selected, such that each child node is made of a group of homogeneous values of the selected attribute. Note that no split is performed if the adjusted p value of the best input attribute is not less than a certain split threshold. This procedure stops also when one of the following conditions is fulfilled:

(1) Maximum tree depth is reached.
(2) Minimum number of cases in a node for being a parent is reached, so it can not be split any further.
(3) Minimum number of cases in a node for being a child node is reached.

CHAID handles missing values by treating them all as a single valid category. CHAID does not perform pruning.

6.1.5 *QUEST*

The QUEST (Quick, Unbiased, Efficient Statistical Tree) algorithm supports univariate and linear combination splits [Loh and Shih (1997)]. For each split, the association between each input attribute and the target attribute is computed using the ANOVA F-test or Levene's test (for ordinal and continuous attributes) or Pearson's chi-square (for nominal attributes). An ANOVA F-statistic is computed for each attribute. If the largest F-statistic exceeds a predefined threshold value, the attribute with the largest F-value is selected to split the node. Otherwise, Levene's test for unequal variances is computed for every attribute. If the largest Levene is greater than a predefined threshold value, the attribute with the largest Levene value is used to split the node. If no attribute exceeded either threshold, the node is split using the attribute with the largest ANOVA F-value.

If the target attribute is multinomial, two-means clustering is used to create two super-classes. The attribute that obtains the highest association with the target attribute is selected for splitting. Quadratic Discriminant Analysis (QDA) is applied to find the optimal splitting point for the input attribute. QUEST has negligible bias and yields a binary decision tree. Ten-fold cross-validation is used to prune the trees.

6.1.6 *Reference to Other Algorithms*

Table 6.1 describes other decision tree algorithms available in the literature. Although there are many other algorithms which are not included in this table, nevertheless, most are a variation of the algorithmic framework presented above. A profound comparison of the above algorithms and many others has been conducted in [Lim *et al.* (2000)].

6.1.7 *Advantages and Disadvantages of Decision Trees*

Several advantages of the decision tree as a classification tool appear in the literature:

(1) Decision trees are self-explanatory and when compacted they are also easy to follow. That is to say, if the decision tree has a reasonable number of leaves it can be grasped by non-professional users. Furthermore, since decision trees can be converted to a set of rules, this sort of representation is considered as comprehensible.

(2) Decision trees can handle both nominal and numeric input attributes.

Table 6.1   Additional Decision Tree Inducers.

Algorithm	Description	Reference
CAL5	Designed specifically for numerical-valued attributes	[Muller and Wysotzki (1994)]
FACT	An earlier version of QUEST. Uses statistical tests to select an attribute for splitting each node and then uses discriminant analysis to find the split point.	[Loh and Vanichsetakul (1988)]
LMDT	Constructs a decision tree based on multivariate tests which are linear combinations of the attributes.	[Brodley and Utgoff (1995)]
T1	A one-level decision tree that classifies instances using only one attribute. Missing values are treated as a "special value". Support both continuous an nominal attributes.	[Holte (1993)]
PUBLIC	Integrates the growing and pruning by using MDL cost in order to reduce the computational complexity.	[Rastogi and Shim (2000)]
MARS	A multiple regression function is approximated using linear splines and their tensor products.	[Friedman (1991)]

(3) Decision tree representation is rich enough to represent any discrete-value classifier.
(4) Decision trees can handle datasets that may have errors.
(5) Decision trees can deal with handle datasets that may have missing values.
(6) Decision trees are considered to be a nonparametric method, i.e., decisions tress do not include any assumptions about the space distribution and on the classifier structure.
(7) When classification cost is high, decision trees may be attractive in that they ask only for the values of the features along a single path from the root to a leaf.

Among the disadvantages of decision trees are:

(1) Most of the algorithms (like ID3 and C4.5) require that the target attribute will have only discrete values.

(2) As decision trees use the "divide and conquer" method, they tend to perform well if a few highly relevant attributes exist, but less so if many complex interactions are present. One of the reasons for this happening is that other classifiers can compactly describe a classifier that would be very challenging to represent using a decision tree. A simple illustration of this phenomenon is the replication problem of decision trees [Pagallo and Huassler (1990)]. Since most decision trees divide the instance space into mutually exclusive regions to represent a concept, in some cases the tree should contain several duplications of the same subtree in order to represent the classifier. The replication problem forces duplication of subtrees into disjunctive concepts For instance, if the concept follows the following binary function: $y = (A_1 \cap A_2) \cup (A_3 \cap A_4)$ then the minimal univariate decision tree that represents this function is illustrated in Figure 6.1. Note that the tree contains two copies of the same subtree.

(3) The greedy characteristic of decision trees leads to another disadvantage that should be pointed out. The over-sensitivity to the training set, to irrelevant attributes and to noise [Quinlan (1993)] make decision trees especially unstable: a minor change in one split close to the root will change the whole subtree below. Due to small variations in the training set, the algorithm may choose an attribute which is not truly the best one.

(4) The fragmentation problem causes partitioning of the data into smaller fragments. This usually happens if many features are tested along the path. If the data splits approximately equally on every split, then a univariate decision tree cannot test more than $O(logn)$ features. This puts decision trees at a disadvantage for tasks with many relevant features. Note that replication always implies fragmentation, but fragmentation may happen without any replication

(5) Another problem refers to the effort needed to deal with missing values [Friedman *et al.* (1996)]. While the ability to handle missing values is considered to be advantage, the extreme effort which is required to achieve it is considered a drawback. The correct branch to take is unknown if a feature tested is missing, and the algorithm must employ special mechanisms to handle missing values. In order to reduce the occurrences of tests on missing values, C4.5 penalizes the information gain by the proportion of unknown instances and then splits these instances into subtrees. CART uses a much more complex scheme of surrogate features.

(6) The myopic nature of most of the decision tree induction algorithms is reflected by the fact that the inducers look only one level ahead. Specifically, the splitting criterion ranks possible attributes based on their immediate descendants. Such strategy prefers tests that score high in isolation and may overlook combinations of attributes. Using deeper lookahead strategies is considered to be computationally expensive and has not proven useful.

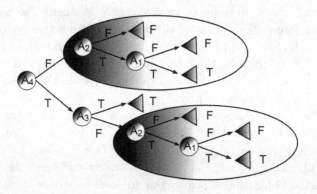

Fig. 6.1   Illustration of Decision Tree with Replication.

6.1.8 *Oblivious Decision Trees*

Oblivious decision trees are those in which all nodes at the same level test the same feature. Despite its restriction, oblivious decision trees are effective for feature selection. [Almuallim and Dietterich (1994)] as well as [Schlimmer (1993)] have proposed a forward feature selection procedure by constructing oblivious decision trees, whereas [Langley and Sage (1994)] suggested backward selection using the same means. [Kohavi and Sommerfield (1998)] have shown that oblivious decision trees can be converted to a decision table. Recently [Maimon and Last (2000)] suggested a new algorithm IFN (Information Fuzzy Network) for constructing oblivious decision trees. Based on information theory, the main advantage of IFN is it compactness. In regular decision trees, like CART the height of a decision tree may exceed the number of input attributes. In IFN the height of a decision tree will never exceed the number of input attributes.

Figure 6.2 illustrates a typical oblivious decision tree with four input features: Glucose level (G), Age (A), Hypertension (H) and Pregnant (P) and the Boolean target feature representing whether that patient suffers from diabetes. Each layer is uniquely associated with an input feature by representing the interaction of that feature and the input features of the previous layers. The number that appears in the terminal nodes indicates the number of instances that fit this path. For example, regarding patients whose glucose level is less than 107 and whose age is greater than 50, ten are positively diagnosed with diabetes while two are not diagnosed with diabetes.

The principal difference between the oblivious decision tree and a regular decision tree structure is the constant ordering of input attributes at every terminal node of the oblivious decision tree. This latter property is necessary for minimizing the overall subset of input attributes (resulting in dimensionality reduction). The arcs that connect the terminal nodes and the nodes of the target layer are labelled with the number of records that fit this path.

An oblivious decision tree is usually built by a greedy algorithm, which tries to maximize the mutual information measure in every layer. The recursive search for explaining attributes is terminated when there is no attribute that explains the target with statistical significance.

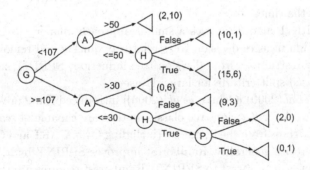

Fig. 6.2   Illustration of Oblivious Decision Tree.

6.1.9   *Decision Trees Inducers for Large Datasets*

With the recent growth in the amount of data collected by information systems there is a need for decision trees that can handle large datasets. [Catlett (1991)] has examined two methods for efficiently growing decision trees from a large database by reducing the computation complexity required for induction. However, the Catlett method requires that all data will be loaded into the main memory before induction. Namely, the largest dataset that can be induced is bounded by the memory size. [Fifield (1992)] suggests parallel implementation of the ID3 algorithm. However, like Catlett it assumes that all dataset can fit in the main memory. [Chan and Stolfo (1997)] suggest partioning the datasets into several disjointed datasets so that each dataset is loaded separately into the memory and used to induce a decision tree. The decision trees are then combined to create a single classifier. However, the experimental results indicate that partition may reduce the classification performance. This means that the classification accuracy of the combined decision trees is not as good as the accuracy of a single decision tree induced from the entire dataset.

The SLIQ algorithm [Mehta *et al.* (1996)] does not require loading the entire dataset into the main memory. Instead it uses a secondary memory (disk). In other words, a certain instance is not necessarily resident in the main memory all the time. While SLIQ creates a single decision tree from the entire dataset, this method also has an upper limit for the largest dataset that can be processed. Because it uses a data structure that scales with the dataset size, this data structure must be resident in the main memory all the time.

The SPRINT algorithm uses a similar approach [Shafer *et al.* (1996)]. This algorithm induces decision trees relatively quickly and removes all of the memory restrictions from decision tree induction. SPRINT scales any impurity-based split criteria for large datasets.

Gehrke *et al.*(2000) [Gehrke *et al.* (2000)] introduced RainForest; a unifying framework for decision tree classifiers that are capable of scaling any specific algorithms from the literature (including C4.5, CART and CHAID). In addition to its generality, RainForest improves SPRINT by a factor of three. However, in contrast to SPRINT, RainForest requires a certain minimum amount of main memory proportional to the set of distinct values in a column of the input relation. This requirement, though, is considered modest and reasonable.

Other decision tree inducers for large datasets can be found in the works of [Alsabti *et al.* (1998)], [Freitas and Lavington (1998)] and [Gehrke *et al.* (1999)].

6.1.10 *Online Adaptive Decision Trees*

A classification scheme called online adaptive decision trees (OADT) was proposed by [Basak (2004)]. As with the decision trees, OADT is a tree-structured network which is capable of online learning like neural networks. This leads to better generalization scores.

The fact that OADT can only handle two-class classification tasks with a given structure is a major drawback. The ExOADT algorithm [Basak (2006)] can handle multiclass classification tasks and is able to perform function approximation. ExOADT is structurally similar to OADT extended with a regression layer.

6.1.11 *Lazy Tree*

In lazy tree algorithms learning is delayed until the query point is observed [Friedman *et al.* (1996)]. An ad hoc decision tree (actually a rule) is constructed just to classify a certain instance. The LazyDT algorithm constructs the best decision tree for each test instance. In practice, only a path needs to be constructed. A caching scheme makes the algorithm run fast.

With the LazyDT algorithm, a single decision tree built from the training set offers a compromise: the test at the root of each subtree is chosen to be the best split on average. This "average" approach can lead to many irrelevant splits for a given test instance, thus fragmenting the data unnecessarily. Such fragmentation reduces the significance of tests at lower levels since they are based on fewer instances. Classification paths, built for a specific instance may be much shorter and hence may provide a better explanation.

A generic pseudo-code of the LazyDT algorithm is described in Figure 6.3. The lazy decision tree algorithm, which gets the test instance as part of the input, follows a separate-and-classify methodology: a test is selected and the sub-problem containing the instances with the same test outcome as the given instance is then solved recursively.

Require: x (an unlabelled instance I to classify), S (training set)

Ensure: A label for instance x

1: If all instances in S have label l, then return l.

2: if all instances in S have the same feature values, return the majority class in S .

3: select a test A and let v be the value of the test on the instance x. recursively apply the algorithm to the set of instances in S with $A = v$.

Fig. 6.3   The LazyDT Algorithm.

6.1.12   *Option Tree*

Regular decision trees make a single test at each node and trace a single path corresponding to test outcomes until a leaf is reached and a prediction is made. Option decision trees (also known as and-or trees), first introduced by [Buntine (1992)], generalize regular decision trees by allowing option nodes in addition to decision nodes; such nodes make it possible to conduct several possible tests instead of the commonly used single test. Classification is similar to regular decision trees, except that a rule is applied to option nodes to combine the predictions of the children nodes.

There are several reasons for using option trees. Option decision trees can reduce the error of decision trees in handling real-world problems by combining multiple options. This is similar to what we find when implementing ensemble methods that learn multiple models and combine the predictions. However, unlike ensemble methods, an option decision tree yields a single tree, which is a compact representation of many possible trees and which can be easily interpreted by humans. The myopic nature of top-down classification tree inducers and the stability of the classifiers are the reasons for the option decision trees improved performance compared to regular decision trees.

Figure 6.4 illustrates an option tree. Recall that the task is to classify mortgage applications into: approved ("A"), denied ("D") or manual underwriting ("M"). The tree looks like any other decision tree with a supplement of an option node, which is denoted as a rectangle. If years at current job (YRSJOB) is greater than or equals two years, then there are two options to choose from. Each option leads to a different subtree that separately solve the problem and make a classification.

In order to classify a new instance with an option tree, it is required to weight the labels predicted by all children of the option node. For example,

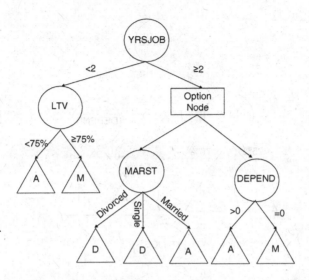

Fig. 6.4   Illustration of Option Tree.

in order to classify an instance with YRSJOB=3, MARST="Married" and
DEPEND=3, we need to combine the fifth leaf and the sixth leaf (from left
to right), resulting in the class "A" (since both are associated with class
"A"). On the other hand, in order to classify an instance with YRSJOB=3,
MARST="Single" and DEPEND=3, then we need to combine the fourth
leaf and sixth leaf, resulting in either class "A" or "D". Since in simple
majority voting, the final class is selected arbitrarily, it never makes sense
to create an option node with two children; Consequently the minimum
number of choices for an option node is three. Nevertheless, assuming
that a probability vector is associated with each leaf, it is possible to use
a Bayesian combination to obtain a non-arbitrary selection. In fact the
model presented in Figure 6.4 can be seen as combining the two regular
decision trees presented in Figure 6.5.

TDDTOP is a Top-Down Decision-Tree (TDDT) inducer which is quite
similar to C4.5 but with the additional ability to create option nodes [Ko-
havi and Kunz (1997)]. The principal modication to the basic TDDT algorithm is that instead of always selecting a single test, when several tests
evaluate close to the best test, the TDDTOP algorithm creates an option
node. All the data is sent to each child of an option node, which then splits
the data according to its predetermined test. As for the pruning phase, the

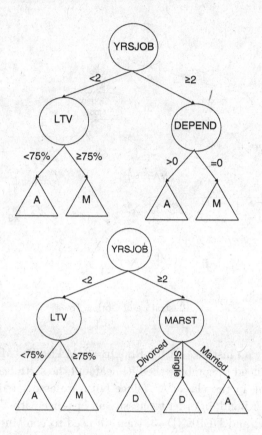

Fig. 6.5 Illustration of two Regular Trees which are equivalent to the Option Tree presented in Figure 6.4.

C4.5 pruning algorithm was modified so that the pessimistic error of an option node was the average of the pessimistic errors of its children.

6.2   Lookahead

The splitting criteria in regular top-down decision tree inducers is usually greedy and local. Fixed-depth lookahead search is a standard technique for improving greedy algorithms. More extensive search quickly leads to intolerable time consumption. Moreover, limited lookahead search does not produce significantly better decision trees [Murthy and Salzberg (1995)]. On average, it produces trees with approximately the same generalization error and size as greedy induction. In fact pruning methods are usually at least as beneficial as limited lookahead.

Figure 6.6 specifies an algorithm of lookahead splitting criterion by wrapping a regular splitting criterion (denoted as SimpleSplitCriterion). Note that the proposed algorithm performs a lookahead of *Depth* levels.

Require: S - training set, $f(a)$ - a function of the input attributes values, $SimpleSplitCriterion$ - a splitting criterion function, $Depth$ - the lookahead depth.

Ensure: The lookahead criterion value

1: **if** $Depth = 1$ **then**
2:     return SimpleSplitCriterion(S,f(A))
3: **end if**
4: Split S into subsets $S_1,...,S_k$ according to the values of f(A).
5: **for all** subset S_i **do**
6:     Find a function $g(A)$ of the input attributes values which gets the best value v_i of $LookAhead(S_i, g(A), SimpleSplitCriterion, Depth - 1)$
7: **end for**
8: Return weighted average of v_i

Fig. 6.6   Algorithm for calculating lookahead splitting criterion.

LSID3 [Esmeir and Markovitch (2004)], a variation of the well known ID3 algorithm, invests more resources for making better split decisions. For every possible candidate split, LSID3 estimates the size of the resulting subtree, and prefers the one with the smallest expected size. For this purpose it uses a sample of the space of trees rooted at the evaluated attribute. The sample is obtained by selecting attributes with a probability proportional to its information gain.

6.3   Oblique Decision Trees

Regular top-down decision trees inducers, such as C4.5, use only a single attribute in each node. Consequently these algorithms are partitioning the instance space using only axis-parallel separating surfaces (typically, hyperplanes). Several cases presented in the literature use multivariate splitting criteria.

In multivariate splitting criteria, several attributes may participate in a single node split test. Obviously, finding the best multivariate criteria is more complicated than finding the best univariate split. Furthermore, although this type of criteria may dramatically improve the trees performance, these criteria are much less popular than the univariate criteria.

Figure 6.7 presents a typical algorithmic framework for top-down inducing of oblique decision trees. Note that this algorithm is very similar to that presented in Figure 2.1. But, instead of looking for a split with a single attribute, it looks for the best function of the input attributes. In each iteration, the algorithm considers the partition of the training set using the outcome of a discrete function of the input attributes. The selection of the most appropriate function is made according to some splitting measures. After the selection of an appropriate split, each node further subdivides the training set into smaller subsets, until no split gains sufficient splitting measures or a stopping criterion is satisfied. Because there are endless functions, the main challenge is to decide on which functions the algorithm should concentrate.

Most of the Multivariate Splitting Criteria are based on the linear combination of the input attributes. In this case the algorithm constructs hyperplanes that are oblique, that is, not parallel to a coordinate axis. Figure 6.8 illustrates an Oblique Decision Tree. The left node in the second level tests a linear combination of the two input attributes $3 \cdot YRSJOB - 2 \cdot DEPEND$. It is reasonable to assume that oblique decision trees would require several less planes then a regular decision tree, resulting in a smaller tree.

Finding the best linear combination can be performed using greedy search ([Breiman *et al.* (1984)], [Murthy (1998)]); linear programming ([Duda and Hart (1973)], [Bennett and Mangasarian (1994)]); linear discriminant analysis ([Duda and Hart (1973)], [Friedman (1977)], [Sklansky and Wassel (1981)], [Lin and Fu (1983)],[Loh and Vanichsetakul (1988)], [John (1996)] and others ([Utgoff (1989a)], [Lubinsky (1993)], [Sethi and Yoo (1994)]).

Growing of oblique decision trees was first proposed as a linear combination extension to the CART algorithm. This extension is known as the CART-LC [Biermann *et al.* (1982)]. OC1 (oblique classifier 1) is an inducer of oblique decision trees designed for training sets with numeric instances [Murthy *et al.* (1994)]. OC1 builds the oblique hyperplanes by using a linear combinations of one or more numeric attributes at each internal node; these trees then partition the space of examples with both oblique and axis-parallel hyperplanes.

TreeGrowing (S,A,y) Where: S - Training Set
A - Input Feature Set y - Target Feature
Create a new tree T with a single root node.
IF One of the Stopping Criteria is fulfilled THEN
    Mark T as a leaf with the most
    common value of y in S as a label.
ELSE
    Find a discrete function $f(A)$ of the input
        attributes values such that splitting S
        according to $f(A)$'s outcomes $(v_1,\ldots,v_n)$ gains
        the best splitting metric.
    IF best splitting metric > threshold THEN
        Label t with $f(A)$
        FOR each outcome v_i of $f(A)$:
            Set $Subtree_i$= TreeGrowing $(\sigma_{f(A)=v_i}S, A, y)$.
            Connect the root node of t_T to $Subtree_i$ with
                an edge that is labelled as v_i
        END FOR
    ELSE
        Mark the root node in T as a leaf with the most
            common value of y in S as a label.
    END IF
END IF RETURN T

Fig. 6.7 Top-Down Algorithmic Framework for Oblique Decision Trees Induction.

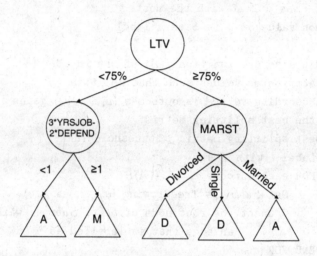

Fig. 6.8   Illustration of Oblique Decision Tree.

Chapter 7

Decision Forests

7.1 Overview

Ensemble methodology, which builds a predictive model by integrating multiple models, can be used for improving prediction performance and researchers from various disciplines such as statistics, machine learning, pattern recognition, and data mining have seriously explored the use of ensemble methodology. This chapter presents an updated survey of ensemble methods in classification tasks, describing the various combining methods, ensemble diversity generators and ensemble size determination.

7.2 Introduction

Supervised methods are methods that attempt to discover relationships between the input attributes and the target attribute. The relationship discovered is represented in a structure referred to as a model. Usually models can be used for predicting the value of the target attribute knowing the values of the input attributes. It is useful to distinguish between two main supervised models: classification models (classifiers) and regression models.

Regression models map the input space into a real-valued domain, whereas classifiers map the input space into predefined classes. For instance, classifiers can be used to classify mortgage consumers into good (fully payback the mortgage on time) and bad (delayed payback).

In a typical supervised learning problem, a training set of labeled examples is given and the goal is to form a description that can be used to predict previously unseen examples.

The main idea of an ensemble methodology is to combine a set of models, each of which solves the same original task, in order to obtain a better composite global model, with more accurate and reliable estimates or decisions than can be obtained from using a single model. The idea of building a predictive model by integrating multiple models has been under investigation for a long time.

The history of ensemble methods starts as early as 1977 with Tukeys twicing, an ensemble of two linear regression models [Buhlmann and Yu (2003)]. Ensemble methods can be also used for improving the quality and robustness of clustering algorithms [Dimitriadou *et al.* (2003)]. Nevertheless, in this chapter we focus on classifier ensembles.

In the past few years, experimental studies conducted by the machine learning community show that combining the outputs of multiple classifiers reduces the generalization error [Domingos (1996); Quinlan (1996); Bauer and Kohavi (1999); Opitz and Maclin (1999)]. Ensemble methods are very effective, mainly due to the phenomenon that various types of classifiers have different "inductive biases" [Geman *et al.* (1995); Mitchell (1997)]. Indeed, ensemble methods can effectively make use of such diversity to reduce the variance-error [Tumer and Ghosh (1999); Ali and Pazzani (1996)] without increasing the bias-error. In certain situations, an ensemble can also reduce bias-error, as shown by the theory of large margin classifiers [Bartlett and Shawe-Taylor (1998)].

The ensemble methodology is applicable in many fields such as: finance [Leigh *et al.* (2002)]; bioinformatics [Tan *et al.* (2003)]; medicine [Mangiameli *et al.* (2004); Park and Cho (2003); Walsh *et al.* (2004)]; cheminformatics [Merkwirth *et al.* (2004)]; manufacturing [Maimon and Rokach (2004)]; geography [Bruzzone *et al.* (2004)] and pattern recognition [Pang *et al.* (2003)].

Given the potential usefulness of ensemble methods, it is not surprising that a vast number of methods is now available to researchers and practitioners. Several surveys on ensemble are available in the literature, such as [Clemen (1989)] for forecasting methods or [Dietterich (2000b)] for machine learning. Nevertheless, this survey proposes an updated and profound description of issues related to ensemble of classifiers. This chapter aims to organize all significant methods developed in this field into a coherent and unified catalog.

A typical ensemble framework for classification tasks contains the following building blocks:

(1) Training set - A labeled dataset used for ensemble training. In semi-

supervised methods of ensemble generation, such as ASSEMBLE [Bennett *et al.* (2002)], unlabeled instances can be also used for the creation of the ensemble.

(2) Inducer – The inducer is an induction algorithm that obtains a training set and forms a classifier that represents the generalized relationship between the input attributes and the target attribute.
(3) Ensemble generator – This component is responsible for generating the diverse classifiers.
(4) Combiner - The combiner is responsible for combining the classifications of the various classifiers.

We use the notation $M_i = I(S_i)$ for representing a classifier M_i which was induced by inducer I on a training set S_i. The notation of $M_t, \alpha_t; t = 1, \ldots, T$ represents an ensemble of T classifiers.

The nature of each building block and the relation between them characterizes the ensemble framework design. The following list describes the main properties.

(1) Classifier dependency — During the classifier training how does each classifier affect the other classifiers? Classifiers may be dependent or independent.
(2) Diversity generator — In order to make the ensemble more effective, there should be some sort of diversity between the classifiers [Kuncheva (2005)]. Diversity may be obtained through different presentations of the input data, as in bagging, variations in learner design, or by adding a penalty to the outputs to encourage diversity.
(3) Ensemble size — The number of classifiers in the ensemble and how the undesirable classifiers are removed from the ensemble.
(4) Inducer usage — This property indicates the relation between the ensemble generator and the inducer used. Some ensemble have been specifically designed for a certain inducer and can not been used for other inducers.
(5) Combiner usage — This property specifies the relation between the ensemble generator and the combiner.
(6) Training data overlap — This property indicates which portion of the input data, used to induce a certain classifier, was also used to train other classifiers.

The issues of classifier dependency and diversity are very closely linked. More specifically, it can be argued that any effective method for generating diversity results in dependent classifiers (otherwise obtaining diversity is just luck). Nevertheless, as we will explain later one can independently create the classifiers and then, as a post-processing step, select the most diverse classifiers. Naturally there might be other properties which can be used to differentiate an ensemble scheme. We begin by surveying various combination methods. Following that we discuss and describe each one of the above mentioned properties in details.

7.3 Combination Methods

There are two main methods for combining classifiers: weighting methods and meta-learning. The weighting methods are best suited for problems where the individual classifiers perform the same task and have comparable success or when we would like to avoid problems associated with added learning (such as overfitting or long training time).

7.3.1 *Weighting Methods*

When combining classifiers with weights, a classifier's classification has a strength proportional to its assigned weight. The assigned weight can be fixed or dynamically determined for the specific instance to be classified.

7.3.1.1 *Majority Voting*

In this combining scheme, a classification of an unlabeled instance is performed according to the class that obtains the highest number of votes (the most frequent vote). This method is also known as the plurality vote (PV) or the basic ensemble method (BEM). This approach has frequently been used as a combining method for comparing newly proposed methods.

Mathematically it can be written as:

$$class(x) = \underset{c_i \in dom(y)}{\arg\max} \left(\sum_k g\left(y_k(x), c_i\right) \right) \tag{7.1}$$

where $y_k(x)$ is the classification of the k'th classifier and $g(y, c)$ is an indicator function defined as:

$$g(y, c) = \begin{cases} 1 & y = c \\ 0 & y \neq c \end{cases} \tag{7.2}$$

Note that in case of a probabilistic classifier, the crisp classification $y_k(x)$ is usually obtained as follows:

$$y_k(x) = \underset{c_i \in dom(y)}{\arg\max} \, \hat{P}_{M_k}(y = c_i \,|\, x) \tag{7.3}$$

where M_k denotes classifier k and $\hat{P}_{M_k}(y = c \,|\, x)$ denotes the probability of y obtaining the value c given an instance x.

7.3.1.2 *Performance Weighting*

The weight of each classifier can be set proportional to its accuracy performance on a validation set [Opitz and Shavlik (1996)]:

$$\alpha_i = \frac{(1 - E_i)}{\sum\limits_{j=1}^{T} (1 - E_j)} \tag{7.4}$$

where E_i is a normalization factor which is based on the performance evaluation of classifier i on a validation set.

7.3.1.3 *Distribution Summation*

The idea of the distribution summation combining method is to sum up the conditional probability vector obtained from each classifier [Clark and Boswell (1991)]. The selected class is chosen according to the highest value in the total vector. Mathematically, it can be written as:

$$Class(x) = \underset{c_i \in dom(y)}{\arg\max} \sum_k \hat{P}_{M_k}(y = c_i \,|\, x) \tag{7.5}$$

7.3.1.4 *Bayesian Combination*

In the Bayesian combination method the weight associated with each classifier is the posterior probability of the classifier given the training set [Buntine (1990)].

$$Class(x) = \operatorname*{argmax}_{c_i \in dom(y)} \sum_k P(M_k \,|S) \cdot \hat{P}_{M_k}(y = c_i \,|x) \qquad (7.6)$$

where $P(M_k \,|S)$ denotes the probability that the classifier M_k is correct given the training set S. The estimation of $P(M_k \,|S)$ depends on the classifier's representation. To estimate this value for decision trees the reader is referred to [Buntine (1990)].

7.3.1.5 Dempster–Shafer

The idea of using the Dempster–Shafer theory of evidence [Buchanan and Shortliffe (1984)] for combining classifiers has been suggested in [Shilen (1990)]. This method uses the notion of basic probability assignment defined for a certain class c_i given the instance x:

$$bpa(c_i, x) = 1 - \prod_k \left(1 - \hat{P}_{M_k}(y = c_i \,|x)\right) \qquad (7.7)$$

Consequently, the selected class is the one that maximizes the value of the belief function:

$$Bel(c_i, x) = \frac{1}{A} \cdot \frac{bpa(c_i, x)}{1 - bpa(c_i, x)} \qquad (7.8)$$

where A is a normalization factor defined as:

$$A = \sum_{\forall c_i \in dom(y)} \frac{bpa(c_i, x)}{1 - bpa(c_i, x)} + 1 \qquad (7.9)$$

7.3.1.6 Vogging

The idea behind the vogging approach (Variance Optimized Bagging) is to optimize a linear combination of base-classifiers so as to aggressively reduce variance while attempting to preserve a prescribed accuracy [Derbeko et al. (2002)]. For this purpose, Derbeko et al. implemented the Markowitz Mean-Variance Portfolio Theory that is used for generating low variance portfolios of financial assets.

7.3.1.7 *Naïve Bayes*

Using Bayes' rule, one can extend the naïve Bayes idea for combining various classifiers:

$$Class(x) = \underset{\substack{c_j \in dom(y) \\ \hat{P}(y=c_j) > 0}}{\operatorname{argmax}} \hat{P}(y=c_j) \cdot \prod_{k=1} \frac{\hat{P}_{M_k}(y=c_j \,|x)}{\hat{P}(y=c_j)} \qquad (7.10)$$

7.3.1.8 *Entropy Weighting*

The idea in this combining method is to give each classifier a weight that is inversely proportional to the entropy of its classification vector.

$$Class(x) = \underset{c_i \in dom(y)}{\operatorname{argmax}} \sum_{\substack{k:c_i = \operatorname{argmax}_{c_j \in dom(y)} \hat{P}_{M_k}(y=c_j|x)}} E(M_k, x) \qquad (7.11)$$

where:

$$E(M_k, x) = -\sum_{c_j} \hat{P}_{M_k}(y=c_j \,|x) \log \left(\hat{P}_{M_k}(y=c_j \,|x) \right) \qquad (7.12)$$

7.3.1.9 *Density-based Weighting*

If the various classifiers were trained using datasets obtained from different regions of the instance space, it might be useful to weight the classifiers according to the probability of sampling x by classifier M_k, namely:

$$Class(x) = \underset{c_i \in dom(y)}{\operatorname{argmax}} \sum_{\substack{k:c_i = \operatorname{argmax}_{c_j \in dom(y)} \hat{P}_{M_k}(y=c_j|x)}} \hat{P}_{M_k}(x) \qquad (7.13)$$

The estimation of $\hat{P}_{M_k}(x)$ depends on the classifier representation and can not always be estimated.

7.3.1.10 *DEA Weighting Method*

Recently there has been attempt to use the data envelop analysis (DEA) methodology [Charnes *et al.* (1978)] in order to assign weights to different classifiers [Sohn and Choi (2001)]. These researchers argue that the weights should not be specified according to a single performance measure, but should be based on several performance measures. Because there is a trade-off among the various performance measures, the DEA is employed in order to figure out the set of efficient classifiers. In addition, DEA provides inefficient classifiers with the benchmarking point.

7.3.1.11 *Logarithmic Opinion Pool*

According to the logarithmic opinion pool [Hansen (2000)], the selection of the preferred class is performed according to:

$$Class(x) = \underset{c_j \in dom(y)}{\operatorname{argmax}} e^{\sum_k \alpha_k \cdot \log(\hat{P}_{M_k}(y=c_j|x))} \tag{7.14}$$

where α_k denotes the weight of the k-th classifier, such that:

$$\alpha_k \geq 0; \sum \alpha_k = 1 \tag{7.15}$$

7.3.1.12 *Gating Network*

Figure 7.1 illustrates an n-expert structure. Each expert outputs the conditional probability of the target attribute given the input instance. A gating network is responsible for combining the various experts by assigning a weight to each network. These weights are not constant but are functions of the input instance x. The gating network selects one or a few experts (classifiers) which appear to have the most appropriate class distribution for the example. In fact each expert specializes on a small portion of the input space.

An extension to the basic mixture of experts, known as hierarchical mixtures of experts (HME), has been proposed in [Jordan and Jacobs (1994)]. This extension decomposes the space into sub-spaces, and then recursively decomposes each sub-space into sub-spaces.

Variations of the basic mixture of experts methods have been developed to accommodate specific domain problems. A specialized modular networks called the Meta-p_i network has been used to solve the vowel-speaker problem [Hampshire and Waibel (1992); Peng et al. (1996)]. There have been other extensions, such as nonlinear gated experts for time-series [Weigend et al. (1995)]; revised modular network for predicting the survival of AIDS patients [Ohno-Machado and Musen (1997)]; and a new approach for combining multiple experts for improving handwritten numeral recognition [Rahman and Fairhurst (1997)].

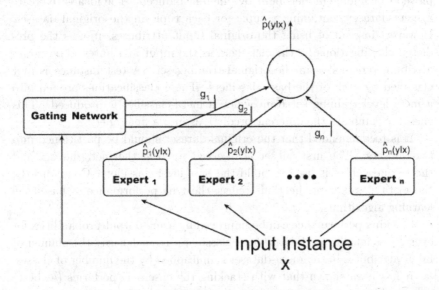

Fig. 7.1 Illustration of n-Expert Structure.

7.3.1.13 *Order Statistics*

Order statistics can be used to combine classifiers [Tumer and Ghosh (2000)]. These combiners offer the simplicity of a simple weighted combination method together with the generality of meta-combination methods (see the following section). The robustness of this method is helpful when there are significant variations among classifiers in some part of the instance space.

7.3.2 *Meta-combination Methods*

Meta-learning means learning from the classifiers produced by the inducers and from the classifications of these classifiers on training data. The following sections describe the most well-known meta-combination methods.

7.3.2.1 *Stacking*

Stacking is a technique for achieving the highest generalization accuracy [Wolpert (1992)]. By using a meta-learner, this method tries to induce which classifiers are reliable and which are not. Stacking is usually employed to combine models built by different inducers. The idea is to create a meta-dataset containing a tuple for each tuple in the original dataset. However, instead of using the original input attributes, it uses the predicted classifications by the classifiers as the input attributes. The target attribute remains as in the original training set. A test instance is first classified by each of the base classifiers. These classifications are fed into a meta-level training set from which a meta-classifier is produced. This classifier combines the different predictions into a final one.

It is recommended that the original dataset should be partitioned into two subsets. The first subset is reserved to form the meta-dataset and the second subset is used to build the base-level classifiers. Consequently, the meta-classifier predications reflect the true performance of base-level learning algorithms.

Stacking performance can be improved by using output probabilities for every class label from the base-level classifiers. In such cases, the number of input attributes in the meta-dataset is multiplied by the number of classes.

It has been shown that with stacking the ensemble performs (at best) comparably to selecting the best classifier from the ensemble by cross-validation [Džeroski and Ženko (2004)]. In order to improve the existing stacking approach, they employed a new multi-response model tree to learn at the meta-level and empirically showed that it performs better than existing stacking approaches and better than selecting the best classifier by cross-validation.

The SCANN (for Stacking, Correspondence Analysis and Nearest Neighbor) combining method [Merz (1999)] uses the strategies of stacking and correspondence analysis. Correspondence analysis is a method for geometrically modelling the relationship between the rows and columns of a matrix whose entries are categorical. In this context Correspondence Analysis is used to explore the relationship between the training examples and their classification by a collection of classifiers.

A nearest neighbor method is then applied to classify unseen examples. Here, each possible class is assigned coordinates in the space derived by correspondence analysis. Unclassified examples are mapped into the new space, and the class label corresponding to the closest class point is assigned to the example.

7.3.2.2 *Arbiter Trees*

According to Chan and Stolfo's approach [Chan and Stolfo (1993)], an arbiter tree is built in a bottom-up fashion. Initially, the training set is randomly partitioned into k disjoint subsets. The arbiter is induced from a pair of classifiers and recursively a new arbiter is induced from the output of two arbiters. Consequently for k classifiers, there are $\log_2(k)$ levels in the generated arbiter tree.

The creation of the arbiter is performed as follows. For each pair of classifiers, the union of their training dataset is classified by the two classifiers. A selection rule compares the classifications of the two classifiers and selects instances from the union set to form the training set for the arbiter. The arbiter is induced from this set with the same learning algorithm used in the base level. The purpose of the arbiter is to provide an alternate classification when the base classifiers present diverse classifications. This arbiter, together with an arbitration rule, decides on a final classification outcome, based upon the base predictions. Figure 7.2 shows how the final classification is selected based on the classification of two base classifiers and a single arbiter.

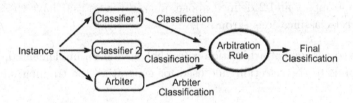

Fig. 7.2   A Prediction from Two Base Classifiers and a Single Arbiter.

The process of forming the union of data subsets; classifying it using a pair of arbiter trees; comparing the classifications; forming a training set; training the arbiter; and picking one of the predictions, is recursively performed until the root arbiter is formed. Figure 7.3 illustrate an arbiter tree created for $k = 4$. $T_1 - T_4$ are the initial four training datasets from which four classifiers $M_1 - M_4$ are generated concurrently. T_{12} and T_{34} are the training sets generated by the rule selection from which arbiters are produced. A_{12} and A_{34} are the two arbiters. Similarly, T_{14} and A_{14} (root arbiter) are generated and the arbiter tree is completed.

There are several schemes for arbiter trees; each is characterized by a

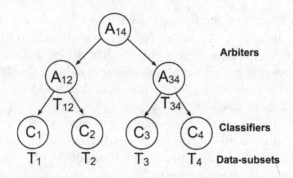

Fig. 7.3   Sample Arbiter Tree.

different selection rule. Here are three versions of selection rules:

- Only instances with classifications that disagree are chosen (group 1).
- Like group 1 defined above, plus instances where their classifications agree but are incorrect (group 2).
- Like groups 1 and 2 defined above, plus instances that have the same correct classifications (group 3).

Of the two versions of arbitration rules that have been implemented, each corresponds to the selection rule used for generating the training data at that level:

- For selection rule 1 and 2, a final classification is made by a majority vote of the classifications of the two lower levels and the arbiter's own classification, with preference given to the latter.
- For selection rule 3, if the classifications of the two lower levels are not equal, the classification made by the sub-arbiter based on the first group is chosen. In case this is not true and the classification of the sub-arbiter constructed on the third group equals those of the lower levels, then this is the chosen classification. In any other case, the classification of the sub-arbiter constructed on the second group is chosen. In fact it is possible to achieve the same accuracy level as in the single mode applied to the entire dataset but with less time and memory requirements [Chan and Stolfo (1993)]. More specifically it has been shown that this meta-learning strategy required only around 30% of the memory used by

the single model case. This last fact, combined with the independent nature of the various learning processes, make this method robust and effective for massive amounts of data. Nevertheless, the accuracy level depends on several factors such as the distribution of the data among the subsets and the pairing scheme of learned classifiers and arbiters in each level. The decision regarding any of these issues may influence performance, but the optimal decisions are not necessarily known in advance, nor initially set by the algorithm.

7.3.2.3 *Combiner Trees*

The way combiner trees are generated is very similar to arbiter trees. Both are trained bottom-up. However, a combiner, instead of an arbiter, is placed in each non-leaf node of a combiner tree [Chan and Stolfo (1997)]. In the combiner strategy, the classifications of the learned base classifiers form the basis of the meta-learner's training set. A composition rule determines the content of training examples from which a combiner (meta-classifier) will be generated. In classifying an instance, the base classifiers first generate their classifications and based on the composition rule, a new instance is generated. The aim of this strategy is to combine the classifications from the base classifiers by learning the relationship between these classifications and the correct classification. Figure 7.4 illustrates the result obtained from two base classifiers and a single combiner.

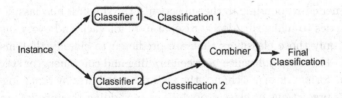

Fig. 7.4 A Prediction from Two Base Classifiers and a Single Combiner.

Two schemes for composition rules were proposed. The first one is the stacking scheme. The second is like stacking with the addition of the instance input attributes. It has been shown that the stacking scheme per se does not perform as well as the second scheme [Chan and Stolfo (1995)]. Although there is information loss due to data partitioning, combiner trees can sustain the accuracy level achieved by a single classifier. In a few cases, the single classifier's accuracy was consistently exceeded.

7.3.2.4   Grading

This technique uses "graded" classifications as meta-level classes [Seewald and Furnkranz (2001)]. The term "graded" is used in the sense of classifications that have been marked as correct or incorrect. The method transforms the classification made by the k different classifiers into k training sets by using the instances k times and attaching them to a new binary class in each occurrence. This class indicates whether the k–th classifier yielded a correct or incorrect classification, compared to the real class of the instance.

For each base classifier, one meta-classifier is learned whose task is to classify when the base classifier will misclassify. At classification time, each base classifier classifies the unlabeled instance. The final classification is derived from the classifications of those base classifiers that are classified to be correct by the meta-classification schemes. In case several base classifiers with different classification results are classified as correct, voting, or a combination considering the confidence estimates of the base classifiers, is performed. Grading may be considered as a generalization of cross-validation selection [Schaffer (1993)], which divides the training data into k subsets, builds $k - 1$ classifiers by dropping one subset at a time and then uses it to find a misclassification rate. Finally, the procedure simply chooses the classifier corresponding to the subset with the smallest misclassification. Grading tries to make this decision separately for each and every instance by using only those classifiers that are predicted to classify that instance correctly. The main difference between grading and combiners (or stacking) is that the former does not change the instance attributes by replacing them with class predictions or class probabilities (or adding them to it). Instead it modifies the class values. Furthermore, in grading several sets of meta-data are created, one for each base classifier. Several meta-level classifiers are learned from those sets.

The main difference between grading and arbiters is that arbiters use information about the disagreements of classifiers for selecting a training set; grading uses disagreement with the target function to produce a new training set.

7.4 Classifier Dependency

This property indicates whether the various classifiers are dependent or independent. In a dependent framework the outcome of a certain classifier affects the creation of the next classifier. Alternatively each classifier is built independently and their results are combined in some fashion. Some researchers refer to this property as "the relationship between modules" and distinguish between three different types: successive, cooperative and supervisory [Sharkey (1996)]. Roughly speaking, "successive" refers to "dependent" while "cooperative" refers to "independent". The last type applies to those cases in which one model controls the other model.

7.4.1 *Dependent Methods*

In dependent approaches for learning ensembles, there is an interaction between the learning runs. Thus it is possible to take advantage of knowledge generated in previous iterations to guide the learning in the next iterations. We distinguish between two main approaches for dependent learning, as described in the following sections [Provost and Kolluri (1997)].

7.4.1.1 *Model-guided Instance Selection*

In this dependent approach, the classifiers that were constructed in previous iterations are used for manipulating the training set for the following iteration (see Figure 7.5). One can embed this process within the basic learning algorithm. These methods usually ignore all data instances on which their initial classifier is correct and only learn from misclassified instances.

The most well known model-guided instance selection is boosting. Boosting (also known as arcing adaptive resampling and combining) is a general method for improving the performance of a weak learner (such as classification rules or decision trees). The method works by repeatedly running a weak learner (such as classification rules or decision trees), on various distributed training data. The classifiers produced by the weak learners are then combined into a single composite strong classifier in order to achieve a higher accuracy than the weak learners classifiers would have had.

Freund and Schapire (1996) introduced the AdaBoost algorithm. The main idea of this algorithm is to assign a weight in each example in the training set. In the beginning, all weights are equal, but in every round,

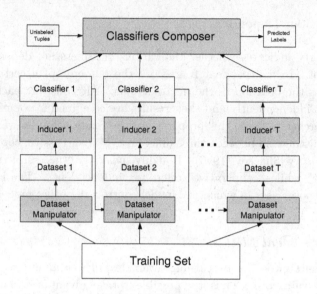

Fig. 7.5　Model–guided Instance Selection Diagram.

the weights of all misclassified instances are increased while the weights of correctly classified instances are decreased. As a consequence, the weak learner is forced to focus on the difficult instances of the training set. This procedure provides a series of classifiers that complement one another.

The pseudo-code of the AdaBoost algorithm is described in Figure 7.6. The algorithm assumes that the training set consists of m instances, labeled as -1 or +1. The classification of a new instance is made by voting on all classifiers $\{M_t\}$, each having a weight of α_t. Mathematically, it can be written as:

$$H(x) = sign(\sum_{t=1}^{T} \alpha_t \cdot M_t(x)) \qquad (7.16)$$

For using the boosting algorithm with decision trees, the decision tree inducer should be able to handle weighted instances. Some decision trees inducers (such as C4.5) can provide different treatments to different instances. This is performed by weighting the contribution of each instance in the analysis according to a provided weight (between 0 and 1). If weighted instances are used, then one may obtain probability vectors in the leaf nodes that consist of irrational numbers. This can be explained by the fact that

Require: I (a weak inducer), T (the number of iterations), S (training set)

Ensure: $M_t, \alpha_t; t = 1, \ldots, T$

1: $t \leftarrow 1$
2: $D_1(i) \leftarrow 1/m; i = 1, \ldots, m$
3: **repeat**
4:    Build Classifier M_t using I and distribution D_t
5:    $\varepsilon_t \leftarrow \sum\limits_{i:M_t(x_i) \neq y_i} D_t(i)$
6:    **if** $\varepsilon_t > 0.5$ **then**
7:       $T \leftarrow t - 1$
8:       exit Loop.
9:    **end if**
10:   $\alpha_t \leftarrow \frac{1}{2}\ln(\frac{1-\varepsilon_t}{\varepsilon_t})$
11:   $D_{t+1}(i) = D_t(i) \cdot e^{-\alpha_t y_t M_t(x_i)}$
12:   Normalize D_{t+1} to be a proper distribution.
13:   $t++$
14: **until** $t > T$

Fig. 7.6   The AdaBoost Algorithm

counting weighted instances is not necessarily summed up with an integer number.

The basic AdaBoost algorithm, described in Figure 7.6, deals with binary classification. Freund and Schapire (1996) describe two versions of the AdaBoost algorithm (AdaBoost.M1, AdaBoost.M2), which are equivalent for binary classification and differ in their handling of multiclass classification problems. Figure 7.7 describes the pseudo-code of AdaBoost.M1. The classification of a new instance is performed according to the following equation:

$$H(x) = \underset{y \in dom(y)}{\operatorname{argmax}}\left(\sum_{t:M_t(x)=y} \log \frac{1}{\beta_t} \right) \qquad (7.17)$$

where β_t is defined in Figure 7.7.

All boosting algorithms presented here assume that the weak inducers which are provided can cope with weighted instances. If this is not the case, an unweighted dataset is generated from the weighted data by a resampling technique. Namely, instances are chosen with a probability according to their weights (until the dataset becomes as large as the original training set).

Require: I (a weak inducer), T (the number of iterations), S (the training set)

Ensure: $M_t, \beta_t; t = 1, \ldots, T$

1: $t \leftarrow 1$

2: $D_1(i) \leftarrow 1/m; i = 1, \ldots, m$

3: **repeat**

4:     Build Classifier M_t using I and distribution D_t

5:     $\varepsilon_t \leftarrow \displaystyle\sum_{i:M_t(x_i) \neq y_i} D_t(i)$

6:     **if** $\varepsilon_t > 0.5$ **then**

7:        $T \leftarrow t - 1$

8:        exit Loop.

9:     **end if**

10:    $\beta_t \leftarrow \dfrac{\varepsilon_t}{1 - \varepsilon_t}$

11:    $D_{t+1}(i) = D_t(i) \cdot \begin{cases} \beta_t & M_t(x_i) = y_i \\ 1 & Otherwise \end{cases}$

12:    Normalize D_{t+1} to be a proper distribution.

13:    $t++$

14: **until** $t > T$

Fig. 7.7   The AdaBoost.M.1 Algorithm.

Boosting seems to improve performance for two main reasons:

(1) It generates a final classifier whose error on the training set is small by combining many hypotheses whose error may be large.
(2) It produces a combined classifier whose variance is significantly lower than those produced by the weak learner.

On the other hand, boosting sometimes leads to a deterioration in generalization performance. According to Quinlan (1996), the main reason for boosting's failure is overfitting. The objective of boosting is to construct a composite classifier that performs well on the data, but a large number of iterations may create a very complex composite classifier, that is significantly less accurate than a single classifier. A possible way to avoid overfitting is by keeping the number of iterations as small as possible. It has been shown that boosting approximates a large margin classifier such as the SVM [Rudin *et al.* (2004)].

Another important drawback of boosting is that it is difficult to understand. The resulting ensemble is considered to be less comprehensible since the user is required to capture several classifiers instead of a single classifier. Despite the above drawbacks, Breiman (1996) refers to the boosting idea as the most significant development in classifier design of the Nineties.

7.4.1.2 *Incremental Batch Learning*

In this method the classification produced in one iteration is given as "prior knowledge" to the learning algorithm in the following iteration. The learning algorithm uses the current training set together with the classification of the former classifier for building the next classifier. The classifier constructed at the last iteration is chosen as the final classifier.

7.4.2 *Independent Methods*

In independent ensemble methodology, the original dataset is partitioned into several subsets from which multiple classifiers are induced. (Please see Figure 7.8). The subsets created from the original training set may be disjointed (mutually exclusive) or overlapping. A combination procedure is then applied in order to produce a single classification for a given instance. Since the method for combining the results of induced classifiers is usually independent of the induction algorithms, it can be used with different inducers at each subset. Moreover, this methodology can be easily parallelized. These independent methods aim either at improving the predictive power of classifiers or decreasing the total execution time. The following sections describe several algorithms that implement this methodology.

7.4.2.1 *Bagging*

The most well-known independent method is bagging (bootstrap aggregating). The method aims to increase accuracy by creating an improved composite classifier, I^*, by amalgamating the various outputs of learned classifiers into a single prediction.

Figure 7.9 presents the pseudo-code of the bagging algorithm [Breiman (1996)]. Each classifier is trained on a sample of instances taken with a replacement from the training set. Usually each sample size is equal to the size of the original training set.

Note that since sampling with replacement is used, some of the original instances of S may appear more than once in S_t and some may not be included at all. To classify a new instance, each classifier returns the class

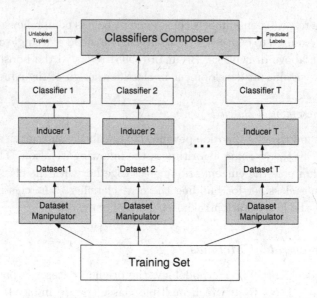

Fig. 7.8   Independent methods.

Require: I (an inducer), T (the number of iterations), S (the training set), μ (the subsample size).
Ensure: $M_t; t = 1, \ldots, T$
1: $t \leftarrow 1$
2: **repeat**
3:     $S_t \leftarrow$ Sample μ instances from S with replacement.
4:     Build classifier M_t using I on S_t
5:     $t + +$
6: **until** $t > T$

Fig. 7.9   The bagging algorithm.

prediction for the unknown instance. The composite bagged classifier, I^*, returns the class that has been predicted most often (voting method). The result is that bagging produces a combined model that often performs better than the single model built from the original single data. Breiman (1996) notes that this is true especially for unstable inducers because bagging can eliminate their instability. In this context, an inducer is considered unstable if perturbing the learning set can cause significant changes in the constructed classifier.

Bagging, like boosting, is a technique for improving the accuracy of a classifier by producing different classifiers and combining multiple models. They both use a kind of voting for classification in order to combine the outputs of the different classifiers of the same type. In boosting, unlike bagging, each classifier is influenced by the performance of those built before with the new classifier trying to pay more attention to errors that were made in the previous ones and to their performances. In bagging, each instance is chosen with equal probability, while in boosting, instances are chosen with a probability proportional to their weight. Furthermore, according to Quinlan (1996), as mentioned above, bagging requires that the learning system should not be stable, where boosting does not preclude the use of unstable learning systems, provided that their error rate can be kept below 0.5.

7.4.2.2 *Wagging*

Wagging is a variant of bagging [Bauer and Kohavi (1999)] in which each classifier is trained on the entire training set, but each instance is stochastically assigned a weight. Figure 7.10 presents the pseudo-code of the wagging algorithm.

In fact bagging can be considered to be wagging with allocation of weights from the Poisson distribution (each instance is represented in the sample a discrete number of times). Alternatively, it is possible to allocate the weights from the exponential distribution, because the exponential distribution is the continuous valued counterpart to the Poisson distribution [Webb (2000)].

Require: I (an inducer), T (the number of iterations), S (the training set), d (weighting distribution).
Ensure: $M_t; t = 1, \ldots, T$
1: $t \leftarrow 1$
2: **repeat**
3:     $S_t \leftarrow S$ with random weights drawn from d.
4:     Build classifier M_t using I on S_t
5:     $t + +$
6: **until** $t > T$

Fig. 7.10   The Wagging Algorithm.

7.4.2.3   *Random Forest*

A random forest ensemble (also known as random subspace) [Breiman (2001)] uses a large number of individual, unpruned decision trees which are created by randomizing the split at each node of the decision tree. Each tree is likely to be less accurate than a tree created with the exact splits. But, by combining several of these "approximate" trees in an ensemble, we can improve the accuracy, often doing better than a single tree with exact splits.

The individual trees are constructed using the algorithm presented in Figure 7.11. The input parameter N represents the number of input variables that will be used to determine the decision at a node of the tree. This number should be much less than the number of attributes in the training set. Note that bagging can be thought of as a special case of random forests obtained when N is set to the number of attributes in the original training set. The IDT in Figure 7.11 represents any top-down decision tree induction algorithm with the following modification: the decision tree is not pruned and at each node, rather than choosing the best split among all attributes, the IDT randomly samples N of the attributes and chooses the best split from among those variables. The classification of an unlabeled instance is performed using majority vote.

Require: IDT (a decision tree inducer), T (the number of iterations), S (the training set), μ (the subsample size). N (number of attributes used in each node)

Ensure: $M_t; t = 1, \ldots, T$

1: $t \leftarrow 1$
2: **repeat**
3:    $S_t \leftarrow$ Sample μ instances from S with replacement.
4:    Build classifier M_t using $IDT(N)$ on S_t
5:    $t + +$
6: **until** $t > T$

Fig. 7.11   The random forest algorithm.

There are other ways to obtain random forests. For example, instead of using all the instances to determine the best split point for each feature, a sub-sample of the instances is used [Kamath and Cantu-Paz (2001)]. This sub-sample varies with the feature. The feature and split value that optimize the splitting criterion are chosen as the decision at that node.

Since the split made at a node is likely to vary with the sample selected, this technique results in different trees which can be combined in ensembles.

Another method for randomization of the decision tree through histograms was proposed by [Kamath *et al.* (2002)]. The use of histograms has long been suggested as a way of of making the features discrete, while reducing the time to handle very large datasets. Typically, a histogram is created for each feature, and the bin boundaries used as potential split points. The randomization in this process is expressed by selecting the split point randomly in an interval around the best bin boundary.

Although the random forest was defined for decision trees, this approach is applicable to all types of classifiers. One important advantage of the random forest method is its ability to handle a very large number of input attributes [Skurichina and Duin (2002)]. Another important feature of the random forest is that it is fast.

7.4.2.4 *Cross-validated Committees*

This procedure creates k classifiers by partitioning the training set into k-equal-sized sets and training, in turn, on all but the i-th set. This method, first used by Gams (1989), employed 10-fold partitioning. Parmanto *et al.* (1996) have also used this idea for creating an ensemble of neural networks. Domingos (1996) used cross-validated committees to speed up his own rule induction algorithm RISE, whose complexity is $O(n^2)$, making it unsuitable for processing large databases. In this case, partitioning is applied by predetermining a maximum number of examples to which the algorithm can be applied at once. The full training set is randomly divided into approximately equal-sized partitions. RISE is then run on each partition separately. Each set of rules grown from the examples in partition p is tested on the examples in partition $p + 1$, in order to reduce overfitting and to improve accuracy.

7.5 Ensemble Diversity

In an ensemble, the combination of the output of several classifiers is only useful if they disagree about some inputs [Tumer and Ghosh (1996)].

Creating an ensemble in which each classifier is as different as possible while still being consistent with the training set is theoretically known to be an important feature for obtaining improved ensemble performance [Krogh and Vedelsby (1995)]. According to [Hu (2001)], diversified classifiers lead to uncorrelated errors, which in turn improve classification accuracy.

In the regression context, the bias-variance-covariance decomposition has been suggested to explain why and how diversity between individual models contribute toward overall ensemble accuracy. Nevertheless, in the classification context, there is no complete and agreed upon theory [Brown *et al.* (2005)]. More specifically, there is no simple analogue of variance-covariance decomposition for the zero-one loss function. Instead, there are several ways to define this decomposition. Each way has its own assumptions.

Sharkey [Sharkey (1999)] suggested a taxonomy of methods for creating diversity in ensembles of neural networks. More specifically, Sharkey's taxonomy refers to four different aspects: the initial weights; the training data used; the architecture of the networks; and the training algorithm used.

Brown et al. [Brown *et al.* (2005)] suggest a different taxonomy which consists of the following branches: varying the starting points within the hypothesis space; varying the set of hypotheses that are accessible by the ensemble members (for instance by manipulating the training set); and varying the way each member traverses the space.

In this paper we suggest the following taxonomy. Note however that the components of this taxonomy are not mutually exclusive, namely, there are a few algorithms which combine two of them.

(1) Manipulating the Inducer – We manipulate the way in which the base inducer is used. More specifically each ensemble member is trained with an inducer that is differently manipulated.
(2) Manipulating the Training Sample – We vary the input that is used by the inducer for training. Each member is trained from a different training set.
(3) Changing the target attribute representation – Each classifier in the ensemble solve a different target concept.
(4) Partitioning the search space – Each member is trained on a different search subspace.
(5) Hybridization – Diversity is obtained by using various base inducers or ensemble strategies.

7.5.1 *Manipulating the Inducer*

A simple method for gaining diversity is to manipulate the inducer used for creating the classifiers. Below we survey several strategies to gain this diversity.

7.5.1.1 *Manipulation of the Inducer's Parameters*

The base inducer usually can be controlled by a set of parameters. For example, the well known decision tree inducer C4.5 has the confidence level parameter that greatly affect learning.

In the neural network community, there were several attempts to gain diversity by using different number of nodes. Nevertheless, these researches concludes that variation in numbers of hidden nodes is not effective method of creating diversity in neural network ensembles. Nevertheless the CNNE algorithm which simultaneously determines the ensemble size along with the number of hidden nodes in individual NNs, has shown encouraging results.

Another effective approach for ANNs is to use several network topologies. For instance the Addemup algorithm [Opitz and Shavlik (1996)] uses genetic algorithm to select the network topologies composing the ensemble. Addemup trains with standard backpropagation, then selects groups of networks with a good error diversity according to the measurement of diversity.

7.5.1.2 *Starting Point in Hypothesis Space*

Some inducers can gain diversity by starting the search in the Hypothesis Space from different points. For example the simplest way to manipulate the back-propagation inducer is to assign different initial weights to the network [Kolen and Pollack (1991)]. Experimental study indicate that the resulting networks differed in the number of cycles in which they took to converge upon a solution, and in whether they converged at all. While it is very simple way to gain diversity, it is now generally accepted that it is not sufficient for achieving good diversity [Brown *et al.* (2005)].

7.5.1.3 *Hypothesis Space Traversal*

These techniques alter the way the inducer traverses the space, thereby leading different classifiers to converge to different hypotheses [Brown *et al.* (2005)]. We differentiate between two techniques for manipulating the space traversal for gaining diversity: Random and Collective-Performance.

Random-based strategy

The idea in this case is to "inject randomness" into the inducers in order to increase the independence among the ensemble's members. Ali and Pazzani [Ali and Pazzani (1996)] propose to change the rule learning HYDRA algorithm in the following way: Instead of selecting the best literal at each stage (using, for instance, an information gain measure), the literal is selected randomly such that its probability of being selected is proportional to its measured value. A similar idea has been implemented for C4.5 decision trees [Dietterich (2000a)]. Instead of selecting the best attribute in each stage, it selects randomly (with equal probability) an attribute from the set of the best 20 attributes. MCMC (Markov Chain Monte Carlo) methods can also be used for introducing randomness in the induction process [Neal (1993)].

Collective-Performance-based strategy

In this case the evaluation function used in the induction of each member is extended to include a penalty term that encourages diversity. The most studied penalty method is the Negative Correlation Learning [Liu (2005); Brown and Wyatt (2003); Rosen (1996)]. The idea of negative correlation learning is to encourage different individual classifiers in the ensemble to represent different subspaces of the problem. While simultaneously creating the classifiers, the classifiers may interact with each other in order to specialize (for instance by using a correlation penalty term in the error function to encourage such specialization).

7.5.2 *Manipulating the Training Samples*

In this method, each classifier is trained on a different variation or subset of the original dataset. This method is useful for inducers whose variance-error factor is relatively large (such as decision trees and neural networks). That is to say, small changes in the training set may cause a major change in the obtained classifier. This category contains procedures such as bagging, boosting and cross-validated committees.

7.5.2.1 *Resampling*

The distribution of tuples among the different classifier could be random as in the bagging algorithm or in the arbiter trees. Other methods distribute the tuples based on the class distribution such that the class distribution in each subset is approximately the same as that in the entire dataset. It has been shown that proportional distribution as used in combiner trees [Chan and Stolfo (1993)] can achieve higher accuracy than random distribution.

Instead of perform sampling with replacement, some methods (like AdaBoost or Wagging) manipulate the weights that are attached to each instance in the training set. The base inducer should be capable to take these weights into account. Recently a novel framework was proposed in which each instance contributes to the committee formation with a fixed weight, while contributing with different individual weights to the derivation of the different constituent classifiers [Christensen *et al.* (2004)]. This approach encourages model diversity without biasing the ensemble inadvertently towards any particular instance.

7.5.2.2 *Creation*

The DECORATE algorithm [Melville and Mooney (2003)] is a dependent approach in which the ensemble is generated iteratively, learning a classifier at each iteration and adding it to the current ensemble. The first member is created by using the base induction algorithm on the original training set. The successive classifiers are trained on an artificial set that combines tuples from the original training set and also on some fabricated tuples. In each iteration, the input attribute values of the fabricated tuples are generated according to the original data distribution. On the other hand, the target values of these tuples are selected so as to differ maximally from the current ensemble predictions. Comprehensive experiments have demonstrated that this technique is consistently more accurate than the base classifier, Bagging and Random Forests. Decorate also obtains higher accuracy than boosting on small training sets, and achieves comparable performance on larger training sets.

7.5.2.3 *Partitioning*

Some argue that classic ensemble techniques (such as boosting and bagging) have limitations on massive datasets, because the size of the dataset can become a bottleneck [Chawla *et al.* (2004)]. Moreover, it is suggested that partitioning the datasets into random, disjoint partitions will not only overcome the issue of exceeding memory size, but will also lead to creating an ensemble of diverse and accurate classifiers, each built from a disjoint partition but with the aggregate processing all of the data. This can improve performance in a way that might not be possible by subsampling. In fact, empirical studies have shown that the performance of the multiple disjoint partition approach is equivalent to the performance obtained by popular ensemble techniques such as bagging. More recently a framework for building thousands of classifiers that are trained from small subsets of data in a distributed environment was proposed [Chawla *et al.* (2004)]. It has been empirically shown that this framework is fast, accurate, and scalable.

Clustering techniques can be used to partitioning the sample. The CBCD (cluster-based concurrent decomposition) algorithm first clusters the instance space by using the K-means clustering algorithm. Then, it creates disjoint sub-samples using the clusters in such a way that each sub-sample is comprised of tuples from all clusters and hence represents the entire dataset. An inducer is applied in turn to each sub-sample. A voting mechanism is used to combine the classifiers classifications. Experimental study indicates that the CBCD algorithm outperforms the bagging algorithm.

7.5.3 *Manipulating the Target Attribute Representation*

In methods that manipulate the target attribute, instead of inducing a single complicated classifier, several classifiers with different and usually simpler representations of the target attribute are induced. This manipulation can be based on an aggregation of the original target's values (known as *Concept Aggregation*) or more complicated functions (known as *Function Decomposition*).

Classical concept aggregation replaces the original target attribute with a function, such that the domain of the new target attribute is smaller than the original one.

Concept aggregation has been used to classify free text documents into predefined topics [Buntine (1996)]. This application suggests breaking the topics up into groups (co-topics) and then, instead of predicting the document's topic directly, classifying the document into one of the co-topics. Another model is then used to predict the actual topic in that co-topic.

A general concept aggregation algorithm called *Error-Correcting Output Coding* (ECOC) which converts multi-class problems into multiple, two-class problems has been suggested by [Dietterich and Bakiri (1995)]. A classifier is built for each possible binary partition of the classes. Experiments show that ECOC improves the accuracy of neural networks and decision trees on several multi-class problems from the UCI repository.

The idea to convert K class classification problems into K-two class classification problems has been proposed by [Anand *et al.* (1995)]. Each problem considers the discrimination of one class to the other classes. Lu and Ito [Lu and Ito (1999)] extend Anand's method and propose a new method for manipulating the data based on the class relations among the training data. By using this method, they divide a K class classification problem into a series of $K(K-1)/2$ two-class problems where each problem considers the discrimination of one class to each one of the other classes. The researchers used neural networks to examine this idea.

Function decomposition was originally developed in the Fifties and Sixties for designing switching circuits. It was even used as an evaluation mechanism for checker playing programs [Samuel (1967)]. This approach was later improved by [Biermann *et al.* (1982)]. Recently the machine learning community has adopted this approach. A manual decomposition of the problem and an expert-assisted selection of examples to construct rules for the concepts in the hierarchy was studied in [Michie (1995)]. Compared to standard decision tree induction techniques, structured induction exhibits about the same degree of classification accuracy with the increased transparency and lower complexity of the developed models. A general-purpose function decomposition approach for machine learning was proposed in [Zupan *et al.* (1998)]. According to this approach, attributes are transformed into new concepts in an iterative manner to create a hierarchy of concepts. A different function decomposition which can be applied in data mining is the Bi-Decomposition [Long (2003)]. In this approach the original function is decomposed into two decomposition functions that are connected by a two-input operator called a "gate". Each of the decomposition functions depends on fewer variables than the original function. Recursive bidecomposition represents a function as a structure of interconnected gates.

7.5.4 *Partitioning the Search Space*

The idea is that each member in the ensemble explores a different part of the search space. Thus, the original instance space is divided into several sub-spaces. Each sub-space is considered independently and the total model is a (possibly soft) union of such simpler models.

When using this approach, one should decide if the subspaces will overlap. At one extreme, the original problem is decomposed into several mutually exclusive sub-problems, such that each subproblem is solved using a dedicated classifier. In such cases, the classifiers may have significant variations in their overall performance over different parts of the input space [Tumer and Ghosh (2000)]. At the other extreme, each classifier solves the same original task. In such cases, "If the individual classifiers are then appropriately chosen and trained properly, their performances will be (relatively) comparable in any region of the problem space. [Tumer and Ghosh (2000)]". However, usually the sub-spaces may have soft boundaries, namely sub-spaces are allowed to overlap.

There are two popular approaches for search space manipulations: divide and conquer approaches and feature subset-based ensemble methods.

7.5.4.1   *Divide and Conquer*

In the neural-networks community, Nowlan and Hinton [Nowlan and Hinton (1991)] examined the mixture of experts (ME) approach, which partitions the instance space into several subspaces and assigns different experts (classifiers) to the different subspaces. The subspaces, in ME, have soft boundaries (i.e., they are allowed to overlap). A gating network then combines the experts' outputs and produces a composite decision.

Some researchers have used clustering techniques to partition the space. The basic idea is to partition the instance space into mutually exclusive subsets using K-means clustering algorithm. An analysis of the results shows that the proposed method is well suited for datasets of numeric input attributes and that its performance is influenced by the dataset size and its homogeneity.

NBTree [Kohavi (1996)] is an instance space decomposition method that induces a decision tree and a Naïve Bayes hybrid classifier. Naïve Bayes, which is a classification algorithm based on Bayes' theorem and a Naïve independence assumption, is very efficient in terms of its processing time. To induce an NBTree, the instance space is recursively partitioned according to attributes values. The result of the recursive partitioning is a decision tree whose terminal nodes are Naïve Bayes classifiers. Since subjecting a terminal node to a Naïve Bayes classifier means that the hybrid classifier may classify two instances from a single hyper-rectangle region into distinct classes, the NBTree is more flexible than a pure decision tree. In order to decide when to stop the growth of the tree, NBTree compares two alternatives in terms of error estimation - partitioning into a hyper-rectangle region and inducing a single Naïve Bayes classifier. The error estimation is calculated by cross-validation, which significantly increases the overall processing time. Although NBTree applies a Naïve Bayes classifier to decision tree terminal nodes, classification algorithms other than Naïve Bayes are also applicable. However, the cross-validation estimations make the NBTree hybrid computationally expensive for more time-consuming algorithms such as neural networks.

More recently Cohen et al. [Cohen *et al.* (2007)] generalizes the NBTree idea and examines a decision-tree framework for space decomposition. According to this framework, the original instance-space is hierarchically partitioned into multiple subspaces and a distinct classifier (such as neural network) is assigned to each subspace. Subsequently, an unlabeled, previously-unseen instance is classified by employing the classifier that was assigned to the subspace to which the instance belongs.

The divide and conquer approach includes many other specific methods such as local linear regression, CART/MARS, adaptive subspace models, etc [Johansen and Foss (1992); Ramamurti and Ghosh (1999); Holmstrom *et al.* (1997)].

7.5.4.2 *Feature Subset-based Ensemble Methods*

Another less common strategy for manipulating the search space is to manipulate the input attribute set. Feature subset based ensemble methods are those that manipulate the input feature set for creating the ensemble members. The idea is to simply give each classifier a different projection of the training set. Tumer and Oza. Feature subset-based ensembles potentially facilitate the creation of a classifier for high dimensionality data sets without the feature selection drawbacks mentioned above. Moreover, these methods can be used to improve the classification performance due to the reduced correlation among the classifiers. Bryll *et al.* also indicate that the reduced size of the dataset implies faster induction of classifiers. Feature subset avoids the class under-representation which may happen in instance subsets methods such as bagging. There are three popular strategies for creating feature subset-based ensembles: random-based, reduct-based and collective-performance-based strategy.

Random-based strategy

The most straightforward techniques for creating feature subset-based ensemble are based on random selection. Ho [Ho (1998)] creates a forest of decision trees. The ensemble is constructed systematically by pseudo-randomly selecting subsets of features. The training instances are projected to each subset and a decision tree is constructed using the projected training samples. The process is repeated several times to create the forest. The classifications of the individual trees are combined by averaging the conditional probability of each class at the leaves (distribution summation). Ho shows that simple random selection of feature subsets may be an effective technique because the diversity of the ensemble members compensates for their lack of accuracy.

Bay [Bay (1999)] proposed using simple voting in order to combine outputs from multiple KNN (K-Nearest Neighbor) classifiers, each having access only to a random subset of the original features. Each classifier employs the same number of features. A technique for building ensembles of simple Bayesian classifiers in random feature subsets was also examined [Tsymbal and Puuronen (2002)] for improving medical applications.

Reduct-based strategy

A reduct is defined as the smallest feature subset which has the same predictive power as the whole feature set. By definition, the size of the ensembles that were created using reducts are limited to the number of features. There have been several attempts to create classifier ensembles by combining several reducts. Wu *et al.* introduce the worst-attribute-drop-first algorithm to find a set of significant reducts and then combine them using naïve Bayes.

Collective-Performance-based strategy

Cunningham and Carney [Cunningham and Carney (2000)] introduced an ensemble feature selection strategy that randomly constructs the initial ensemble. Then, an iterative refinement is performed based on a hill-climbing search in order to improve the accuracy and diversity of the base classifiers. For all the feature subsets, an attempt is made to switch (include or delete) each feature. If the resulting feature subset produces a better performance on the validation set, that change is kept. This process is continued until no further improvements are obtained. Similarly, Zenobi and Cunningham [Zenobi and Cunningham (2001)] suggest that the search for the different feature subsets will not be solely guided by the associated error but also by the disagreement or ambiguity among the ensemble members.

Tsymbal *et al.* [Tsymbal *et al.* (2004)] compare several feature selection methods that incorporate diversity as a component of the fitness function in the search for the best collection of feature subsets. This study shows that there are some datasets in which the ensemble feature selection method can be sensitive to the choice of the diversity measure. Moreover, no particular measure is superior in all cases.

Gunter and Bunke [Gunter and Bunke (2004)] suggest employing a feature subset search algorithm in order to find different subsets of the given features. The feature subset search algorithm not only takes the performance of the ensemble into account, but also directly supports diversity of subsets of features.

Combining genetic search with ensemble feature selection was also examined in the literature. Opitz and Shavlik [Opitz and Shavlik (1996)] applied GAs to ensembles using genetic operators that were designed explicitly for hidden nodes in knowledge-based neural networks. In a later research, Opitz [Opitz (1999)] used genetic search for ensemble feature selection. This genetic ensemble feature selection (GEFS) strategy begins by creating an initial population of classifiers where each classifier is generated by randomly selecting a different subset of features. Then, new candidate classifiers are continually produced by using the genetic operators of crossover and mutation on the feature subsets. The final ensemble is composed of the most fitted classifiers.

Feature set partitioning

Feature set partitioning is a particular case of feature subset-based ensembles in which the subsets are pairwise disjoint subsets. At the same time, feature set partitioning generalizes the task of feature selection which aims to provide a single representative set of features from which a classifier is constructed. Feature set partitioning, on the other hand, decomposes the original set of features into several subsets and builds a classifier for each subset. Thus, a set of classifiers is trained such that each classifier employs a different subset of the original feature set. Subsequently, an unlabelled instance is classified by combining the classifications of all classifiers.

Several researchers have shown that the partitioning methodology can be appropriate for classification tasks with a large number of features [Kusiak (2000)]. The search space of a feature subset-based ensemble contains the search space of feature set partitioning, and the latter contains the search space of feature selection. Mutually exclusive partitioning has some important and helpful properties:

(1) There is a greater possibility of achieving reduced execution time compared to non-exclusive approaches. Since most learning algorithms have computational complexity that is greater than linear in the number of features or tuples, partitioning the problem dimensionality in a mutually exclusive manner means a decrease in computational complexity [Provost and Kolluri (1997)].

(2) Since mutual exclusiveness entails using smaller datasets, the classifiers obtained for each sub-problem are smaller in size. Without the mutually exclusive restriction, each classifier can be as complicated as the classifier obtained for the original problem. Smaller classifiers contribute to comprehensibility and ease in maintaining the solution.

(3) According to Bay [Bay (1999)], mutually exclusive partitioning may help avoid some error correlation problems that characterize feature subset based ensembles. However Sharkey [Sharkey (1996)] argues that mutually exclusive training sets do not necessarily result in low error correlation. This point is true when each sub-problem is representative.

(4) In feature subset-based ensembles, different classifiers might generate contradictive classifications using the same features. This inconsistency in the way a certain feature can affect the final classification may increase mistrust among end-users. We claim that end-users can grasp mutually exclusive partitioning much easier.

(5) The mutually exclusive approach encourages smaller datasets which are generally more practicable. Some data mining tools can process only limited dataset sizes (for instance, when the program requires that the entire dataset will be stored in the main memory). The mutually exclusive approach can ensure that data mining tools can be scaled fairly easily to large data sets [Chan and Stolfo (1997)].

In the literature there are several works that deal with feature set partitioning. In one research, the features are grouped according to the feature type: nominal value features, numeric value features and text value features [Kusiak (2000)]. A similar approach was also used for developing the linear Bayes classifier [Gama (2000)]. The basic idea consists of aggregating the features into two subsets: the first subset containing only the nominal features and the second only the continuous features.

In another research, the feature set was decomposed according to the target class [Tumer and Ghosh (1996)]. For each class, the features with low correlation relating to that class were removed. This method was applied on a feature set of 25 sonar signals where the target was to identify the meaning of the sound (whale, cracking ice, etc.). Feature set partitioning has also been used for radar-based volcano recognition [Cherkauer (1996)]. The researcher manually decomposed a feature set of 119 into 8 subsets. Features that were based on different image processing operations were grouped together. As a consequence, for each subset, four neural networks with different sizes were built. A new combining framework for feature set partitioning has been used for text-independent speaker identification [Chen *et al.* (1997)]. Other researchers manually decomposed the features set of a certain truck backer-upper problem and reported that this strategy has important advantages [Jenkins and Yuhas (1993)].

The feature set decomposition can be obtained by grouping features based on pairwise mutual information, with statistically similar features assigned to the same group [Liao and Moody (2000)]. For this purpose one can use an existing hierarchical clustering algorithm. As a consequence, several feature subsets are constructed by selecting one feature from each group. A neural network is subsequently constructed for each subset. All networks are then combined.

In statistics literature, the well-known feature-oriented ensemble algorithm is the MARS algorithm [Friedman (1991)]. In this algorithm, a multiple regression function is approximated using linear splines and their tensor products. It has been shown that the algorithm performs an ANOVA decomposition, namely, the regression function is represented as a grand total of several sums. The first sum is of all basic functions that involve only a single attribute. The second sum is of all basic functions that involve exactly two attributes, representing (if present) two-variable interactions. Similarly, the third sum represents (if present) the contributions from three-variable interactions, and so on.

A general framework that searches for helpful feature set partitioning structures has also been proposed [Rokach and Maimon (2005b)]. This framework nests many algorithms, two of which are tested empirically over a set of benchmark datasets. The first algorithm performs a serial search while using a new Vapnik-Chervonenkis dimension bound for multiple oblivious trees as an evaluating scheme. The second algorithm performs a multi-search while using a wrapper evaluating scheme. This work indicates that feature set decomposition can increase the accuracy of decision trees.

7.5.5 *Multi-Inducers*

In Multi-Inducer strategy, diversity is obtained by using different types of inducers [Michalski and Tecuci (1994)]. Each inducer contains an explicit or implicit bias [Mitchell (1980)] that leads it to prefer certain generalizations over others. Ideally, this multi-inducer strategy would always perform as well as the best of its ingredients. Even more ambitiously, there is hope that this combination of paradigms might produce synergistic effects, leading to levels of accuracy that neither atomic approach by itself would be able to achieve.

Most research in this area has been concerned with combining empirical approaches with analytical methods (see for instance [Towell and Shavlik (1994)]. Woods et al. [Woods *et al.* (1997)] combine four types of base inducers (decision trees, neural networks, k-nearest neighbor, and quadratic Bayes). They then estimate local accuracy in the feature space to choose the appropriate classifier for a given new unlabled instance. Wang et al. [Wang *et al.* (2004)] examined the usefulness of adding decision trees to an ensemble of neural networks. The researchers concluded that adding a few decision trees (but not too many) usually improved the performance. Langdon et al. [Langdon *et al.* (2002)] proposed using Genetic Programming to find an appropriate rule for combining decision trees with neural networks.

The model class selection (MCS) system fits different classifiers to different subspaces of the instance space, by employing one of three classification methods (a decision-tree, a discriminant function or an instance-based method). In order to select the classification method, MCS uses the characteristics of the underlined training-set, and a collection of expert rules. Brodley's expert-rules were based on empirical comparisons of the methods' performance (i.e., on prior knowledge).

The NeC4.5 algorithm, which integrates decision tree with neural networks [Zhou and Jiang (2004)], first trains a neural network ensemble. Then, the trained ensemble is employed to generate a new training set by replacing the desired class labels of the original training examples with the output from the trained ensemble. Some extra training examples are also generated from the trained ensemble and added to the new training set. Finally, a C4.5 decision tree is grown from the new training set. Since its learning results are decision trees, the comprehensibility of NeC4.5 is better than that of neural network ensembles.

Using several inducers can solve the dilemma which arises from the "no free lunch" theorem. This theorem implies that a certain inducer will be successful only insofar its bias matches the characteristics of the application domain [Brazdil *et al.* (1994)]. Thus, given a certain application, the practitioner need to decide which inducer should be used. Using the multi-inducer obviate the need to try each one and simplifying the entire process.

7.5.6   Measuring the Diversity

As stated above, it is usually assumed that increasing diversity may decrease ensemble error [Zenobi and Cunningham (2001)].   For regression problems, *variance* is usually used to measure diversity [Krogh and Vedelsby (1995)]. In such cases it can be easily shown that the ensemble error can be reduced by increasing ensemble diversity while maintaining the average error of a single model.

In classification problems, a more complicated measure is required to evaluate the diversity. There have been several attempts to define diversity measure for classification tasks.

In the neural network literature two measures are presented for examining diversity:

- Classification coverage: An instance is covered by a classifier, if it yields a correct classification.
- Coincident errors: A coincident error amongst the classifiers occurs when more than one member misclassifies a given instance.

Based on these two measures, Sharkey (1997) defined four diversity levels:

- Level 1 - No coincident errors and the classification function is completely covered by a majority vote of the members.
- Level 2 - Coincident errors may occur, but the classification function is completely covered by majority vote.
- Level 3 - A majority vote will not always correctly classify a given instance, but at least one ensemble member always correctly classifies it.
- Level 4 - The function is not always covered by the members of the ensemble.

Brown et al. [Brown *et al.* (2005)] claim that the above four-level scheme provides no indication of how typical the error behaviour described by the assigned diversity level is. This claim, especially, holds when the ensemble exhibits different diversity levels on different subsets of instance space.

There are other more quantative measures which categorize these measures into two types [Brown *et al.* (2005)]: pairwise and non-pairwise. Pairwise measures calculate the average of a particular distance metric between all possible pairings of members in the ensemble, such as Q-statistic [Brown *et al.* (2005)] or kappa-statistic [Margineantu and Dietterich (1997)]. The non-pairwise measures either use the idea of entropy (such as [Cunningham and Carney (2000)]) or calculate a correlation of each ensemble member with the averaged output. The comparison of several measures of diversity has resulted in the conclusion that most of them are correlated [Kuncheva and Whitaker (2003)].

7.6 Ensemble Size

7.6.1 *Selecting the Ensemble Size*

An important aspect of ensemble methods is to define how many component classifiers should be used. There are several factors that may determine this size:

- Desired accuracy — In most cases, ensembles containing ten classifiers are sufficient for reducing the error rate [Hansen (1990)]. Nevertheless, there is empirical evidence indicating that: when AdaBoost uses decision trees, error reduction is observed in even relatively large ensembles containing 25 classifiers [Opitz and Maclin (1999)]. In disjoint partitioning approaches, there may be a trade-off between the number of subsets and the final accuracy. The size of each subset cannot be too small because sufficient data must be available for each learning process to produce an effective classifier.
- Computational cost — Increasing the number of classifiers usually increases computational cost and decreases their comprehensibility. For that reason, users may set their preferences by predefining the ensemble size limit.
- The nature of the classification problem - In some ensemble methods, the nature of the classification problem that is to be solved, determines the number of classifiers. For instance in the ECOC algorithm the number of classes determine the ensemble size.
- Number of processors available — In independent methods, the number of processors available for parallel learning could be put as an upper bound on the number of classifiers that are treated in paralleled process.

There three methods that are used to determine the ensemble size, as described by the following subsections.

7.6.2 *Pre Selection of the Ensemble Size*

This is the most simple way to determine the ensemble size. Many ensemble algorithms have a controlling parameter such as "number of iterations", which is can be set by the user. Algorithms such as Bagging belong to this category. In other cases the nature of the classification problem determine the number of members (such as in the case of ECOC).

7.6.3 *Selection of the Ensemble Size while Training*

There are ensemble algorithms that try to determine the best ensemble size while training. Usually as new classifiers are added to the ensemble these algorithms check if the contribution of the last classifier to the ensemble performance is still significant. If it is not, the ensemble algorithm stops. Usually these algorithms also have a controlling parameter which bounds the maximum size of the ensemble.

An algorithm that decides when a sufficient number of classification trees have been created was recently proposed [Banfield *et al.* (2007)]. The algorithm uses the out-of-bag error estimate, and is shown to result in an accurate ensemble for those methods that incorporate bagging into the construction of the ensemble. Specifically, the algorithm works by first smoothing the out-of-bag error graph with a sliding window in order to reduce the variance. After the smoothing has been completed, the algorithm takes a larger window on the smoothed data points and determines the maximum accuracy within that window. It continues to process windows until the maximum accuracy within a particular window no longer increases. At this point, the stopping criterion has been reached and the algorithm returns the ensemble with the maximum raw accuracy from within that window.

7.6.4 *Pruning — Post Selection of the Ensemble Size*

As in decision tree induction, it is sometimes useful to let the ensemble grow freely and then prune the ensemble in order to get more effective and compact ensembles. Post selection of the ensemble size allows ensemble optimization for such performance metrics as accuracy, cross entropy, mean precision, or the ROC area. Empirical examinations indicate that pruned ensembles may obtain a similar accuracy performance as the original ensemble [Margineantu and Dietterich (1997)]. In another empirical study that was conducted in order to understand the affect of ensemble sizes on ensemble accuracy and diversity, it has been shown that it is feasible to keep a small ensemble while maintaining accuracy and diversity similar to those of a full ensemble [Liu et al., 2004].

The pruning methods can be divided into two groups: pre-combining pruning methods and post-combining pruning methods.

7.6.4.1 *Pre-combining Pruning*

Pre-combining pruning is performed before combining the classifiers. Classifiers that seem to perform well are included in the ensemble. Prodromidis et al. [Prodromidis *et al.* (1999)] present three methods for pre-combining pruning: based on an individual classification performance on a separate validation set, diversity metrics, the ability of classifiers to classify correctly specific classes.

In attribute bagging, classification accuracy of randomly selected m-attribute subsets is evaluated by using the wrapper approach and only the classifiers constructed on the highest ranking subsets participate in the ensemble voting.

7.6.4.2 *Post-combining Pruning*

In post-combining pruning methods, we remove classifiers based on their contribution to the collective.

Prodromidis examines two methods for post-combining pruning assuming that the classifiers are combined using meta-combination method: Based on decision tree pruning and the correlation of the base classifier to the unpruned meta-classifier.

A forward stepwise selection procedure can be used in order to select the most relevant classifiers (that maximize the ensemble's performance) among thousands of classifiers [Caruana *et al.* (2004)]. It has been shown that for this purpose one can use feature selection algorithms. However, instead of selecting features one should select the ensemble's members [Liu et al., 2004].

One can also rank the classifiers according to their ROC performance. Then, they suggest to plot a graph where the Y- axis displays a performance measure of the integrated classification. The X-axis presents the number of classifiers that participated in the combination. i.e., the first best classifiers from the list are combined by voting (assuming equal weights for now) with the rest getting zero weights. The ensemble size is chosen when there are several sequential points with no improvement.

The GASEN algorithm was developed for selecting the most appropriate classifiers in a given ensemble [Zhou *et al.* (2002)]. In the initialization phase, GASEN assigns a random weight to each of the classifiers. Consequently, it uses genetic algorithms to evolve those weights so that they can characterize to some extent the fitness of the classifiers in joining the ensemble. Finally, it removes from the ensemble those classifiers whose weight is less than a predefined threshold value.

Recently a revised version of the GASEN algorithm called GASEN-b has been suggested [Zhou and Tang (2003)]. In this algorithm, instead of assigning a weight to each classifier, a bit is assigned to each classifier indicating whether it will be used in the final ensemble. In an experimental study the researchers showed that ensembles generated by a selective ensemble algorithm, which selects some of the trained C4.5 decision trees to make up an ensemble, may be not only smaller in size but also stronger in the generalization than ensembles generated by non-selective algorithms.

A comparative study of pre combining and post combining methods when meta-combining methods are used has been performed in [Prodromidis *et al.* (1999)]. The results indicate that the post-combining pruning methods tend to perform better in this case.

7.7   Cross-Inducer

This property indicates the relation between the ensemble technique and the inducer used.

Some implementations are considered as an inducer-dependent type, namely these ensemble generators which use intrinsic inducer, have been developed specifically for a certain inducer. They can neither work nor guarantee effectiveness in any other induction method. For instance, the works of [Hansen (1990); Lu and Ito (1999); Sharkey (1996)] were developed specifically for neural networks. The works of [Breiman (2001); Rokach and Maimon (2005b)] were developed specifically for decision trees.

Other implementations are considered to be the inducer-independent type. These implementations can be performed on any given inducer and are not limited to a specific inducer like the inducer-dependent.

7.8   Multistrategy Ensemble Learning

Multistrategy ensemble learning combines several ensemble strategies. It has been shown that this hybrid approach increases the diversity of ensemble members.

MultiBoosting, an extension to AdaBoost expressed by adding wagging-like features [Webb (2000)], can harness both AdaBoost's high bias and variance reduction with wagging's superior variance reduction. Using C4.5 as the base learning algorithm, MultiBoosting, significantly more often than the reverse, produces decision committees with lower error than either AdaBoost or wagging. It also offers the further advantage over AdaBoost of suiting parallel execution. MultiBoosting has been further extended by adding the stochastic attribute selection committee learning strategy to boosting and wagging [Webb and Zheng (2004)]. The latter's research has shown that combining ensemble strategies would increase diversity at the cost of a small increase in individual test error resulting in a trade-off that reduced overall ensemble test error.

Another multistrategy method suggests to create the ensemble by decomposing the original classification problem into several smaller and more manageable sub-problems. This multistrategy uses an elementary decomposition framework that consists of five different elementary decompositions: Concept Aggregation, Function, Sample, Space and Feature Set. The concept of elementary decomposition can be used to obtain a complicated decomposition by using the elementary decomposition concept recursively. Given a certain problem, the procedure selects the most appropriate elementary decomposition (if any) to that problem. A suitable decomposer then decomposes the problem and provides a set of sub-problems. A similar procedure is performed on each sub-problem until no beneficial decomposition is anticipated. The selection of the best elementary decomposition for a given problem is performed by using a meta-learning approach.

7.9   Which Ensemble Method Should be Used?

Recent research has experimentally evaluated bagging and seven other randomization-based approaches for creating an ensemble of decision tree classifiers [Banfield *et al.* (2007)]. Statistical tests were performed on experimental results from 57 publicly available datasets. When cross-validation comparisons were tested for statistical significance, the best method was statistically more accurate than bagging on only eight of the 57 datasets. Alternatively, examining the average ranks of the algorithms across the group of datasets, Banfield found that boosting, random forests, and randomized trees is statistically significantly better than bagging.

7.10   Open Source for Decision Trees Forests

There are two open source software packages which can be used for creating decision trees forests. Both systems, which are free, are distributed under the terms of the GNU General Public License.

- The OpenDT [Banfield (2005)] package has the ability to output trees very similar to C4.5, but has added functionality for ensemble creation. In the event that the attribute set randomly chosen provides a negative information gain, the OpenDT approach is to randomly rechoose attributes until a positive information gain is obtained, or no further split is possible. This enables each test to improve the purity of the resultant leaves. The system is written in Java.
- The Weka package [Frank et. al (2005)] is an organized collection of state-of-the-art machine learning algorithms and data preprocessing tools. The basic way of interacting with these methods is by invoking them from the command line. However, convenient interactive graphical user interfaces are provided for data exploration, for setting up large-scale experiments on distributed computing platforms, and for designing configurations for streamed data processing. These interfaces constitute an advanced environment for experimental data mining. Weka includes many decision tree learners: decision stumps, ID3, a C4.5 clone called "J48," trees generated by reduced error pruning, alternating decision trees, and random trees and forests thereof, including random forests, bagging, boosting, and stacking.

Chapter 8

Incremental Learning of Decision Trees

8.1 Overview

To reflect new data that has become available, most decision trees inducers must be rebuilt from scratch. This is time-consuming and expensive and several researchers have addressed the issue of updating decision trees incrementally. Utgoff [Utgoff (1989b); Utgoff (1997)], for example, presents several methods for incrementally updating decision trees while [Crawford (1989)] describes an extension to the CART algorithm that is capable of inducing incremental changes.

8.2 The Motives for Incremental Learning

In the ever-changing world of information technology there are two fundamental problems to be addressed:

- Vast quantities of digital data continue to grow at staggering rates. In organizations such as e-commerce sites, large retailers and telecommunication corporations, data increases of gigabytes per day are not uncommon. While this data could be extremely valuable to these organizations, the tremendous volume makes it virtually impossible to extract useful information. This is due to the fact that KDD systems in general, and traditional data mining algorithms in particular, are limited by several crippling factors. These factors, referred to as computational resources, are the size of the sample to be processed, running time and memory. As a result, most of the available data is unused which leads to underfitting. While there is enough data to model a compound phenomenon, there is no capability for fully utilizing this

131

data and unsatisfactorily simple models are produced.

- Most machine learning algorithms, among them those underlying the data mining process assume that the data, which needs to be learned (training data), serves as a random sample drawn from a stationary distribution. (These algorithms include CART (Breiman et al. (1984)), ID3 (Quinlan, J.R., (1986)), C4.5 (Quinlan, J.R., 1986)), IFN (Maimon and Last (2000)) and very fast decision tree (VFDT) (Domingos and Hulten (2000).) The assumption is unfortunately violated by the majority of databases and data streams available for mining today. These databases accumulate over large periods of time, with the underlying processes generating them changing respectively and at times quite drastically. This occurrence is known as concept drift. According to [Domingos and Hulten (2001)] "in many cases... it is more accurate to assume that data was generated by ... a concept function with time-varying parameters." Incorrect models are learned by the traditional data mining algorithms when these mistakenly assume that the underlying concept is stationary, when it is, in fact, drifting. This may serve to degrade the predictive performance of the models.

A prime example of systems which may have to deal with the aforementioned problems are on-line learning systems, which use continuous incoming batches of training examples to induce rules for a classification task. Two instances in which these systems are currently utilized are credit card fraud detection and real-time monitoring of manufacturing processes.

As a result of the above mentioned problems it is now common practice to mine a sub-sample of the available data or to mine for a model drastically simpler than the data could support. Ideally, the KDD systems will function continuously, constantly processing data received so that potentially valuable information is never lost. In order to achieve this goal, many methods have been developed. Termed incremental (online) learning methods, these methods aim to extract patterns from changing streams of data.

8.3 The Inefficiency Challenge

According to [Domingos and Hulten (2001)], incremental learning algorithms suffer from numerous inadequacies from the KDD point of view. Whereas some of these algorithms are relatively efficient, they do not guarantee that the model that emerges will be similar to the one obtained by learning on the same data in the non-incremental (batch) methods. Other incremental learning algorithms produce the same model as the batch version, but at a higher cost in efficiency, which may mean longer training times.

In order to overcome this trade-off, Domingos and Hulten (2000) proposed VFDT a decision-tree learning method which is aimed at learning online from high-volume data streams by using sub-sampling of the entire data stream generated by a stationary process. This method uses constant time per example and constant memory and can incorporate tens of thousands of examples per second using off-the-shelf hardware. This method involves learning by seeing each example only once; there is no necessity for storing them. As a result it is possible to directly mine online data sources. The sample size is determined in VFDT from distribution-free Hoeffding bounds to guarantee that its output is asymptotically nearly identical to that of a conventional learner.

8.4   The Concept Drift Challenge

The second problem, centered around concept drift, is also addressed by incremental learning methods that have been adapted to work effectively with continuous, time-changing data streams. Black and Hickey (1999) identified several important sub-tasks involved in handling drift within incremental learning methods. The two most fundamental sub-tasks are identifying that drift is occurring and updating classification rules in the light of this drift.

Time-windowing is one of the most known and acceptable approaches for dealing with these tasks. The basic concept of this approach is the repeated application of a learning algorithm to a sliding window, which contains a certain amount (either constant or changing) of examples. As new examples arrive, they are placed into the beginning of the window. A corresponding number of examples are removed from the end of the window. The latest model is the one used for future prediction of incoming instances until concept drift is detected. At this point the learner is reapplied on the last window of instances and a new model is built.

FLORA, the time-windowing approach developed by [Widmer and Kubat (1996)] describes a family of incremental algorithms for learning in the presence of drift. This method uses a currently trusted window of examples as well as stored, old concept hypothesis description sets which are reactivated if they seem to be valid again. The first realization of this framework of this family of incremental algorithms is FLORA2, which maintains a dynamically adjustable window of the latest training examples. The method of adjusting the size of the window is known as WAH (window adjustment heuristic). Whenever a concept drift is suspected as a result of a drop in predictive accuracy, the size of the window is decreased by disposing of the oldest examples. The window size is left unchanged if the concept appears to be stable. If concept drift remains uncertain, none of the examples are forgotten, and thus the window size is gradually increased until a stable concept description can be formed. As long as a relatively low rate of concept drift is preserved this strategy of window adjustment can detect radical changes in the underlying concept efficiently.

FLORA3 stores concepts for later use and reassesses their utility when a context change is perceived. FLORA4 is designed to be exceptionally robust with respect to noise in the training data since it is very difficult in incremental learning to distinguish between slight irregularities due to noise and actual concept drift. Both of these algorithms serve as an extension of FLORA2.

According to [Domingos and Hulten (2001)], as long as the window size is small relative to the rate of concept drift, the time-windowing procedure assures availability of a model reflecting the current concept generating the data. However, if the window is too small, this may result in insufficient examples to satisfactorily learn the concept. Furthermore, the computational cost of reapplying a learner may be prohibitively high, especially if examples arrive at a rapid rate and the concept changes quickly.

To meet these challenges, Domingos and Hulten (2001) proposed an efficient algorithm for mining decision trees from continuously changing data streams. Called CVFDT (concept-adapting very fast decision trees learner), the algorithm is based on the ultra-fast VFDT decision tree learner. CVFDT, a VFDTn extension, maintains VFDTs speed and accuracy advantages but adds the ability to detect and respond to changes in the example-generating process.

Like other systems with this capability, CVFDT works by keeping its model consistent with a sliding window of examples. However, it does not need to learn a new model from scratch every time a new example arrives; instead, it updates the sufficient statistics at its nodes by incrementing the counts corresponding to the new example and by decrementing the counts corresponding to the oldest example in the window (which now must be forgotten). This will statistically have no effect if the underlying concept is stationary. If the concept is changing, however, some splits that previously passed the Hoeffding test will no longer do so because an alternative attribute now has higher gain. In this case, CVFDT begins to grow an alternative sub-tree with the new best attribute at its root. When this alternate sub-tree becomes more accurate on new data than the old one, the new one replaces the old sub-tree. CVFDT learns a model which is similar in accuracy to the one that would be learned by reapplying VFDT to a moving window of examples every time a new example arrives, but with $O(1)$ complexity per example, as opposed to $O(w)$, where w is the size of the window.

Last (2001) presented an online classification system. The induced concept is represented in the form of an info-fuzzy network (IFN), a tree-like classification model. The proposed system, called OLIN (on-line information network) receives a continuous stream of data and repeatedly constructs a new network from a sliding window of the latest examples. Concurrently, the system dynamically adapts the size of the training window and the frequency of model re-construction to the current rate of concept drift. The dynamic adaptation consists of the increase of the update cycle when the concept appears stable, and the reduction in size of the training window whenever concept drift is detected. These two qualities work towards conserving computer resources. Once concept drift is detected (by an unexpected rise in the classification error rate), the size of the training window is re-calculated by using the principles of information theory and statistics.

The latest model classifies the examples that arrive before the subsequent network reconstruction. Though the cumulative accuracy of models produced by OLIN may be somewhat lower than the accuracy of an incremental system that does not forget past examples, it still tends to be higher than the accuracy acquired with a fixed-size sliding window.

Black and Hickey (1999) offer a new approach to handling the aforementioned sub-tasks dealing with drift within incremental learning methods. Instead of utilizing the time-windowing approach presented thus far, they employ a new purging mechanism to remove examples that are no longer valid while retaining valid examples, regardless of age. As a result, the example base grows, thus assisting good classification. Black and Hickey describe an algorithm called CD3, which utilizes ID3 with post-pruning, based on the time-stamp attribute relevance or TSAR approach.

In this approach, the time-stamp is treated as an attribute, and its value is added as an additional input attribute to the examples description, later to be used in the induction process. Consequently, if the time-stamp attribute appears in the decision tree, the implication is that it is relevant to classification. This, in turn, means that drift has occurred. Routes where the value of the time-stamp attribute refers to the old period (or periods) represent invalid rules. When the process is stable for a sufficiently long period, the time-stamp attribute should not appear in any path of the tree.

The CD3 algorithm sustains a set of examples regarded as valid. This set, referred to as the current example base, must be updated before another round of learning can take place. Using invalid rules extracted from the CD3 tree, any example whose description matches (i.e. is covered by) that of an invalid rule can be removed from the current example set. This process of deletion is referred to as purging the current example set.

Chapter 9

Feature Selection

9.1 Overview

Dimensionality (i.e., the number of dataset attributes or groups of attributes) constitutes a serious obstacle to the efficiency of most induction algorithms, primarily because induction algorithms are computationally intensive. Feature selection is an effective way to deal with dimensionality.

The objective of feature selection is to identify those features in the dataset which are important, and discard others as irrelevant and redundant. Since feature selection reduces the dimensionality of the data, data mining algorithms can be operated faster and more effectively by using feature selection. The reason for the improved performance is mainly due to a more compact, easily interpreted representation of the target concept [George and Foster (2000)]. We differentiate between three main strategies for feature selection: filter, wrapper and embedded [Blum and Langley (1997)].

9.2 The "Curse of Dimensionality"

High dimensionality of the input (that is, the number of attributes) increases the size of the search space in an exponential manner and thus increases the chance that the inducer will find spurious classifiers that are not valid in general. It is well known that the required number of labeled samples for supervised classification increases as a function of dimensionality [Jimenez and Landgrebe (1998)]. [Fukunaga (1990)] showed that the required number of training samples is linearly related to the dimensionality for a linear classifier and to the square of the dimensionality for a quadratic classifier. In terms of nonparametric classifiers like decision trees, the situation is even more severe. It has been estimated that as the number of dimensions increases, the sample size needs to increase exponentially in order to have an effective estimate of multivariate densities ([Hwang *et al.* (1994)].

This phenomenon is usually referred to as the "curse of dimensionality". Bellman (1961) was the first to coin this term, while working on complicated signal processing issues. Techniques like decision trees inducers that are efficient in low dimensions fail to provide meaningful results when the number of dimensions increases beyond a "modest" size. Furthermore, smaller classifiers, involving fewer features (probably less than 10), are much more understandable by humans. Smaller classifiers are also more appropriate for user-driven data mining techniques such as visualization.

Most methods for dealing with high dimensionality focus on Feature Selection techniques, i.e. selecting a single subset of features upon which the inducer (induction algorithm) will run, while ignoring the rest. The selection of the subset can be done manually by using prior knowledge to identify irrelevant variables or by using proper algorithms.

In the last decade, many researchers have become increasingly interested in feature selection. Consequently many feature selection algorithms have been proposed, some of which have reported as displaying remarkable improvements in accuracy Since the subject is too broad to survey here, readers seeking further information about recent developments, should see: [Langley (1994); Liu and Motoda (1998)].

A number of linear dimension reducers have been developed over the years. The linear methods of dimensionality reduction include projection pursuit [Friedman and Tukey (1973)]; factor analysis [Kim and Mueller (1978)]; and principal components analysis [Dunteman (1989)]. These methods are not aimed directly at eliminating irrelevant and redundant features, but are rather concerned with transforming the observed variables into a small number of "projections" or "dimensions". The underlying assumptions are that the variables are numeric and the dimensions can be expressed as linear combinations of the observed variables (and vice versa). Each discovered dimension is assumed to represent an unobserved factor and thus provide a new way of understanding the data (similar to the curve equation in the regression models).

The linear dimension reducers have been enhanced by constructive induction systems that use a set of existing features and a set of predefined constructive operators to derive new features [Pfahringer (1994); Ragavan and Rendell (1993)]. These methods are effective for high dimensionality applications only if the original domain size of the input feature can be decreased dramatically.

On the one hand, feature selection can be used as a preprocessing step before building a decision tree. On the other hand, the decision tree can be used as a feature selector for other induction methods.

At first glance, it seems redundant to use feature selection as a pre-process phase for the training phase. Decision trees inducers, as opposed to other induction methods, incorporate in their training phase a built-in feature selection mechanism. Indeed, all criteria described in Section 4.1 are criteria for feature selection.

Still, it is well known that correlated and irrelevant features may degrade the performance of decision trees inducers. This phenomenon can be explained by the fact that feature selection in decision trees is performed on one attribute at a time and only at the root node over the entire decision space. In subsequent nodes, the training set is divided into several sub-sets and the features are selected according to their local predictive power [Perner (2001)]. Geometrically it means that the selection of features is done in orthogonal decision subspaces, which do not necessarily represent the distribution of the entire instance space. It has been shown that the predictive performance of decision trees could be improved with an appropriate feature pre-selection phase. Moreover using feature selection can reduce the number of nodes in the tree making it more compact.

Formally, the problem of feature subset selection can be defined as follows [Jain *et al.* (1997)]: Let A be the original set of features, with cardinality n. Let d represent the desired number of features in the selected subset B, $B \subseteq A$. Let the feature selection criterion function for the set B be represented by $J(B)$. Without any loss of generality, a lower value of J is considered to be a better feature subset (for instance if J represents the generalization error). The problem of feature selection is to find an optimal subset B that solves the following optimization problem:

$$
\begin{aligned}
& \min J(Z) \\
& s.t. \\
& Z \subseteq A \\
& |Z| = d
\end{aligned}
\tag{9.1}
$$

An exhaustive search would require examining all $\frac{n!}{d! \cdot (n-d)!}$ possible d-subsets of the feature set A.

9.3   Techniques for Feature Selection

Feature selection techniques can be used in many applications from choosing the most important social-economic parameters for determining whatever a person can return a bank loan to dealing an with chemical process and selecting the best set of ingredients.

The filter approach operates independently of the data mining method employed subsequently - undesirable features are filtered out of the data before the learning of a filtering threshold begins. These fileterning algorithms use heuristics based on general characteristics of the data to evaluate the merit of feature subsets. A sub-category of filter methods, refered to as rankers, includes methods that employ some criterion to score each feature and provide a ranking. From this ordering, several feature subsets can be chosen manually.

The wrapper approach [Kohavi and John (1998)] uses a learning algorithm as a black box along with a statistical re-sampling technique such as cross-validation to select the best feature subset according to some predictive measure.

The *embedded* approach [Guyon and Elisseeff] is similar to the wrapper approach in the sense that the features are specifically selected for a certain learning algorithm. . However, in the embedded approach the features are selected in the process of learning.

While most of the feature selection methods have been applied to supervised methods (such as classification and regression) there are important works that deals with unsupervised methods [Wolf and Shashua (2005)].

Feature selection algorithms search through the space of feature subsets in order to find the best subset. This subset search has four major properties [Langley (1994)]:

- Starting Point - Selecting a point in the feature subset space from which to begin the search can affect the direction of the search.
- Search Organization - A comprehensive search of the feature subspace is prohibitive for all but a small initial number of features.
- Evaluation Strategy - How feature subsets are evaluated (filter, wrapper and ensemble).
- Stopping Criterion - A feature selector must decide when to stop searching through the space of feature subsets.

The next sections provide detailed description of feature selection techniques for each property described above.

9.3.1 *Feature Filters*

Filter methods, the earliest approaches for feature selection, use general properties of the data in order to evaluate the merit of feature subsets. As a result, filter methods are generally much faster and practical than wrapper methods, especially for use on data of high dimensionality.

9.3.1.1 *FOCUS*

The FOCUS algorithm is originally designed for attributes with Boolean domains [Almuallim and Dietterich (1994)]. FOCUS exhaustively searches the space of feature subsets until every combination of feature values is associated with one value of the class. After selecting the subset, it passed to the *ID*3 algorithm which constructs a decision tree.

9.3.1.2 *LVF*

Similar algorithm to FOCUS is the LVF algorithm [Liu and Setiono (1996)]. LVF is consistency-driven and can handle noisy domains if the approximate noise level is known a-priori. During every round of implemention, LVF generates a random subset from the feature subset space. If the chosen subset is smaller than the current best subset, the inconsistency rate of the dimensionally reduced data described by the subset is compared with the inconsistency rate of the best subset. If the subset is at least as consistent as the best subset, the subset replaces the best subset.

9.3.1.3 *Using One Learning Algorithm as a Filter for Another*

Some works have explored the possibility of using a learning algorithm as a pre-processor to discover useful feature subsets for a primary learning algorithm. Cardie (1995) describes the application of decision tree algorithms for selecting feature subsets for use by instance based learners. In [Provan and Singh (1996)], a greedy oblivious decision tree algorithm is used to select features to construct a Bayesian network. Holmes and Nevill-Manning (1995) apply Holte's (1993) 1R system in order to estimate the predictive accuracy of individual features. A program for inducing decision table majority classifiers used for selecting features is presented in [Pfahringer (1995)].

DTM (decision table majority) classifiers are restricted to returning stored instances that are exact matches with the instance to be classified. When no instances are returned, the most prevalent class in the training data is used as the predicted class; otherwise, the majority class of all matching instances is used. In such cases, the minimum description length principle (MDL) guides the search by estimating the cost of encoding a decision table and the training examples it misclassifies with respect to a given feature subset. The features in the final decision table are then used with other learning algorithms.

9.3.1.4 *An Information Theoretic Feature Filter*

There are many filters techniques that are based on information theory and probabilistic reasoning [Koller and Sahami (1996)]. The rationale behind this approach is that, since the goal of an induction algorithm is to estimate the probability distributions over the class values, given the original feature set, feature subset selection should attempt to remain as close to these original distributions as possible.

9.3.1.5 *An Instance Based Approach to Feature Selection – RE-LIEF*

RELIEF [Kira and Rendell (1992)] uses instance based learning to assign a relevance weight to each feature. The weight for each feature reflects its ability to single out the class values. The features are ranked by its weights and chosen by using a user-specified threshold. RELIEF randomly chooses instances from the training data. For every instance, RELIEF samples the nearest instance of the same class (nearest hit) and finds the opposite class (nearest miss). The weight for each feature is updated according to how well its values differentiate the sampled instance from its nearest hit and nearest miss. A feature will gain a high weight if it differentiates between instances from different classes and has the same value for instances of the same class.

9.3.1.6 *Simba and G-flip*

The SIMBA (iterative search margin based algorithm) technique introduces the idea of measuring the quality of a set of features by the margin it induces. To overcome the drawback of iterative search, a greedy feature flip algorithm G-flip is used [Gilad-Bachrach *et al.* (2004)] for maximizing the margin function of a subset. The algorithm constantly iterates over the feature set and updates the set of chosen features. During each iteration G-flip decides to eliminate or include the current feature to the selected subset by evaluating the margin with and without this feature.

9.3.1.7 *Contextual Merit Algorithm*

The contextual merit (CM) algorithm [Hong (1997)] uses a merit function based upon weighted distances between examples which takes into account complete feature correlation's to the instance class. This approach assumes that features should be weighted according to their discrimination power regarding instances that are close to each other (based on the Euclidean distance) but which are associated with different classes. The CM approach has been used to select features for decision trees and an experimental study shows that feature subset selection can help to improve the prediction accuracy of the induced classifier [Perner (2001)].

The notation $d_{r,s}^i$ represents the distance between the value of feature i in the instances r and s (i.e. the distance between $x_{r,i}$ and $x_{s,i}$). For numerical attributes, the distance is $min(1, \frac{x_{r,i} - x_{s,i}}{t_i})$ where t_i is usually 0.5 of the value range of the attribute i. For nominal attributes, the distance is 0 if $x_{r,i} = x_{s,i}$, and 1 otherwise. The contextual merit for attribute i is calculated as $M_i = \sum_{r=1}^m \sum_{s \in \{(x,y) \in S | y_i \neq y_r\}} w_{r,s}^i d_{r,s}^i$ where m is the training set size, $\{(x,y) \in S | y_i \neq y_r\}$ is the set of instances associated with a different class than the instance r, and $w_{r,s}^i$ is a weighting factor.

9.3.2 *Using Traditional Statistics for Filtering*

9.3.2.1 *Mallows Cp*

This method minimizes the mean square error of prediction [Mallows (1973)]:

$$C_p = \frac{RSS_\gamma}{\hat{\sigma}_{FULL}^2} + 2q_\gamma - nC_p = \frac{RSS_\gamma}{\hat{\sigma}_{FULL}^2} + 2q_\gamma - n \qquad (9.2)$$

where, RSS_γ is the residual sum of squares for the γth model and σ_{FULL}^2 is the usual unbiased estimate of σ^2 based on the full model.

The goal is to find the subset which has minimum Cp.

9.3.2.2 *AIC, BIC and F-ratio*

AIC (Akaike Information Criterion) and BIC (Bayesian Information Criterion) are criteria for choosing a subset of features. Letting $\hat{l}_\gamma$ denote the maximum log likelihood of the γth model, AIC selects the model which maximizes $(\hat{l}_\gamma - q_\gamma)$ whereas BIC selects the model which maximizes $(\hat{l}_\gamma - (logn)q_\gamma 2)$.

For the linear model, many of the popular selection criteria are a penalized sum of squares criterion that can provide a unified framework for comparisons. This criterion selects the subset model that minimizes:

$$RSS_\gamma / \hat{\sigma}^2 + Fq_\gamma \tag{9.3}$$

where F is a preset "dimensionality penalty". The above penalizes $RSS\gamma/\sigma 2$ by F times $q\gamma$, the dimension of the γth model. AIC and minimum Cp are equivalent, corresponding to $F = 2$, and BIC is obtained by $F = logn$. Using a smaller penalty, AIC and minimum Cp will select larger models than BIC (unless n is very small).

9.3.2.3 *Principal Component Analysis (PCA)*

Principal component analysis (PCA) is linear dimension reduction technique [Jackson (1991)]. PCA based on the covariance matrix of the variables, is a second-order method. PCA seeks to reduce the dimension of the data by finding a few orthogonal linear combinations (the PCs) of the original features with the largest variance. The first PC, s_1, is the linear combination with the largest variance. We have $s_1 = x^T w_1$, where the p-dimensional coefficient vector $w_1 = (w_{1,1}, \ldots, w_1, p)^T$ solves:

$$w_1 = \arg \max_{\|w=1\|} Var\left\{x^T w\right\} \tag{9.4}$$

The second PC is the linear combination with the second largest variance and orthogonal to the first PC, and so on. There are as many PCs as the number of original features. For many datasets, the first several PCs explain most of the variance, so that the rest can be ignored with minimal loss of information.

9.3.2.4 *Factor Analysis (FA)*

Factor analysis (FA), a linear method based on the second-order data summaries, assumes that the measured features depend on some unknown factors. Typical examples include features defined as various test scores of individuals that might to be related to a common intelligence factor. The goal of FA is to find out such relations, and thus it can be used to reduce the dimension of datasets following the factor model.

9.3.2.5 *Projection Pursuit*

Projection pursuit (PP) is a linear method which is more computationally intensive than second-order methods. Given a projection index that defines the merit of a direction, the algorithm looks for the directions that optimize that index. As the Gaussian distribution is the least interesting distribution, projection indices usually measure some aspect of non-Gaussianity.

9.3.3 **Wrappers**

The wrapper strategy for feature selection uses an induction algorithm to evaluate feature subsets. The motivation for this strategy is that the induction method that will eventually use the feature subset should provide a better predictor of accuracy than a separate measure that has an entirely different inductive bias [Langley (1994)].

Feature wrappers are often better than filters since they are tuned to the specific interaction between an induction algorithm and its training data. Nevertheless, they tend to be much slower than feature filters because they must repeatedly perform the induction algorithm.

9.3.3.1 *Wrappers for Decision Tree Learners*

The wrapper general framework for feature selection, has two degrees of feature relevance definitions that are used by the wrapper to discover relevant features [John *et al.* (1994)]. A feature X_i is said to be strongly relevant to the target concept(s) if the probability distribution of the class values, given the full feature set, changes when X_i is eliminated. A feature X_i is said to be weakly relevant if it is not strongly relevant and the probability distribution of the class values, given some subset which contains X_i, changes when X_i is removed. All features that are not strongly or weakly relevant are irrelevant.

Vafaie and De Jong (1995) and Cherkauer and Shavlik (1996) have both applied genetic search strategies in a wrapper framework in order to improve the performance of decision tree learners. Vafaie and De Jong (1995) present a system that has two genetic algorithm driven modules. The first performs feature selection while the second module performs constructive induction, which is the process of creating new attributes by applying logical and mathematical operators to the original features.

9.4 Feature Selection as a Means of Creating Ensembles

The main idea of ensemble methodology is to combine a set of models, each of which solves the same original task, in order to obtain a better composite global model, with more accurate and reliable estimates or decisions than can be obtained from using a single model. Some of the drawbacks of wrappers and filters can be solved by using ensemble. As mentioned above filters perform less than wrappers. Due to the voting process, noisy results are filtered. Secondly, the drawback of wrappers which "cost" computing time is solved by operating a group of filters. The idea of building a predictive model by integrating multiple models has been under investigation for a long time.

Ensemble feature selection methods [Opitz (1999)] extend traditional feature selection methods by looking for a set of feature subsets that will promote disagreement among the base classifiers. Simple random selection of feature subsets may be an effective technique for ensemble feature selection because the lack of accuracy in the ensemble members is compensated for by their diversity [Ho (1998)]. Tsymbal and Puuronen (2002) presented a technique for building ensembles of simple Bayes classifiers in random feature subsets.

The hill climbing ensemble feature selection strategy [Cunningham and Carney (2000)], randomly constructs the initial ensemble. Then, an iterative refinement is performed based on hill-climbing search in order to improve the accuracy and diversity of the base classifiers. For all the feature subsets, an attempt is made to switch (include or delete) each feature. If the resulting feature subset produces better performance on the validation set, that change is kept. This process is continued until no further improvements are obtained.

The GEFS (Genetic Ensemble Feature Selection) [Opitz (1999)] uses genetic search for ensemble feature selection. This strategy begins with creating an initial population of classifiers where each classifier is generated by randomly selecting a different subset of features. Then, new candidate classifiers are continually produced by using the genetic operators of crossover and mutation on the feature subsets. The final ensemble is composed of the most fitted classifiers.

Another method for creating a set of feature selection solutions using a genetic algorithm was proposed by [Oliveira *et al.* (2003)]. They create a Pareto-optimal front in relation to two different objectives: accuracy on a validation set and number of features. Following that they select the best feature selection solution.

In the statistics literature, the most well known feature oriented ensemble algorithm is the MARS algorithm [Friedman (1991)]. In this algorithm, a multiple regression function is approximated using linear splines and their tensor products.

Tuv and Torkkola (2005) examined the idea of using ensemble of classifiers such as decision trees in order to create a better feature ranker. They showed that this ensemble can be very effective in variable ranking for problems with up to a hundred thousand input attributes. Note that this approach uses inducers for obtaining the ensemble by concentrating on wrapper feature selectors.

9.5 Ensemble Methodology as a Means for Improving Feature Selection

The ensemble methodology can be employed as a filter feature selector. More specifically, the selected subset is a weighted average of subsets obtained from various filter methods [Rokach *et al.* (2007),].

The problem of feature selection ensemble is that of finding the best feature subset by combining a given set of feature selectors such that if a specific inducer is run on it, the generated classifier will have the highest possible accuracy. Formally the optimal feature subset with respect to a particular inducer [Kohavi (1996)] is defined as:

Definition 9.1 *Given an inducer I, a training set S with input feature set $A = \{a_1, a_2, ..., a_n\}$ and target feature y from a fixed and unknown distribution D over the labeled instance space, the subset $B \subseteq A$ is said to be optimal if the expected generalization error of the induced classifier $I(\pi_{B \cup y} S)$ will be minimized over the distribution D.*

where $\pi_{B\cup y}S$ represents the corresponding projection of S and $I(\pi_{B\cup y}S)$ represent a classifier which was induced by activating the induction method I onto dataset $\pi_{B\cup y}S$.

Definition 9.2 *Given an inducer I, a training set S with input feature set $A = \{a_1, a_2, ..., a_n\}$ and target feature y from a fixed and unknown distribution D over the labeled instance space, and an optimal subset B, a Feature Selector FS is said to be consistent if it selects an attribute $a_i \in B$ with probability $p > \frac{1}{2}$ and it selects an attribute $a_j \notin B$ with probability $q < \frac{1}{2}$.*

Definition 9.3 *Given a set of feature subsets $B_1, ..., B_\omega$ the majority combination of features subsets is a single feature subset that contains any attribute a_i such that $f_c(a_i, B_1, ..., B_\omega) > \frac{\omega}{2}$ where $f_c(a_i, B_1, ..., B_\omega) = \sum\limits_{j=1}^{\omega} g(a_i, B_j)$ and $g(a_i, B_j) = \begin{cases} 1 \ a_i \in B_j \\ 0 \ otherwise \end{cases}$*

The last definition refers to a simple majority voting, in which attribute a_i is included in the combined feature subset if it appears in at least half of the base feature subsets $B_1, ..., B_\omega$, where ω is the number of base feature subsets. Note that $f_c(a_i, B_1, ..., B_\omega)$ counts the number of base feature subsets in which a_i is included.

Lemma 9.1 *A majority combination of feature subsets obtained from a given a set of independent and consistent feature selectors $FS_1, ..., FS_\omega$ (where ω is the number of feature selectors) converges to the optimal feature subset when $\omega \to \infty$.*

Proof. For ensuring that for attributes for which $a_i \in B$ are actually selected we need to show that:

$$\lim_{\omega \to \infty, p > 1/2} p\left(f_c(a_i) > \frac{\omega}{2}\right) = 1 \tag{9.5}$$

We denote by $p_{j,i} > 1$ the probability of FS_j to select a_i. We denote by $p_i = \min(p_{j,i})$. Note that $p_i > \frac{1}{2}$. Because the feature selectors are independent we can use approximation binomial distribution, i.e.:

$$\lim_{\omega \to \infty} p\left(f_c(a_i) > \frac{\omega}{2}\right) \leq \lim_{\omega \to \infty, p_i > 1/2} \sum_{k=0}^{\frac{\omega}{2}} \binom{\omega}{k} p_i^k (1 - p_i)^{\omega-k} \tag{9.6}$$

Due to the fact that $\omega \to \infty$ we can use the central limit theorem in which, $\mu = \omega p_i, \sigma = \sqrt{\omega p_i(1 - p_i)}$:

$$\lim_{\omega \to \infty, p_i > 1/2} p\left(Z > \frac{\sqrt{\omega}(1/2 - p_i)}{\sqrt{p_i(1 - p_i)}}\right) = p(Z > -\infty) = 1 \qquad (9.7)$$

For ensuring that for attributes for which $a_i \notin B$ are actually selected we need to show that:

$$\lim_{\omega \to \infty} p\left(f_c(a_i) < \frac{\omega}{2}\right) = 0 \qquad (9.8)$$

We denote by $q_{j,i} < 1/2$ the probability of FS_j to select a_i. We denote by $q_i = \max(q_{j,i})$. Note that $q_i < \frac{1}{2}$. Because the feature selectors are independent we can use approximation binomial distribution, i.e.:

$$\lim_{\omega \to \infty} p\left(f_c(a_i) < \frac{\omega}{2}\right) \geq \lim_{\omega \to \infty, q_i < 1/2} \sum_{k=0}^{\frac{\omega}{2}} \binom{\omega}{k} q_i^k (1 - q_i)^{\omega - k} \qquad (9.9)$$

Due to the fact that $\omega \to \infty$ we can use the central limit theorem again this time: $\mu = \omega q_i, \sigma = \sqrt{\omega q_i(1 - q_i)}$:

$$\lim_{\omega \to \infty, q_i < 1/2} \sum_{k=0}^{\frac{\omega}{2}} \binom{\omega}{k} q_i^k (1 - q_i)^{\omega - k} = \lim_{\omega \to \infty, q_i < 1/2} p\left(Z > \frac{\frac{\omega}{2} - q_i \omega}{\sqrt{\omega q_i(1 - q_i)}}\right) =$$

$$\lim_{\omega \to \infty, q_i < 1/2} p\left(Z > \frac{\sqrt{\omega}(1/2 - q_i)}{\sqrt{q_i(1 - q_i)}}\right) = p(Z > \infty) = 0 \qquad (9.10)$$

$$\square$$

9.5.1 *Independent Algorithmic Framework*

Roughly speaking, the feature selectors in the ensemble can be created dependently or independently. In the dependent framework, the outcome of a certain feature selector affects the creation of the next feature selector. Alternatively, each feature selector is built independently; the resulted features subsets are then combined in some fashion. Here we concentrate on an independent framework. Figure 9.1 presents the proposed algorithmic framework. This simple framework receives as an input the following arguments:

(1) A Training set (S) – A labeled dataset used for feature selectors.
(2) A set of feature selection algorithms $\{FS_1, \ldots, FS_\xi\}$ – A feature selection algorithm is an algorithm that obtains a training set and outputs a subset of relevant features. Recall that we employ non-wrapper and non-ranker feature selectors.
(3) Ensemble Size (ω)
(4) Ensemble generator (G) – This component is responsible for generating a set of ω pairs of feature selection algorithms and their corresponding training sets. We refer to G as a class that implements a method called "genrateEnsemble".
(5) Combiner (C) – The combiner is responsible for creating the subsets and combining them into a single subset. We refer to C as a class that implements the method "combine".

The proposed algorithm simply uses the ensemble generator to create a set of feature selection algorithm pairs and their corresponding training sets. Then it calls the combine method in C to execute the feature selection algorithm on its corresponding dataset. The various feature subsets are then combined into a single subset.

Require: $S, \{FS_1, \ldots, FS_\xi\}, G, C$
Ensure: A combined feature subset.
1: $(S_1, FS_1), \ldots, (S_\omega, FS_\omega) =$G.genrateEnsemble$(S, (FS_1, \ldots, FS_\xi), \omega)$
2: Return C.combine $(\{(S_1, FS_1), \ldots, (S_\omega, FS_\omega)\})$

Fig. 9.1   Pseudo-code of Independent Algorithmic Framework for Feature Selection

9.5.2   *Combining Procedure*

We begin by describing two implementations for the combiner component. In the literature there are two ways of combining the results of the ensemble members: weighting methods and meta-learning methods. Here we concentrate on weighting methods. The weighting methods are best suited for problems where the individual members have comparable success or when we would like to avoid problems associated with added learning (such as over-fitting or long training time).

9.5.2.1 *Simple Weighted Voting*

Figure 9.2 presents an algorithm for selecting a feature subset based on the weighted voting of feature subsets. As this is an implementation of the abstract combiner used in Figure 9.1, the input of the algorithm is a set of pairs; every pair is built from one feature selector and a training set. After executing the feature selector on its associated training set to obtain a feature subset, the algorithm employs some weighting method and attaches a weight to every subset. Finally it uses a weighted voting to decide which attribute should be included in the final subset. We considered the following methods for weighting the subsets:

(1) **Majority Voting** – In this weighting method the same weight is attached to every subset such that the total weights is 1, i.e. if there are ω subsets then the weight is simply $1/\omega$. Note that the inclusion of a certain attribute in the final result requires that this attribute will appear in at least $\omega/2$ subsets. This method should have a low false positive rate, because selecting an irrelevant attribute will take place only if at least $\omega/2$ feature selections methods will decide to select this attribute.

(2) **"Take-It-All"** – In this weighting method all subsets obtain a weight that is greater than 0.5. This leads to the situation in which any attribute that has been in at least one of the subsets will be included in the final result. This method should have a low false negative rate, because losing a relevant attribute will take place only if all feature selections methods will decide to filter out this attribute.

(3) **"Smaller is Heavier"** – The weight for each selector is defined by its bias to the smallest subset. Selectors that tend to provide small subsetss will gain more weight than selectors that tend to provide large subsets. This approach is inspired by the fact that the precision rate of selectors tend to decrease as the size of the subset increases. This approach can be used to avoid noise caused by feature selectors that tend to select most of the possible attributes. More specifically the weights are defined as:

$$w_i = \frac{|B_i|}{\sum_{j=1}^{\omega} |B_j|} \Bigg/ \sum_{k=1}^{\omega} \frac{|B_k|}{\sum_{j=1}^{\omega} |B_j|} \qquad (9.11)$$

Require: $\{(S_1, FS_1), \ldots, (S_\omega, FS_\omega)\}$
Ensure: A Combined feature subset
1: **for all** $(S_i, FS_i) \in F$ **do**
2:    $B_i = \text{FS}_i.\text{getSelectedFeatures}(S_i)$
3: **end for**
4: $\{w_1, \ldots, w_\omega\} = getWeight(\{B_1, ..., B_\omega\})$
5: $B \leftarrow \emptyset$
6: **for all** $a_j \in A$ **do**
7:    totalWeight=0
8:    **for** $i = 1$ to ω **do**
9:      **if** $a_j \in B_i$ **then**
10:        totalWeight $\leftarrow$ totalWeight+W_i
11:      **end if**
12:    **end for**
13:    **if** totalWeight> 0.5 **then**
14:      $B \leftarrow B \cup a_j$
15:    **end if**
16: **end for**
17: Return B

Fig. 9.2   Pseudo-code of combining procedure

9.5.2.2 *Naïve Bayes Weighting using Artificial Contrasts*

Using the Bayesian approach a certain attribute should be filtered out if: $P(a_i \notin B | B_1, ..., B_\omega) > 0.5$ or $P(a_i \notin B | B_1, ..., B_\omega) > P(a_i \in B | B_1, ..., B_\omega)$ where $B \subseteq A$ denote the set of relevant features. By using the Bayes Theorem we obtain:

$$P(a_i \notin B | B_1, ..., B_\omega) = \frac{P(B_1, ..., B_\omega | a_i \notin B)P(a_i \notin B)}{P(B_1, ..., B_\omega)} \quad (9.12)$$

However, since calculating the above probability as is might be difficult, we use the naive Bayes combination. This is a well-known combining method due to its simplicity and its relatively outstanding results. According to the naive Bayes assumption, the results of the feature selectors are independent given the fact that the attribute ai is not relevant. Thus, using this assumption we obtain:

$$\frac{P(B_1, ..., B_\omega \, | a_i \notin B) P(a_i \notin B)}{P(B_1, ..., B_\omega)} = \frac{P(a_i \notin B) \prod\limits_{j=1}^{\omega} P(B_j \, | a_i \notin B)}{P(B_1, ..., B_\omega)} \tag{9.13}$$

Using Bayes theorem again:

$$\frac{P(a_i \notin B) \prod\limits_{j=1}^{\omega} P(B_j | a_i \notin B)}{P(B_1, ..., B_\omega)} = \frac{P(a_i \notin B) \prod\limits_{j=1}^{\omega} \frac{P(a_i \notin B | B_j)}{P(a_i \notin B)} P(B_j)}{P(B_1, ..., B_\omega)} =$$
$$\frac{\prod\limits_{j=1}^{\omega} P(B_j) \prod\limits_{j=1}^{\omega} P(a_i \notin B | B_j)}{P(B_1, ..., B_\omega) \cdot P^{\omega-1}(a_i \notin B)}. \tag{9.14}$$

Thus a certain attribute should be filtered out if:

$$\frac{\prod\limits_{j=1}^{\omega} P(B_j) \prod\limits_{j=1}^{\omega} P(a_i \notin B | B_j)}{P(B_1, ..., B_\omega) \cdot P^{\omega-1}(a_i \notin B)} > \frac{\prod\limits_{j=1}^{\omega} P(B_j) \prod\limits_{j=1}^{\omega} P(a_i \in B | B_j)}{P(B_1, ..., B_\omega) \cdot P^{\omega-1}(a_i \in B)} \tag{9.15}$$

or after omitting the common term from both sides:

$$\frac{\prod\limits_{j=1}^{\omega} P(a_i \notin B | B_j)}{P^{\omega-1}(a_i \notin B)} > \frac{\prod\limits_{j=1}^{\omega} P(a_i \in B | B_j)}{P^{\omega-1}(a_i \in B)} \tag{9.16}$$

Assuming that the a-priori probability for a_i to be relevant is equal to that of not being relevant:

$$\prod\limits_{j=1}^{\omega} P(a_i \notin B | B_j) > \prod\limits_{j=1}^{\omega} P(a_i \in B | B_j) \tag{9.17}$$

Using the complete probability theorem:

$$\prod\limits_{j=1}^{\omega} P(a_i \notin B | B_j) > \prod\limits_{j=1}^{\omega} (1 - P(a_i \notin B | B_j)) \tag{9.18}$$

Because we are using non-ranker feature selectors the above probability is estimated using:

$$P(a_i \notin B \,|B_j) \approx \begin{cases} P(a \notin B \,|a \in B_j) \ if \ a_i \in B_j \\ P(a \notin B \,|a \notin B_j) \ if \ a_i \notin B_j \end{cases} \qquad (9.19)$$

Note that $P(a \notin B \,|a \in B_j)$ does not refer to a specific attribute, but to the general bias of the feature selector j. In order to estimate the remaining probabilities, we are adding to the dataset a set of ϕ contrast attributes that are known to be truly irrelevant and analyzing the number of artificial features ϕ_j included in the subset B_j obtained by the feature selector j:

$$P(a \in B_j \,|a \notin B) = \frac{\phi_j}{\phi} \quad ; \quad P(a \notin B_j \,|a \notin B) = 1 - \frac{\phi_j}{\phi} \qquad (9.20)$$

The artificial contrast variables are obtained by randomly permuting the values of the original n attributes across m instances. Generating just random attributes from some simple distribution, such as Normal Distribution, is not sufficient, because the values of original attributes may exhibit some special structure. Using Bayes theorem:

$$P(a \notin B \,|a \in B_j) = \frac{P(a \notin B)P(a \in B_j \,|a \notin B)}{P(a \in B_j)} = \frac{P(a \notin B)}{P(a \in B_j)} \frac{\phi_j}{\phi} \qquad (9.21)$$

$$P(a \notin B \,|a \notin B_j) = \frac{\frac{P(a \notin B)P(a \notin B_j \,|a \notin B)}{P(a \notin B_j)}}{\frac{P(a \notin B)}{1-P(a \in B_j)}\left(1 - \frac{\phi_j}{\phi}\right)} = \qquad (9.22)$$

where $P(a \in B_j) = \frac{|B_j|}{n+\phi}$

9.5.3   Feature Ensemble Generator

In order to make the ensemble more effective, there should be some sort of diversity between the feature subsets. Diversity may be obtained through different presentations of the input data or variations in feature selector design. The following sections describe each one of the different approaches.

9.5.3.1   *Multiple Feature Selectors*

In this approach we simply use a set of different feature selection algorithms. The basic assumption is that since different algorithms have different inductive biases, they will create different feature subsets.

The proposed method can be employed with the correlation-based feature subset selection (CFS) as a subset evaluator [Hall (1999)]. CFS evaluates the worth of a subset of attributes by considering the individual predictive ability of each feature along with the degree of redundancy between them. Subsets of features that are highly correlated with the class while having low inter-correlation are preferred.

At the heart of the CFS algorithm is a heuristic for evaluating the worth or merit of a subset of features. This heuristic takes into account the usefulness of individual features for predicting the class label along with the level of inter-correlation among them. The heuristic is based on the following hypothesis: a good features subset contains features that are highly correlated with the class, but which are uncorrelated with each other.

Equation 9.23 formalizes the feature selection heuristics:

$$M_B = \frac{k\overline{r_{c_f}}}{\sqrt{k + k(k-1)\overline{r_{f_f}}}} \tag{9.23}$$

where M_B is the heuristic "merit" of a feature subset B containing k features; $\overline{r_{c_f}}$ is the average feature-class correlation; and $\overline{r_{f_f}}$ is the average feature-feature correlation.

In order to apply Equation 9.23 to estimate the merit of a feature subset, it is necessary to compute the correlation (dependence) between attributes. For discrete class problems, CFS first discretises numeric features then uses symmetrical uncertainty (a modified information gain measure) to calculates feature-class and feature-feature correlations:

$$SU = \frac{\text{InformationGain}(a_i, a_j, S)}{Entropy(a_i, S) + Entropy(a_j, S)} \tag{9.24}$$

Recall from Section 4.1.3:

$$\text{InformationGain}(a_i, a_j, S) =$$
$$Entropy(a_j, S) - \sum_{v_{i,k} \in dom(a_i)} \frac{\left|\sigma_{a_i = v_{i,k}} S\right|}{|S|} \cdot Entropy(a_j, \sigma_{a_i = v_{i,k}} S) \tag{9.25}$$

$$Entropy(a_i, S) = \sum_{v_{i,k} \in dom(a_i)} -\frac{\left|\sigma_{a_i = v_{i,k}} S\right|}{|S|} \cdot \log_2 \frac{\left|\sigma_{a_i = v_{i,k}} S\right|}{|S|} \tag{9.26}$$

Symmetrical uncertainty is used (rather than simple gain ratio) because it is a symmetric measure and can therefore be used to measure feature-feature correlations where there is no notion of one attribute being the "class" as such.

As for the search organization the following methods can be used: Best First Search; Forward Selection Search; Gain Ratio; Chi-Square; OneR classifier; and Information Gain.

Beside the CFS, other evaluation methods can be considered including, consistency subset evaluator and the the wrapper subset evaluator with simple classifiers (K-nearest neighbors, logistic regression and naïve bayes)

9.5.3.2   *Bagging*

The most well-known independent method is bagging (bootstrap aggregating). In this case, each feature selector is executed on a sample of instances taken with replacement from the training set. Usually each sample size is equal to the size of the original training set. Note that since sampling with a replacement is used, some of the instances may appear more than once in the same sample and some may not be included at all. Although the training samples are different from each other, they are certainly not independent from a statistical point of view.

9.6   Using Decision Trees for Feature Selection

Using decision trees for feature selection has one important advantage known as "anytime". However, for highly dimensional datasets, the feature selection process becomes computationally intensive.

Decision trees can be used to implement a trade-off between the performance of the selected features and the computation time which is required to find a subset. Top-down inducers of decision trees can be considered as anytime algorithms for feature selection, because they gradually improve the performance and can be stopped at any time and provide sub-optimal feature subsets.

Decision trees have been used as an evaluation means for directing the feature selection search. For instance, a hybrid learning methodology that integrates genetic algorithms (GAs) and decision tree inducers in order to find the best feature subset was proposed in [Bala *et al.* (1995)]. A GA is used to search the space of all possible subsets of a large set of candidate discrimination features. In order to evaluate a certain feature subset, a decision tree is trained and its accuracy is used as a measure of fitness for the given feature set, which, in turn, is used by the GA to evolve better feature sets.

9.7 Limitation of Feature Selection Methods

Despite its popularity, the usage of feature selection methodologies for overcoming the obstacles of high dimensionality has several drawbacks:

- The assumption that a large set of input features can be reduced to a small subset of relevant features is not always true; in some cases the target feature is actually affected by most of the input features, and removing features will cause a significant loss of important information.
- The outcome (i.e. the subset) of many algorithms for feature selection (for example, almost any of the algorithms that are based upon the wrapper methodology) is strongly dependent on the training set size. That is, if the training set is small, then the size of the reduced subset will be small also. Consequently, relevant features might be lost. Accordingly, the induced classifiers might achieve lower accuracy compared to classifiers that have access to all relevant features.
- In some cases, even after eliminating a set of irrelevant features, the researcher is left with relatively large numbers of relevant features.
- The backward elimination strategy, used by some methods, is extremely inefficient for working with large-scale databases, where the number of original features is more than 100.

One way to deal with the above mentioned disadvantages is to use a very large training set (which should increase in an exponential manner as the number of input features increases). However, the researcher rarely enjoys this privilege, and even if it does happen, the researcher will probably encounter the aforementioned difficulties derived from a high number of instances.

Practically most of the training sets are still considered "small" not because of their absolute size but rather due to the fact that they contain too few instances given the nature of the investigated problem, namely the instance space size, the space distribution and the intrinsic noise. Furthermore, even if a sufficient dataset is available, the researcher will probably encounter the aforementioned difficulties derived from a high number of records.

Chapter 10

Fuzzy Decision Trees

10.1 Overview

There are two main types of uncertainty in supervised learning: statistical and cognitive. Statistical uncertainty deals with the random behavior of nature and all techniques described in previous chapters can handle the uncertainty that arises (or is assumed to arise) in the natural world from statistical variations or randomness. While these techniques may be appropriate for measuring the likelihood of a hypothesis, they say nothing about the meaning of the hypothesis.

Cognitive uncertainty, on the other hand, deals with human cognition. Cognitive uncertainty can be further divided into two sub-types: vagueness and ambiguity. Ambiguity arises in situations with two or more alternatives such that the choice between them is left unspecified. Vagueness arises when there is a difficulty in making a precise distinction in the world

Fuzzy set theory, first introduced by Zadeh in 1965, deals with cognitive uncertainty and seeks to overcome many of the problems found in classical set theory. For example, a major problem in the early days of control theory is that a small change in input results in a major change in output. This throws the whole control system into an unstable state. In addition there was also the problem that the representation of subjective knowledge was artificial and inaccurate.

Fuzzy set theory is an attempt to confront these difficulties and in this chapter we present some of it basic concepts. The main focus, however, is on those concepts used in the induction process when dealing with fuzzy decision trees. Since fuzzy set theory and fuzzy logic are much broader than the narrow perspective presented here, the interested reader is encouraged to read [Zimmermann (2005)].

159

10.2   Membership Function

In classical set theory, a certain element either belongs or does not belong to a set. Fuzzy set theory, on the other hand, permits the gradual assessment of the membership of elements in relation to a set.

Definition 10.1   Let U be a universe of discourse, representing a collection of objects denoted generically by u. A fuzzy set A in a universe of discourse U is characterized by a membership function μ_A which takes values in the interval $[0, 1]$. Where $\mu_A(u) = 0$ means that u is definitely not a member of A and $\mu_A(u) = 1$ means that u is definitely a member of A.

The above definition can be illustrated on a vague set, that we will label as *young*. In this case the set U is the set of people. To each person in U, we define the degree of membership to the fuzzy set *young*. The membership function answers the question: "To what degree is person u young?". The easiest way to do this is with a membership function based on the person's age. For example Figure 10.1 presents the following membership function:

$$\mu_{Young}(u) = \begin{cases} 0 & age(u) > 32 \\ 1 & age(u) < 16 \\ \frac{32-age(u)}{16} & otherwise \end{cases} \tag{10.1}$$

Given this definition, John, who is 18 years old, has degree of youth of 0.875. Philip, 20 years old, has degree of youth of 0.75. Unlike probability theory, degrees of membership do not have to add up to 1 across all objects and therefore either many or few objects in the set may have high membership. However, an objects membership in a set (such as "young") and the sets complement ("not young") must still sum to 1.

The main difference between classical set theory and fuzzy set theory is that the latter admits to partial set membership. A classical or crisp set, then, is a fuzzy set that restricts its membership values to $\{0,1\}$, the endpoints of the unit interval. Membership functions can be used to represent a crisp set. For example, Figure 10.2 presents a crisp membership function defined as:

$$\mu_{CrispYoung}(u) = \begin{cases} 0 & age(u) > 22 \\ 1 & age(u) \leq 22 \end{cases} \tag{10.2}$$

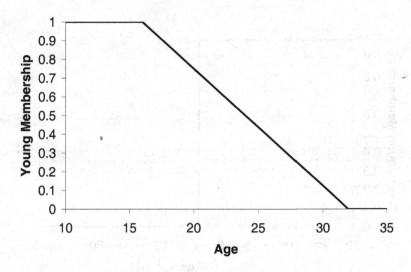

Fig. 10.1 Membership function for the young set.

10.3 Fuzzy Classification Problems

All classification problems we have discussed so far in this chapter assume that each instance takes one value for each attribute and that each instance is classified into only one of the mutually exclusive classes [Yuan and Shaw (1995)].

To illustrate the idea, we introduce the problem of modeling the preferences of TV viewers. In this problem there are three input attributes:

$$A = \{\text{Time of Day,Age Group,Mood}\}$$

and each attribute has the following values:

- dom(Time of Day) = {Morning,Noon,Evening,Night}
- dom(Age Group) = {Young,Adult}
- dom(Mood) = {Happy,Indifferent,Sad,Sour,Grumpy}

The classification can be the movie genre that the viewer would like to watch, such as $C = \{\text{Action,Comedy,Drama}\}$.

All the attributes are vague by definition. For example, peoples feelings of happiness, indifference, sadness, sourness and grumpiness are vague

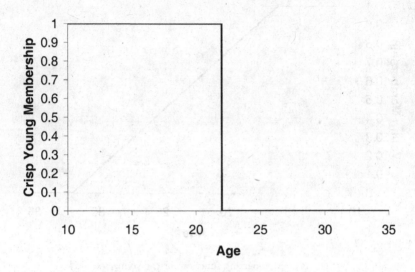

Fig. 10.2   Membership function for the crisp young set.

without any crisp boundaries between them. Although the vagueness of "Age Group" or "Time of Day" can be avoided by indicating the exact age or exact time, a rule induced with a crisp decision tree may then have an artificial crisp boundary, such as "IF Age < 16 THEN action movie". But how about someone who is 17 years of age? Should this viewer definitely not watch an action movie? The viewer preferred genre may still be vague. For example, the viewer may be in a mood for both comedy and drama movies. Moreover, the association of movies into genres may also be vague. For instance the movie "Lethal Weapon" (starring Mel Gibson and Danny Glover) is considered to be both comedy and action movie.

Fuzzy concept can be introduced into a classical problem if at least one of the input attributes is fuzzy or if the target attribute is fuzzy. In the example described above, both input and target attributes are fuzzy. Formally the problem is defined as following[Yuan and Shaw (1995)]:

Each class c_j is defined as a fuzzy set on the universe of objects U. The membership function $\mu_{c_j}(u)$ indicates the degree to which object u belongs to class c_j. Each attribute a_i is defined as a linguistic attribute which takes linguistic values from $dom(a_i) = \{v_{i,1}, v_{i,2}, \ldots, v_{i,|dom(a_i)|}\}$. Each linguistic value $v_{i,k}$ is also a fuzzy set defined on U. The membership $\mu_{v_{i,k}}(u)$ specifies the degree to which object u's attribute a_i is $v_{i,k}$. Recall that the membership of a linguistic value can be subjectively assigned or transferred from numerical values by a membership function defined on the range of the numerical value.

10.4 Fuzzy Set Operations

Like classical set theory, fuzzy set theory includes such operations as union, intersection, complement, and inclusion, but also includes operations that have no classical counterpart, such as the modifiers concentration and dilation, and the connective fuzzy aggregation. Definitions of fuzzy set operations are provided in this section.

Definition 10.2 The membership function of the union of two fuzzy sets A and B with membership functions μ_A and μ_B respectively is defined as the maximum of the two individual membership functions $\mu_{A \cup B}(u) = max\{\mu_A(u), \mu_B(u)\}$.

Definition 10.3 The membership function of the intersection of two fuzzy sets A and B with membership functions μ_A and μ_B respectively is defined as the minimum of the two individual membership functions $\mu_{A \cap B}(u) = min\{\mu_A(u), \mu_B(u)\}$.

Definition 10.4 The membership function of the complement of a fuzzy set A with membership function μ_A is defined as the negation of the specified membership function $\mu_{\overline{A}}(u) = 1 - \mu_A(u)$.

To illustrate these fuzzy operations, we elaborate on the previous example. Recall that John has a degree of youth of 0.875. Additionally John's happiness degree is 0.254. Thus, the membership of John in the set Young $\cup$ Happy would be $max(0.875, 0.254) = 0.875$, and its membership in Young $\cap$ Happy would be $min(0.875, 0.254) = 0.254$.

It is possible to chain operators together, thereby constructing quite complicated sets. It is also possible to derive many interesting sets from chains of rules built up from simple operators. For example John's membership in the set $\overline{Young} \cup$ Happy would be $max(1 - 0.875, 0.254) = 0.254$

The usage of the max and min operators for defining fuzzy union and fuzzy intersection, respectively is very common. However, it is important to note that these are not the only definitions of union and intersection suited to fuzzy set theory.

10.5 Fuzzy Classification Rules

Definition 10.5 The fuzzy subsethood $S(A, B)$ measures the degree to which A is a subset of B.

$$S(A, B) = \frac{M(A \cap B)}{M(A)} \tag{10.3}$$

where $M(A)$ is the *cardinality* measure of a fuzzy set A and is defined as

$$M(A) = \sum_{u \in U} \mu_A(u) \tag{10.4}$$

The subsethood can be used to measure the truth level of the rule of classification rules. For example given a classification rule such as "IF Age is Young AND Mood is Happy THEN Comedy" we have to calculate $S(Hot \cap Sunny, Swimming)$ in order to measure the truth level of the classification rule.

10.6 Creating Fuzzy Decision Tree

There are several algorithms for induction of decision trees. In this section we will focus on the algorithm proposed by [Yuan and Shaw (1995)]. This algorithm can handle the classification problems with both fuzzy attributes and fuzzy classes represented in linguistic fuzzy terms. It can also handle other situations in a uniform way where numerical values can be fuzzified to fuzzy terms and crisp categories can be treated as a special case of fuzzy terms with zero fuzziness. The algorithm uses classification ambiguity as fuzzy entropy. The classification ambiguity, which directly measures the quality of classification rules at the decision node, can be calculated under fuzzy partitioning and multiple fuzzy classes.

The fuzzy decision tree induction consists of the following steps:

- Fuzzifying numeric attributes in the training set.
- Inducing a fuzzy decision tree.
- Simplifying the decision tree.
- Applying fuzzy rules for classification.

10.6.1 *Fuzzifying Numeric Attributes*

When a certain attribute is numerical, it needs to be fuzzified into linguistic terms before it can be used in the algorithm. The fuzzification process can be performed manually by experts or can be derived automatically using some sort of clustering algorithm. Clustering groups the data instances into subsets in such a manner that similar instances are grouped together; different instances belong to different groups. The instances are thereby organized into an efficient representation that characterizes the population being sampled.

Yuan and Shaw (1995) suggest a simple algorithm to generate a set of membership functions on numerical data. Assume attribute a_i has numerical value x from the domain X. We can cluster X to k linguistic terms $v_{i,j}, j = 1, \ldots, k$. The size of k is manually predefined. For the first linguistic term $v_{i,1}$, the following membership function is used:

$$\mu_{v_{i,1}}(x) = \begin{cases} 1 & x \leq m_1 \\ \frac{m_2 - x}{m_2 - m_1} & m_1 < x < m_2 \\ 0 & x \geq m_2 \end{cases} \tag{10.5}$$

For each $v_{i,j}$ when $j = 2, \ldots, k-1$ has a triangular membership function as follows:

$$\mu_{v_{i,j}}(x) = \begin{cases} 0 & x \leq m_{j-1} \\ \frac{x - m_{j-1}}{m_j - m_{j-1}} & m_{j-1} < x \leq m_j \\ \frac{m_{j+1} - x}{m_{j+1} - m_j} & m_j < x < m_{j+1} \\ 0 & x \geq m_{j+1} \end{cases} \tag{10.6}$$

Finally the membership function of the last linguistic term $v_{i,k}$ is:

$$\mu_{v_{i,k}}(x) = \begin{cases} 0 & x \leq m_{k-1} \\ \frac{x - m_{k-1}}{m_k - m_{k-1}} & m_{k-1} < x \leq m_k \\ 1 & x \geq m_k \end{cases} \tag{10.7}$$

Figure 10.3 illustrates the creation of four groups defined on the age attribute: "young", "early adulthood", "middle-aged" and "old age". Note that the first set ("young") and the last set ("old age") have a trapezoidal form which can be uniquely described by the four corners. For example, the "young" set could be represented as $(0, 0, 16, 32)$. In between, all other sets ("early adulthood" and "middle-aged") have a triangular form which can be uniquely described by the three corners. For example, the set "early adulthood" is represented as $(16, 32, 48)$.

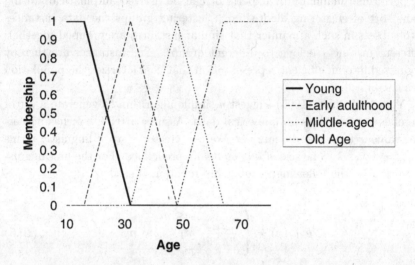

Fig. 10.3   Membership function for various groups in the age attribute.

The only parameters that need to be determined are the set of k centers $M = \{m_1, \ldots, m_k\}$. The centers can be found using the algorithm presented in Figure 10.4. Note that in order to use the algorithm, a monotonic decreasing learning rate function should be provided.

10.6.2   *Inducing of Fuzzy Decision Tree*

The induction algorithm of fuzzy decision tree is presented in Figure 10.5. The algorithm measures the classification ambiguity associated with each attribute and splits the data using the attribute with the smallest classification ambiguity. The classification ambiguity of attribute a_i with linguistic terms $v_{i,j}, j = 1, \ldots, k$ on fuzzy evidence S, denoted as $G(a_i|S)$, is the weighted average of classification ambiguity calculated as:

$$G(a_i|S) = \sum_{j='1}^{k} w(v_{i,j}|S) \cdot G(v_{i,j}|S) \tag{10.8}$$

Require: X - a set of values, $\eta(t)$ - some monotonic decreasing scalar function representing the learning rate.

Ensure: $M = \{m_1, \ldots, m_k\}$

1: Initially set m_i to be evenly distributed on the range of X.

2: $t \leftarrow 1$

3: **repeat**

4:    Randomly draw one sample x from X

5:    Find the closest center m_c to x.

6:    $m_c \leftarrow m_c + \eta(t) \cdot (x - m_c)$

7:    $t \leftarrow t + 1$

8:    $D(X, M) \leftarrow \sum\limits_{x \in X} \min_i \|x - m_i\|$

9: **until** $D(X, M)$ converges

Fig. 10.4   Algorithm for fuzzifying numeric attributes

where $w(v_{i,j} | S)$ is the weight which represents the relative size of $v_{i,j}$ and is defined as:

$$w(v_{i,j} | S) = \frac{M(v_{i,j} | S)}{\sum\limits_{k} M(v_{i,k} | S)} \tag{10.9}$$

The classification ambiguity of $\mathrm{v}_{i,j}$ is defined as $G(v_{i,j} | S) = g(\vec{p}(C | v_{i,j}))$, which is measured based on the possibility distribution vector $\vec{p}(C | v_{i,j}) = \left(p(c_1 | v_{i,j}), \ldots, p\left(c_{|\mathrm{k}|} | v_{i,j}\right) \right)$.

Given $v_{i,j}$, the possibility of classifying an object to class c_l can be defined as:

$$p(c_l | v_{i,j}) = \frac{S(v_{i,j}, c_l)}{\max\limits_{k} S(v_{i,j}, c_k)} \tag{10.10}$$

where $S(A, B)$ is the fuzzy subsethood that was defined in Definition 10.5. The function $g(\vec{p})$ is the possibilistic measure of ambiguity or nonspecificity and is defined as:

$$g(\vec{p}) = \sum\limits_{i=1}^{|\vec{p}|} \left(p_i^* - p_{i+1}^* \right) \cdot \ln(i) \tag{10.11}$$

where $\vec{p}^* = \left(p_1^*, \ldots, p_{|\vec{p}|}^*\right)$ is the permutation of the possibility distribution $\vec{p}$ sorted such that $p_i^* \geq p_{i+1}^*$.

All the above calculations are carried out at a predefined significant level α. An instance will take' into consideration of a certain branch $v_{i,j}$ only if its corresponding membership is greater than α. This parameter is used to filter out insignificant branches.

After partitioning the data using the attribute with the smallest classification ambiguity, the algorithm looks for nonempty branches. For each nonempty branch, the algorithm calculates the truth level of classifying all instances within the branch into each class. The truth level is calculated using the fuzzy subsethood measure $S(A, B)$.

If the truth level of one of the classes is above a predefined threshold β then no additional partitioning is needed and the node become a leaf in which all instance will be labeled to the class with the highest truth level. Otherwise the procedure continues in a recursive manner. Note that small values of β will lead to smaller trees with the risk of underfitting. A higher β may lead to a larger tree with higher classification accuracy. However, at a certain point, higher values β may lead to overfitting.

Require: S - Training Set A - Input Feature Set y - Target Feature
Ensure: Fuzzy Decision Tree
1: Create a new fuzzy tree FT with a single root node.
2: **if** S is empty OR Truth level of one of the classes $\geq \beta$ **then**
3:     Mark FT as a leaf with the most common value of y in S as a label.
4:     Return FT.
5: **end if**
6: $\forall a_i \in A$ find a with the smallest classification ambiguity.
7: **for** each outcome v_i of a **do**
8:     Recursively call procedure with corresponding partition v_i.
9:     Connect the root node to the returned subtree with an edge that is labeled as v_i.
10: **end for**
11: Return FT

Fig. 10.5   Fuzzy decision tree induction

10.7 Simplifying the Decision Tree

Each path of branches from root to leaf can be converted into a rule with the condition part representing the attributes on the passing branches from the root to the leaf and the conclusion part representing the class at the leaf with the highest truth level classification. The corresponding classification rules can be further simplified by removing one input attribute term at a time for each rule we try to simplify. Select the term to remove with the highest truth level of the simplified rule. If the truth level of this new rule is not lower than the threshold β or the truth level of the original rule, the simplification is successful. The process will continue until no further simplification is possible for all the rules.

10.8 Classification of New Instances

In a regular decision tree, only one path (rule) can be applied for every instance. In a fuzzy decision tree, several paths (rules) can be applied for one instance. In order to classify an unlabeled instance, the following steps should be performed [Yuan and Shaw (1995)]:

- Step 1: Calculate the membership of the instance for the condition part of each path (rule). This membership will be associated with the label (class) of the path.
- Step 2: For each class calculate the maximum membership obtained from all applied rules.
- Step 3: An instance may be classified into several classes with different degrees based on the membership calculated in Step 2.

10.9 Other Fuzzy Decision Tree Inducers

There have been several fuzzy extensions to the ID3 algorithm. The UR-ID3 algorithm [Maher and Clair (1993)] starts by building a strict decision tree, and subsequently fuzzifies the conditions of the tree. Tani and Sakoda (1992) use the ID3 algorithm to select effective numerical attributes. The obtained splitting intervals are used as fuzzy boundaries. Regression is then used in each subspace to form fuzzy rules. Cios and Sztandera (1992) use the ID3 algorithm to convert a decision tree into a layer of a feedforward neural network. Each neuron is represented as a hyperplane with a fuzzy boundary. The nodes within the hidden layer are generated until some fuzzy entropy is reduced to zero. New hidden layers are generated until there is only one node at the output layer.

Fuzzy-CART [Jang (1994)] is a method which uses the CART algorithm to build a tree. However, the tree, which is the first step, is only used to propose fuzzy sets of the continuous domains (using the generated thresholds). Then, a layered network algorithm is employed to learn fuzzy rules. This produces more comprehensible fuzzy rules and improves the CART's initial results.

Another complete framework for building a fuzzy tree including several inference procedures based on conflict resolution in rule-based systems and efficient approximate reasoning methods was presented in [Janikow, 1998].

Olaru and Wehenkel (2003) presented a new type of fuzzy decision trees called soft decision trees (SDT). This approach combines tree-growing and pruning, to determine the structure of the soft decision tree. Refitting and backfitting are ised to improve its generalization capabilities. The researchers empirically showed that soft decision trees are significantly more accurate than standard decision trees. Moreover, a global model variance study shows a much lower variance for soft decision trees than for standard trees as a direct cause of the improved accuracy.

Peng (2004) has used FDT to improve the performance of the classical inductive learning approach in manufacturing processes. Peng proposed using soft discretization of continuous-valued attributes. It has been shown that FDT can deal with the noise or uncertainties existing in the data collected in industrial systems.

Chapter 11

Hybridization of Decision Trees with other Techniques

11.1 Introduction

Hybridization in artificial intelligence (AI) involves simultaneously using two or more intelligent techniques in order to handle real world complex problems, involving imprecision, uncertainty and vagueness. Hybridization is frequently practiced in machine learning, to make more powerful and reliable classifiers.

The combination or integration of additional methodologies can be done in any form: by modularly integrating two or more intelligent methodologies, which maintains the identity of each methodology; by fusing one methodology into another; or by transforming the knowledge representation in one methodology into another form of representation characteristic to another methodology.

Hybridization of decision trees with other AI techniques can be performed by using either a decision tree to partition the instance space for other induction techniques or other AI techniques for obtaining a better decision tree.

11.2 A Decision Tree Framework for Instance-Space Decomposition

In the first approach, termed instance-space decomposition (ISD) and involving hybrid decision tree with other inducers, the instance space of the original problem is partitioned into several subspaces using a decision tree with a distinct classifier assigned to each subspace. Subsequently, an unlabeled, previously unseen instance is classified by employing the classifier that was assigned to the subspace to which the instance belongs.

171

In an approach, which Cohen *et al.* (2007) term decision tree ISD, the partition of the instance-space is attained by a decision tree. Along with the decision tree, the ISD method employs another classification method, which classifies the tree's leaves (the tree's leaves represent the different subspaces). Namely, decision tree ISD methods produce decision tree s, in which the leaves are assigned classifiers rather than simple class labels. When a non- decision tree method produces the leaves' classifiers, the composite classifier is sometimes termed a decision tree hybrid classifier.

The term "decision tree hybrid classifier", however, is also used in a broader context, such as in cases where a sub-classification method decides about the growth of the tree and its pruning [Sakar and Mammone (1993)].

There are two basic techniques for implementing decision tree ISD. The first technique is to use some decision tree method to create the tree and then, in a post-growing phase, to attach classifiers to the tree's leaves. The second technique is to consider the classifiers as part of the tree-growing procedure. Potentially, the latter technique can achieve more accurate composite classifiers. On the other hand, it usually requires more computationally intensive procedures.

Carvalho and Freitas [Carvalho and Freitas. (2004)] proposed a hybrid decision tree genetic-algorithm classifier, which grows a decision tree and assigns some of the leaves with class labels and the others with genetic-algorithm classifiers. The leaves with the classifiers are those that have a small number of corresponding instances. A previously unseen instance is subsequently either directly assigned with a class label or is sub-classified by a genetic-algorithm classifier (depending on the leaf to which the instance is sorted). Zhou and Chen [Zhou and Chen (2002)] suggested a method, called hybrid decision tree (HDT). HDT uses the binary information gain ratio criterion to grow a binary decision tree in an instance-space that is defined by the nominal explaining-attributes only. A feed-forward neural network, subsequently classifies the leaves, whose diversity exceeds a predefined threshold. The network only uses the ordinal explaining-attributes.

In this chapter, we focus on the second decision tree ISD technique, which considers the classifiers as part of the decision tree's growth. NBTree is a method which produces a decision tree naive-Bayes hybrid classifier [Kohavi (1996)]. In order to decide when to stop the recursive partition of the instance-space (i.e., stop growing the tree), NBTree compares two alternatives: partitioning the instance-space further on (i.e., continue splitting the tree) versus stopping the partition and producing a single naive Bayes classifier. The two alternatives are compared in terms of their error estimations, which are calculated by a cross-validation procedure. Naive Bayes classification, by itself, is very efficient in terms of its processing time. However, using cross-validation significantly increases the overall computational complexity. Although Kohavi has used naive Bayes, to produce the classifiers, other classification methods are also applicable. However, due to the cross-validation estimations, NBTree becomes computationally expensive for methods that are more time-consuming than naive Bayes (e.g., neural networks).

We describe a simple framework for decision tree ISD, termed decision tree framework for instance space decomposition (DFID). The framework hierarchically partitions the instance space using a top-down (pruning-free) decision tree procedure. Although various DFID implementations use different stopping rules, split-validation examinations and splitting rules, in this chapter we concentrate on a specific DFID method – contrasted populations miner (CPOM). The splitting rule that this method uses – grouped gain ratio – combines the well-accepted gain ratio criterion with a heuristic grouping procedure. CPOM can reduce the processing time while keeping the composite classifier accurate.

Implementations of DFID consist of a decision-tree (as a wrapper) and another embedded classification method (this method can, in principle, also be a decision tree). The embedded classification method generates the multiple classifiers for the tree's leaves. The DFID sequence is illustrated by the pseudo code in Figure 10.1. DFID inputs are: training instances; a list of attributes (which will be examined as candidates for splitting the decision tree); a classification method; and, optionally, (depending on the specific implementation), some additional parameters.

The procedure begins by creating the decision tree's root node. The root represents the entire instance space X. When constructed, each node is attached with a rule which defines the subspace of X that the node represents. The DFID framework considers rules that can be expressed in a conjunctive normal form. A rule may be, for example: "$(A_1 = 3 \lor A_1 = 4) \land A_2 = 1$". DFID then checks whether there should be a split from the root node (i.e., whether X should be partitioned). This check, which uses some stopping rules, is represented, in Figure 10.1 by the general function StoppingCriterion. The function receives some inputs (depending on the specific implementation) and returns a Boolean value that indicates whether the stopping rules are met. If the stopping rules are met, then I is trained using all of the training instances. The classifier that results is attached to the root node and the procedure terminates. If, however, the stopping-rules are not met, then DFID searches for a split, according to some splitting rule, represented in Figure 10.1 by the general function split.

Splits in DFID are based on the values of a certain candidate attribute. We assume that there exists at least a single attribute that can create a split (or otherwise the stopping-rules would have indicated that there should be no more splits).

The function split receives a training set, a set of candidate attributes and optionally some additional inputs. It then returns the attribute upon whose values the split is based and a set of descendents nodes. Recall that upon its creation, each node is attached with a rule, which defines the subspace of X that the node represents. The rules for the descendent nodes are conjunctions of the root's rule and restrictions on the values of the selected attribute. The split that was found may be then subjected to a validation examination, represented, in Figure 10.1 by the general function validate. If a split is found to be invalid, then DFID will search for another split (another attribute). If there are no more candidate attributes, I will be trained using all the training instances and the classifier that results will be attached to the root node. As soon as a valid split is found, the descendent nodes that were created by the split are recursively considered for further splits. Further splits are achieved by the recurrence of DFID. In the recurrence, only a subset of the training instances is relevant (the instances that are actually sorted to the certain descendent node). In addition, the attribute, which defined the current split, is removed from the list of candidate attributes. The descendents are finally linked to their parent (the root). Different DFID implementations may differ in all or some of the procedures that implement the three main framework components – stopping-rules (the function StoppingCriterion), splitting rules (the function split) and split validation examinations (the function validate).

11.2.1 *Stopping Rules*

Stopping rules are checked by the general function StoppingCriterion (Figure 10.1). However, it should be noticed that a negative answer by this function is not the only condition that stops the DFID recurrence; another, and even more natural, condition, is the lack of any valid split.

According to the simple stopping rule that NBTree uses, no splits are considered when there are 30 instances or less in the examined node. Splitting a node with only a few training instances will hardly affect the final accuracy and will lead, on the other hand, to a complex and less comprehensible decision tree (and hence a complex and less comprehensible composite classifier). Moreover, since the classifiers are required to generalize from the instances in their subspaces, they must be trained on samples of sufficient size.

Kohavi's stopping-rule can be revised into a rule that never considers further splits in nodes that correspond to $\beta|S|$ instances or less, where $0 < \beta < 1$ is a proportion and $|S|$ is the number of instances in original training set, S. When using this stopping rule (either in Kohavi's way or in the revised version), a threshold parameter must be provided to DFID as well as to the function StoppingCriterion. Another heuristic stopping rule is never to consider splitting a node, if a single classifier can accurately describe the node's subspace (i.e., if a single classifier which was trained by all of the training instances, and using the classification method appear to be accurate). Practically, this rule can be checked by comparing an accuracy estimation of the classifier to a pre-defined threshold (thus, using this rule requires an additional parameter). The motivation for this stopping rule is that if a single classifier is good enough, why replace it with a more complex tree that also has less generalization capabilities? Finally, as mentioned above, another (inherent) stopping-rule of DFID is the lack of even a single candidate attribute.

11.2.2 *Splitting Rules*

The core question of DFID is how to split nodes. The answer to this question lies in the general function split (Figure 10.1). It should be noted that any splitting rule that is used to grow a pure decision tree, is also suitable in DFID.

Kohavi [Kohavi (1996)] has suggested a new splitting rule, which selects the attribute with the highest value of a measure, which he refers to as the "utility". Kohavi defines the utility as the fivefold cross-validation accuracy estimation of using a naive-Bayes method for classifying the subspaces which will be generated by the considered split.

11.2.3 *Split Validation Examinations*

Since splitting rules, are heuristic, it may be beneficial to regard the splits they produce as recommendations that should be validated. Kohavi [Kohavi (1996)] validated a split by estimating the reduction in error, which is gained by the split and comparing it to a predefined threshold of 5% (i.e., if it is estimated that the split will reduce the overall error rate by only 5% or less, the split is regarded as invalid). In an NBTree, it is enough to examine only the first proposed split in order to conclude that there are no valid splits, if the one examined is invalid. This follows since in an NBTree, the attribute according to which the split is done is the one that maximizes the utility measure, which is strictly increasing with the reduction in error. If a split, in accordance with the selected attribute cannot reduce the accuracy by more than 5%, then no other split can.

We suggest a new split validation procedure. In very general terms, a split according to the values of a certain attribute is regarded as invalid if the subspaces that result from this split are similar enough to be grouped together.

11.3   The CPOM Algorithm

This section presents the contrasted population miner (CPOM), which splits nodes according to a novel splitting rule, termed grouped gain ratio. Generally speaking, this splitting rule is based on the gain ratio criterion (Quinlan, 1993), followed by a grouping heuristic. The gain ratio criterion selects a single attribute from the set of candidate attributes, and the grouping heuristic thereafter groups together subspaces which correspond to different values of the selected attribute.

11.3.1   *CPOM Outline*

CPOM uses two stopping rules. First, the algorithm compares the number of training instances to a pre-defined ratio of the number of instances in the original training set. If the subset is too small, CPOM stops (since it is undesirable to learn from too small a training subset). Secondly, CPOM compares the accuracy estimation of a single classifier to a pre-defined threshold. It stops if the accuracy estimation exceeds the threshold (if a single classifier is accurate enough, there is no point in splitting further on). Therefore, in addition to the inputs in Figure 11.1, CPOM must receive two parameters: β, the minimal ratio of the training instances and acc, the maximal accuracy estimation that will still result in split considerations.

CPOM's split validation procedure is directly based on grouped gain ratio. The novel rule is described in detail, in the following subsection;

however, in general terms, the rule returns the splitting attribute and a set of descendent nodes. The nodes represent subspaces of X that are believed to be different. If the procedure returns just a single descendent node, the split it has generated is regarded as invalid.

11.3.2 *The Grouped Gain Ratio Splitting Rule*

Grouped gain ratio is based on the gain ratio criterion followed by a grouping heuristic. The gain ratio criterion selects a single attribute from a set of candidate attributes. The instance subspace, whose partition we are now considering, may, in principle, be partitioned so that each new sub-subspace will correspond to a unique value of the selected attribute. Group gain ratio avoids this alternative, through heuristically grouping sub-subspaces together. By grouping sub-subspaces together, grouped gain ratio increases the generalization capabilities, since there are more instances in a group of sub-subspaces than there are in the individual sub-subspaces.

Clearly, if we separately train I on each subset and obtain the same exact classifier from each subset, then there is no point in the split, since using this single classifier for the entire instance space is as accurate as using the multiple classifiers; it is also much simpler and understandable, and it can generalize better. The other direction of this argument is slightly less straightforward. If the classifiers that were trained over the training subsets are very different from one another, then none of them can classify X as one, and we can believe that the split is beneficial. Based on this observation, the grouped gain ratio splitting rule groups together subspaces that have similar classifiers.

The intuition regarding the classifier comparisons raises questions of what is similar, what is different and how to compare classifiers? Although there may be multiple classifiers, all of which must be simultaneously compared to each other, we begin answering these questions with the simpler case of exactly two classifiers, using a comparison heuristic, which we refer to as cross-inspection (see Figure 10.2).

Cross-inspection is based on two mutually-exclusive training subsets and a classification method as inputs. The comparison begins by randomly partitioning each subset into a training sub-subset and a test sub-subset. Then, two classifiers are produced, by training the input method, once over each training sub-subset. After producing the two classifiers, the cross-inspection heuristic calculates the error rates of each classifier over each of the test sub-subsets. If the error rate of the first classifier over the first test sub-subset is significantly (with confidence level alpha) different from the error of the first classifier over the second test sub-subset, or vice versa, then the two classifiers are regarded as different. The errors are compared by testing the hypothesis that the errors are generated by the same binomial random variable [Dietterich (1998)].

The cross-inspection heuristic compares only two distinct classifiers. However, in the DFID framework, more than two classifiers must be compared at a time (if the attribute, which was selected by the gain ratio criterion, has more than two possible values). For example, if it is believed that graduate students from different schools behave differently, one may consider splitting according to the school's name. The attribute 'school' can receive multiple values, all of which will have to be compared simultaneously. A successful split will group similar schools together, while different schools will be in different groups. Since an exhaustive search, over all the possible groupings, is unacceptable in terms of complexity, grouped gain ratio (see Figure 10.4) uses a greedy grouping heuristic, which is based on cross-inspection.

The procedure begins by using cross-inspection, to compare all the distinct pairs of classifiers (if there are q classifiers, there are $q(q\text{-}1)/2$ comparisons). For each instance-subspace, the procedure computes the number of instances that belong to subspaces that are similar to it (by definition the similarity by cross-inspection is defined with regard to classifiers rather than subspaces; each subspace, however, is described by a classifier). The classifier that represents the subspace with the largest such number is regarded as the classifier that covers the maximal number of instances. The subspaces of all the instances which are covered by this classifier are grouped together, and the procedure iterates. The heuristic does not explicitly guarantee that any two classifiers in a group are equivalent, but equivalence is assumed to be a transitive relation. The greedy grouping procedure is a simple clustering method and other clustering methods, like graph coloring [Zupan *et al.* (1998)] may also be suitable here. Alternatively one could use the Warshall algorithm [Warshall (1962)] for finding the transitive closure of the comparison matrix, which can be used for calculating $\sup_j$. However, this form of calculation will not be convenient in this case because it will tend to group too much as the following example illustrates.

Cohen *et al.* (2007) demonstrated that CPOM improved the obtained accuracy compared to the examined embedded methods (naive Bayes, back-propagation and C4.5). Not only was CPOM more accurate than other decision tree ISD methods, the grouping heuristic significantly improved the accuracy results, compared to a CPOM variation which does not group. Finally, using three synthetic datasets, CPOM distinguished between different populations in an underlined dataset.

11.4 Induction of Decision Trees by an Evolutionary Algorithm

Evolutionary Algorithms (EAs) are stochastic search algorithms inspired by the concept of Darwinian evolution. The motivation for applying EAs to data mining tasks is that they are robust, adaptive search techniques that perform a global search in the solution space [Freitas (2005)]. Since a well-designed EA continually considers new solutions, it can be viewed as an "anytime" learning algorithm capable of quite quickly producing a good-enough solution. It then continues to search the solution space, reporting the new "best" solution whenever one is found.

Genetic algorithms (GA), a popular type of evolutionary algorithms, have been successfully used for feature selection. Figure 10.5 presents a high level pseudo code of GA adapted from [Freitas (2005)].

Genetic algorithms begin by randomly generating a population of L candidate solutions. Given such a population, a genetic algorithm generates a new candidate solution (population element) by selecting two of the candidate solutions as the parent solutions. This process is termed reproduction. Generally, parents are selected randomly from the population with a bias toward the better candidate solutions. Given two parents, one or more new solutions are generated by taking some characteristics of the solution from the first parent (the "father") and some from the second parent (the "mother"). This process is termed "crossover". For example, in genetic algorithms that use binary encoding of n bits to represent each possible solution, we might randomly select a crossover bit location denoted as o. Two descendant solutions could then be generated. The first descendant would inherit the first o string characteristics from the father and the remaining $n-o$ characteristics from the mother. The second descendant would inherit the first o string characteristics from the mother and the remaining $n-o$ characteristics from the father. This type of crossover is the most common and it is termed one-point crossover. Crossover is not necessarily applied to all pairs of individuals selected for mating: a $P_{crossover}$ probability is used in order to decide whether crossover will be applied. If crossover is not applied, the offspring are simply duplications of the parents.

Finally, once descendant solutions are generated, genetic algorithms allow characteristics of the solutions to be changed randomly in a process known as mutation. In the binary encoding representation, according to a certain probability (P_{mut}), each bit is changed from its current value to the opposite value. Once a new population has been generated, it is decoded and evaluated. The process continues until some termination criterion is satisfied. A GA converges when most of the population is identical, or in other words, when the diversity is minimal.

Based on the pseudo code, one should provide the following ingredients when using a GA algorithm for decision trees: crossover operator, mutation operator, fitness function, a method to create the initial population and a stopping criterion.

Several GA-based systems, which learn decision trees in the top-down manner have been proposed, such as BTGA [Chai *et al.* (1996)], OC1-ES [Cantu-Paz and Kamath (2003)] and DDT-EA [Krtowski (2004)]. Generally, they apply an evolutionary approach to the test search, especially in the form of hyper-planes.

The GDT-EA algorithm [Krtowski and Grze (2005)] that we describe here searches for the whole tree at once in contrast to greedy, top-down approaches. The initial population is generated by applying a standard top-down decision tree inducers but attributes are selected in a dipolar way. Specifically, two instances from different classes are randomly chosen. Then an attribute which differentiates between the two instances is selected.

The Fitness function is composed of two terms: the classification accuracy on the training set and the tree complexity. Specifically, the fitness function, which must be maximized, has the following form:

$$Fitness = Acc - \alpha \cdot S \qquad (11.1)$$

where *Acc* is the classification quality estimated on the learning set; S is the size of the tree (number of nodes); and α - is a parameter which indicate the relative importance of the complexity term. The value of α should be provided by the user by tuning it to the specific problem that is solved.

The algorithm terminates if the fitness of the best individual in the population does not improve during the fixed number of generations. This status indicates, that the algorithm has converged. Additionally, the maximum number of generations is specified, which allows limiting the computation time in case of a slow convergence.

Like many other GAs, the GDT-EA also has two operators: *MutateNode* (for mutation) and *CrossTrees* (for crossover). The first operator MutateN-ode, which is applied with the given probability to every node of the tree, can modify the test or change the node structure. If a non-leaf node is concerned it can be pruned to a leaf or its test can be altered. Specifically, there are four modification options in case of non-leaf node:

- A completely new test is applied with another randomly chosen attribute and threshold,
- A new threshold is randomly chosen without changing the attribute used in the test,
- The current sub-tree is replaced by a sub-tree of an adjacent node.
- The test can be exchanged with another test taken from randomly chosen descendant-nodes.

If a leaf node is to be mutated, then there are two options:

- The leaf node is replaced with a non-leaf node with a new randomly chosen test.
- The leaf node is replaced with a sub-tree generated using an appropriate algorithm.

The CrossTrees operator is equivalent to the standard crossover oper-ator. It alters two solutions by exchanging certain parts of input trees. There are three possible exchange types: two types of sub-tree exchanges and an exchange of only tests. At the beginning, regardless of the type, one node in each tree is randomly chosen. Then the type of exchange between trees is decided.

In the first CrossTree variant, the tests that are associated with the chosen nodes are substituted. This option is valid only when the chosen nodes have the same number of outgoing branches. In the second CrossTree variant, we substitute the sub-trees starting from the chosen nodes. The third CrossTree variant actually combines the first two variants. Branches which start from the chosen nodes are exchanged in random order.

```
DFID (S, A, I)
Where:
S - Training Set
A - Input Feature Set
I - Inducer

Create a tree with a root node;
IF StoppingCriterion(S, A, I) THEN
    Attach the classifier I(S, A) to the root;
ELSE
    A* ← A;
    valid ← FALSE;
    WHILE A* ≠ ∅ and NOT(valid)
            (SplitAtt, nodes) ← split(S, A*);
            IF validate(nodes, SplitAtt, S)  THEN
                valid ← TRUE;
                A ← A − SplitAtt;
                FOR each node ∈ nodes
                    Generate classifier DFID(NodeInstances, A, I);
                    Attach the classifier to node;
                    Link the node to root;
                END FOR
              ELSE
                A* ← A * −SplitAtt;
    END WHILE
    IF NOT (valid) THEN
        Attach the classifier I(S, A) to the root;
    END IF
END IF
RETURN tree;
```

Fig. 11.1 DFID outline: A DFID implementation recursively partitions the instance space of the training set, according to the values of the candidate attributes. As the recursive partition ends, classifiers are attached to the leaves by employing the embedded classification method.

CrossInspection (S_1, S_2, I, α)

Where:

S_1, S_2 - Mutually-exclusive training sets

I - Inducer

α - Confidence level

$S_{11} \leftarrow$ a random sample from S_1;

$S_{12} \leftarrow S_1 - S_{11}$;

$S_{21} \leftarrow$ a random sample from S_2;

$S_{22} \leftarrow S_2 - S_{21}$;

$H_1 \leftarrow I(S_{11})$;

$H_2 \leftarrow I(S_{21})$;

FOR $i, j \in \{1, 2\}$ DO

$\qquad \varepsilon_{i,j} \leftarrow$ accuracy estimation of H_i over $S_{j,2}$;

END FOR

IF $\varepsilon_{1,2}$ is different from $\varepsilon_{1,1}$ with a confidence level α OR

$\qquad \varepsilon_{2,1}$ is different from $\varepsilon_{2,2}$ with a confidence level α THEN

$\qquad$ return FALSE;

ELSE

$\qquad$ return TRUE;

Fig. 11.2 The cross-inspection procedure outline: Searching for statistical significance, the procedure compares the accuracy estimations of two distinct classifiers.

GroupedGainRatio $(S, A, I, root, \alpha)$

Where:

S - Training Set

A - Input Feature Set

I - Inducer

root - the node from which the split is considered

α - confidence level

$A_i \leftarrow$ the attribute from A with the maximal gain ratio;

$S_1, S_2, \ldots, S_{d(i)} \leftarrow$ a partition of S, according to values of A_i;

FOR all $j, k \in \{1, 2, \ldots, d(i)\}$ so that $j \leq k$

    $E_{j,k} \leftarrow$ CrossInspection(S_j, S_k, I, α)

    $E_{k,j} \leftarrow E_{j,k}$;

END FOR

FOR all $j \in \{1, 2, \ldots, d(i)\}$

    $sup_j \leftarrow$ the number of instances in the

            subsets S_k for which $E_{j,k}$=TRUE;

END FOR

$L \leftarrow$ a list of the subsets indices sorted descending by sup_j;

nodes $\leftarrow$ an empty set of nodes

WHILE L is not empty DO

    Create a new node;

    Attach the rule which is a conjecture of the root's rule

        and a disjoint of the values that correspond to

        S_j the first member of L and the members

        S_k for which $E_{j,k}$=TRUE;

    Remove from L any member that is described by the new node;

    Add node to nodes;

END WHILE

RETURN $(A_i, nodes)$

Fig. 11.3   The grouped gain ratio procedure outline. The procedure groups together similar values of a candidate attribute. Similarity is based on the cross-inspection heuristic.

```
GA
Create initial population of individuals
      (candidate solutions)
Compute the fitness of each individual
REPEAT
      Select individuals based on fitness
      Apply genetic operators to selected individuals,
            creating new individuals
      Compute fitness of each of the new individuals
      Update the current population
            (new individuals replace old individuals)
UNTIL (stopping criterion)
```

Fig. 11.4   A Pseudo code for GA.

Chapter 12

Sequence Classification Using Decision Trees

12.1 Introduction

In this chapter we discuss how decision trees can be used for sequence classifications. The new method we present, Cascaded Regular Expression Decision Trees (CREDT), induces a cascaded ensemble of decision trees for classifying sequences patterns. CREDT consists of four main steps: (1) sequence representation: a domain specific task designed to represent sequences as a string of tokens; (2) pattern discovery: the automatic creation of a regular expression pattern from each pair of sequences; (3) pattern selection: applying heuristics to select the best patterns for correct classification; (4) classifier training: training a cascaded decision tree classifier to combine several patterns. The following sections describe each of the above phases.

12.2 Sequence Representation

This step is domain specific and every application might require different preprocessing. Generally the sequences are represented as a string of tokens. Each token may also include attributes that better characterize it. For instance, in order to discover interesting patterns in complicated manufacturing processes, each product manufacturing data is represented as a string of tokens, each token representing a different operation activity. If the makespan factor is unimportant, then the representation is straightforward. For instance, the production sequence 1-5-9-3-2 is represented as the string "B 1 5 9 3 2 F". If the makespan factor is important, then a more complicated representation is required. For this purpose we first need to decide what the desirable time granularity is. Time granularity should be

187

no more than the minimum operation duration in the database.

After deciding what the desirable time granularity is, we can represent the manufacturing process of each product instance as a string. Each time bucket is represented as a single letter. We denote by Σ the alphabet of the manufacturing process. Each letter in Σrepresents the identification of the operation performed in this time bucket. Idle time is also represented by a special letter (for instance "_"). The size of Σ depends on the number of operations that must be encoded. For instance, the string "B 1 1 _ _ _ _ 3 3 3 F" represents a manufacturing sequence with the operation "1" being performed during the first two time buckets. Then, during the four subsequent time buckets, no operations are performed. Three time buckets then follow in which operation "3" is performed.

In addition to the string we may keep for each token its attributes. For instance, we may keep the setting parameters of the machine (such as speed) that participated in the operation "1".

12.3 Pattern Discovery

The term sequence pattern usually refers to a set of short sequences that is precisely specified by some formalism. Following much research that is being carried out now in bioinformatics, we also adopt regular expressions in order to represent sequence patterns. A pattern is defined as any string consisting of a letter of the alphabet Σ and the wild-card character '.'. The wild-card (also known as the "don't care" character) denotes a position that can be occupied by any letter of the alphabet Σ. For instance, the pattern "B 1 1 _ . . _ 3 . 3" can be matched against the following production strings "B 1 1 _ _ _ _ 3 3 3", "B 1 1 _ 2 4 _ 3 1 3", "1 1 _ 7 _ _ 3 4 4", etc. The pattern element ". ∗" denotes an arbitrary string of symbols (possibly of length 0), ".{*3,5*}" to denote any string of between 3 and 5 characters.

In this research we examined two approaches for obtaining the regular expressions: the longest common subsequence and the TEIRESIAS algorithm. Here we describe the first approach, in which we compare any pair of sequences with the same class label. From each pair, we create the longest regular expression that fits the two sequences. For instance, assume we are given the following two sequences:

```
B 1 8 4 2 3 4 F
B 9 1 4 2 7 F
```

Table 12.1 illustrates how the longest regular expression can be extracted from the two strings. Every line in the table refers to a different part in the sequences. The first column enumerates the subsequence part. The following two columns present the subsequences. Note that by concatenating the subsequences, one can obtain the original complete sequence. The last column presents the generalized regular expression pattern that covers these subsequences. For instance, in the first line, since both subsequences contain the character "B" (Begin), the generalized pattern is also "B". In the second line, since the first subsequence is empty (null) and the second subsequence is "9", the generalized subsequence is the regular expression ".{0,1}" meaning that "one or no token" generalized these subsequences. Note that whenever there was an empty subsequence we added a wild card expression with a minimum length of 0 and a maximum length of the compared subsequence. On the other hand, whenever there were two unequal subsequences, we added a wild card expression with the minimum length of the shortest subsequence and the maximum length of the largest sequence.

Table 12.1 Illustration of Longest Common Subsequence Generation

#	Sequence 1	Sequence 2	Pattern
1	B	B	B
2		9	.{0,1}
3	1	1	1
4	8		.{0,1}
5	4 2	4 2	4 2
6	34	7	.{1,2}
7	F	F	F

By concatenating the expressions that appear in the pattern column, we can obtain the following regular expression pattern:

B .{0,1} 1 .{0,1} 4 2 . {1,2} F

In order to find the subsequences in Table 12.1, we use the longest common subsequence algorithm. One way to solve the problem is to convert it into the longest path problem based on the lattice graph. The nodes in the upper horizontal line are labeled with the tokens of the first sequence while the nodes of the first vertical line are labeled with the tokens of the second sequence. In this graph, all horizontal and vertical edges are possible. Additionally, diagonal edges in which the target node has the same horizontal and vertical label, are also available. If the horizontal and vertical edges have zero length, and the diagonal edges have length of one, then the longest common subsequence corresponds to the longest path from the top left corner to the bottom right corner. This graph is acyclic and is frequently solved using dynamic programming. The highlighted path presents one of the longest paths. Note that the destination node of the highlighted diagonal edges (B,1,4,2,F) is used in the regular expression, while the horizontal/vertical edges are converted to the wild-card expression.

12.4   Pattern Selection

Obviously there are many patterns that can be created via the LCS (each pair of sequences with the same class label). In fact, initially too many patterns are created and it is essential to stay within a manageable number of patterns. For example, a training set of 100 sequences from class "A" and 50 sequences of class "B" yielded 100*99/2 + 50*49/2=6175 patterns. In this chapter, we suggest using a two-phase pattern reduction as described in the following sections. In the first phase, we introduce new patterns that are created by merging existing patterns. In the second phase we reduce these sets of patterns using correlation-based feature selection.

12.4.1   *Heuristics for Pattern Selection*

Many of the generated patterns differ only in the distance between the tokens. Grouping such patterns by smoothing distances eliminates many patterns. The proposed simple heuristic for pattern reduction is based on merging two or more patterns into a single pattern. The merging is based on the specific tokens used in each pattern while ignoring the wild-cards. For instance, the "specific token" representation of "B 1 2 .{2,7} 3 F" is "B 1 2 3 F". All patterns with the same "specific token" representation are merged by the smoothing wild-card expressions. This is obtained by taking the minimum and maximum For example, the patterns "B 1 2 .{2,7} 3 F" and "B 1 2 .{3,9} 3 F" and "B 1 .{1,3} 2 .{3,4} 3 F" which all have the same "specific token" representation of "B 1 2 3 F" are generalized using the pattern "B 1 .{0,3} 2 .{2,9} 3 F". Moreover any two or more patterns whose "specific token" representations are different in one position (a Hamming distance of one) are generalized by introducing a wild-card into that position.

12.4.2   *Correlation based Feature Selection*

Feature selection is the process of identifying relevant features in the dataset and discarding everything else as irrelevant and redundant. For this purpose, each "regular expression" pattern represents a different feature. In this work we use a non-ranker filter feature selection algorithm. Filtering means that the selection is performed independently of any learning algorithm. Non-ranker means that the algorithm does not score each pattern but only determines which pattern is relevant and which is not.

In this work we use the correlation-based feature subset selection (CFS) as a subset evaluator. CFS evaluates the worth of a subset of attributes by considering the individual predictive ability of each feature along with the degree of redundancy between them. Subsets of features that are highly correlated with the class while having low inter-correlation are preferred. This approach is useful when there are many correlated patterns (for instance, when one pattern generalizes another pattern).

The CFS algorithm was executed with best-first forward selection. This search strategy searches the space of attribute subsets by greedy hill-climbing augmented with a backtracking facility. It starts with the empty set of attributes and search forward.

12.5   Classifier Training

We are using a decision tree inducer as the base inducer. Using a decision tree as a classifier in this case has several advantages. (1) The sequence is not classified based on a single pattern, but on set of patterns, i.e. this classifier can be used to indicate that a sequence is classified to the label "A" only if it matched two patterns and does not match a third pattern. This is more expressive than the classical approach in which the classification is based on a single pattern. Moreover, in this way, instead of searching for complicated regular expressions, we can search for simple regular expressions and "rely" on the decision tree to combine them. In fact, in some cases, it is possible to express a tree path as a single complicated regular expression; (2) The hierarchical structure of decision tree enforces an order (priority) in the usage of patterns, i.e. given a new sequence, not all patterns should be matched in advance but one pattern at a time based on the specific branch. In this way we inherently obtain a conflict resolution mechanism; (3) As opposed to other classifiers (such as neural networks) the meaning of the classifier can be explained.

12.5.1   *Adjustment of Decision Trees*

Instead of using the C4.5 algorithm as is, we were required to make some adjustment to the splitting criterion. In the problem solved here, there are two types of attributes: the regular expressions (binary attributes indicating if the expression is matched or not) and the attributes that characterize the tokens. Note that the characterizing attributes of the tokens become available only when the corresponding token is matched. For instance, if the token "A" in the sequence has the attribute "var1" then we can use the attribute "var1" in a certain decision node only if a regular expression with the token "A" has appeared in one of its ancestor nodes. This suggests for consideration other criteria than the information gain ratio, such as:

- Select pattern with the largest support – If the support of a pattern is relatively high, then there are sufficient training instances to grow a meaningful sub-tree.
- Select the longest pattern – Longest sequence implies that the dimensionality (namely, the number of characterizing attributes) of the matched training instances is large enough to grow a meaningful sub-tree.

12.5.2   *Cascading Decision Trees*

Studying the training corpuses, the classification errors and patterns selected by the classifier, we noticed that it is possible to create a more powerful ensemble structure than the structure obtained from such a general-purpose ensemble method as Adaboost. More specifically, we noticed that: (1) training set size might be a limiting issue due to the computational complexity of the machine learning algorithms used; (2) in the training and test corpuses there are simple sequences versus compound sequences; and (3) some of the patterns yield very high precision.

These observations, as well as the improvement achieved using the Adaboost method, triggered the idea of constructing a cascade of classifiers. The idea is to build a cascade of classifiers. The selection of tree cascades is due to the fact that in this case we assume the class is binary (positive and negative): The first cascade includes only simple patterns obtained from the negative class, ensuring high precision (very few positive sequences will be classified as negative).

The "errors" of the first cascade "Trained classifier 1", meaning sequences from the negative corpus that were not classified as negative by

"Trained classifier 1", are taken as the negative training corpus for the second cascade classifier (positive corpus remains the same as for the first cascade). The second cascade is of negative patterns (learned from the original corpus of negative sequences). The third cascade classifier includes also positive patterns.

12.6 Application of CREDT in Improving of Information Retrieval of Medical Narrative Reports

In this section, we illustrate how the CREDT algorithm can be used in a real world application of information retrieval. Information retrieval from free text is now an established and well known application with vast popularity among Internet search engines such as Google. The limitations of naïve keyword-based information retrieval are also well understood and many research works are focused around this issue.

We illustrate the CREDT in improving the information retrieval from medical narratives. Medical narratives present some unique problems that are not normally encountered in other kinds of texts. When a physician writes an encounter note, a highly telegraphic form of language may be used. There are often very few (if any) grammatically proper sentences and acronyms and abbreviations are frequently used. Many of these abbreviations and acronyms are highly idiosyncratic and may not be found in a general dictionary.

Information retrieval from medical narratives has many applications: enrollment of patients into clinical trials; detecting adverse events; modern evidence-based practice; and medical research in general. A typical application scenario may involve a hospital-based medical investigator receiving from a pharmaceutical company a patient profile for a planned clinical trial. The profile includes attributes that cannot be used as is in a structured query of the hospital information systems. Example of such a patient profile is: *"Male and female, 18 years and older; Female must not be pregnant; Location of pain must be low back area; Pain must be present for three months or greater; No surgical intervention in the past 12 months nor plans for surgical intervention for the low back pain during the duration of the study"*.

Most of the data needed for locating patients meeting the above profile is stored as electronic medical narratives in the hospital information systems. The medical investigator retrieves such records by a keyword-based search.

The keywords primarily include: diagnostic names, symptoms, procedures, medicine, etc. A useful knowledge source designed for resolving medical terms is the Unified Medical Language System (UMLS) [Lindbergh and Humphreys (1993)].

The common use-case when searching in discharge summaries is looking for patients with specific symptom, for example, *nausea*. The issue of context is very important. Consider the sentence: *"He complained at admission of headache, nausea, vomiting, and neck soreness"* versus *"The patient denies any headache, nausea, vomiting, blurring vision and fever"*. Both sentences will match a naïve keyword-based query containing the term *nausea*. We assume that the person initiating the query is looking for patients with a specific symptom (e.g. *nausea*). For example, the sentence *"The patient states she had fever and chills two nights prior to admission with a nonproductive cough"*, taken from a discharge summary report is a positive example for *fever* and *chills* diagnoses, while another sentence from a discharge report: *"The patient denied any cough, chest pain, urinary symptoms or bowel symptoms"* is a negative example for cough, chest pain, urinary symptoms and bowel symptoms diagnoses.

A search for patients with a specific symptom or set of findings might result in numerous records retrieved. The mere presence of a search term in the text, however, does not imply that retrieved records are indeed relevant to the query. Depending upon the various contexts that a term might have, only a portion of the retrieved records may actually be relevant. Therefore, in addition to excluding negated concepts, there are additional contexts we opt to exclude. For example: *"The patient as well as her daughter were given very clear instructions to call or return for any nausea, vomiting, bleeding, or any unusual symptoms."*; and the sentence: *"The patient could not tolerate the nausea and vomiting associated with Carboplatin"*; *"She is married, lives with her husband and admits to drinking alcohol excessively in the remote past."* ; and more.

To cope with the natural ambiguity that these sentences and the various contexts suggest, we introduce here a new supervised method for inducing a sequence-aware (or sequence sensitive) classifier. First we automatically discover a set of sequence patterns that are described as regular expressions. Then a classifier is induced to classify instances based on their matching the discovered set of sequence patterns. We show the advantages of the new method by applying it to a well-known and well-defined problem in the medical domain. The challenge is to increase information retrieval accuracy from the common 60% baseline naïve search. This improvement is achieved by identifying the context of the query keyword (e.g. medical diagnosis such as nausea) being searched.

The issues encountered in dealing with this problem constitute a special case of context identification in free text, one of the key research problems in the field of text mining. We compare the results obtained using our proposed method to previous works which implement two primary methodologies: knowledge engineering; and machine learning. The knowledge engineering approach is based on handcrafted patterns for identifying the negated context. Such methods yield high accuracy but are labor-intensive, domain specific and tedious to maintain. The more modern methods are based on machine learning techniques. The bag-of-words is considered as one of the prominent machine learning techniques for classification problems. The negative context detection can be formulated as a text classification problem and solved using bag-of-words. The negation problem is closely related to the part-of-speech tagging problem, which is properly solved by frameworks for labeling sequential data, such as hidden Markov model (HMM) and conditional random fields (CRF). In this work we compare our new method to the above mentioned techniques. Our new method is much faster than manual knowledge engineering techniques with matching accuracy. We show that our new method achieves higher accuracy compared to existing methods.

12.6.1 Related Works

The negation problem in medical reports can be solved in various ways. First, in addition to existing general purpose text classification methods that can be used. there are several information extraction methods that can also be implemented. After discussing these methods, we survey specific works regarding the negation problem in general and in the medical domain in particular. Finally, we discuss evaluation measures that can be used for estimating the quality of the solutions.

12.6.1.1 Text Classification

From a comprehensive survey of the methods used for text categorization and which describes recent research trends we see that the machine learning paradigm to automatic classifier construction definitely supersedes the knowledge-engineering approach. Within the machine learning paradigm, a classifier is built by learning from a set of previously classified documents.

The advantages of the machine learning approach are its high degree of effectiveness, a considerable savings in terms of expert manpower, and domain independence.

Since texts cannot be directly interpreted by a classifier or by a classifier-building algorithm, it is necessary to uniformly apply a transformation procedure to the text corpora in order to map a text d_j into a compact representation of its content. In text categorization (TC) a text d_j is usually represented as a vector of term weights $d_j = (w_{1j}, \ldots, w_{|V|j})$ where V is the set of terms (sometimes called features) that occur at least once in at least one document of T_r, and where $0 \leq w_{kj} \leq 1$ represents, loosely speaking, how many term t_k contributes to the semantics of document d_j. Differences among approaches are accounted for by (1) different ways to understand what a term is; (2) different ways to compute term weights. A typical choice for the first alternative is to identify terms with words. Depending on whether weights are binary or not, this approach is often called either the "*set of words*" or the "*bag-of- words*" approach to document representation.

The following example demonstrates the bag-of-words representation applied to our domain. Consider the two sentences: (1) *The patient was therefore admitted to the hospital and started on <MEDICINE> as treatments for <DIAGNOSIS>;* and (2) *The patient was ruled in for <DIAGNOSIS> and started <MEDICINE> for <DIAGNOSIS>.*

One of the main drawbacks of the bag-of-words representation is in its destruction of semantic relations between words; the meaning of word combinations is lost. This representation loses the meaning of important terms such as "*ruled in*". This bag-of-words limitation is especially important for the negation detection.

Another popular choice for text representation is to identify terms with word sequences of length n. This n-gram vector text representation method is used to classify text documents. One option is to select the normalized frequency with which the n-gram occurs in the document as the choice of 2-term weight. Each vector identifies a point in a multidimensional space, and similar documents are expected to have points close to each other. Then the dot product between two histogram vectors is used as a measure of their similarity.

Caropreso et al. (2001) experimented with n-grams for text categorization on the Reuters dataset. They define an n-gram as an alphabetically ordered sequence of n stems of consecutive words in a sentence (after stop words were removed). The authors use both unigrams (bag-of-words) and bigrams as document features. They extract the top-scored features using various feature selection methods including mutual information. Their results indicate that in general bigrams can better predict categories than unigrams.

A regular expression is defined as any string that describes or matches a set of strings according to certain syntax rules. Regular expressions are usually used to give a concise description of a set without having to list all elements. The regular expression consists of a letter of the alphabet and special characters. For example, the set containing the four strings: hat, hit, hot and hut can be described by the pattern "h.t" (or alternatively, it is said that the pattern matches each of the four strings). The wild-card (".") denotes a single position that can be occupied by any letter of the alphabet. The curly brackets are used to indicate a match between min and max of the preceding characters. For instance the pattern "without .{0,10} <diagnosis>" can be matched against the following strings "without < diagnosis >", "without any < diagnosis >", "without serious < diagnosis >", etc.

Regular expressions are used by many text editors and utilities to search and manipulate bodies of text based on certain patterns. Many programming languages support regular expressions for string manipulation. For example, Perl has a powerful regular expression engine built directly into their syntax. In our work we use the Java regular expression implementation (package *java.util.regex*).

The bag-of-words and n-gram representations are actually a special case of the regular expression representation proposed in this work. A regular expression feature such as ".*{0,500} started .{0,500}*" is actually equivalent to the word feature *started* in the bag-of-words representation. The regular expression feature ".*{0,500} ruled in .{0,500}*" matches the bigram representation of the two words phrase *ruled in*. An additional benefit of our proposed regular expressions compared to bag-of-words is in handling compound sentences that include both positive and negative findings. For example, the sentence: *"upon admission showed no <diagnosis_1> but did show extensive <diagnosis_2> and <diagnosis_3> but there were no masses noted"*. The bag-of-words representation of such sentences is problematic since the same features apply to both negative and positive contexts and the algorithm cannot learn to distinguish between them. The regular expressions representation can represent such structural features using the distance and presence of additional diagnosis.

12.6.1.2   *Part-of-speech Tagging*

Part-of-speech tagging (POS tagging) refers to labeling words in a text as corresponding to a particular part of speech based on both its definition, as well as its context—i.e., relationship with adjacent and related words in the text. POS tagging is hard mainly because some words may have multiple part of speech tags and the correct tag depends on the context. POS tags indicate the basic syntactic function of that token, such as noun or verb, as well as other grammatical information, such as number and tense. POS tagging is a fundamental preprocessing step for many other NLP (Natural Language Processing) applications (e.g., syntactic parsing). Typically, POS tags provide general shallow syntactic information to these downstream applications.

Machine learning methods have been shown to be more effective in solving POS tagging than classic NLP methods. POS tagging is closely related to our problem. In fact, the negation detection problem can be regarded as a special case of POS tagging – we define a polarity tag (possible values are Negative and Positive) that is applicable to the <*diagnosis*> terms only. The following sections present sequences labeling frameworks that have been successfully used for POS tagging.

12.6.1.3   *Frameworks for Information Extraction*

A common information extraction (IE) task is to automatically extract entities and relationships from semi-structured or free text. For example, in the medical domain, an IE task is to automatically populate a structured database from a discharge summary report.

Many works in IE propose learning approaches that automatically process free text and overcome the knowledge engineering bottleneck. For example Califf and Moony (1997) proposed the RAPIER system that induces pattern-match rules from rigidly structured text. Such systems focus on extracting entities and relationships. However there is no emphasis on special contexts, such as negation that might totally divert the meaning of the text. Apparently such cases are rare in the corpora used for evaluating the above works (which is not true when dealing with discharge reports where more than 50% of the findings might actually be negated). More recent IE works are focused on hidden Markov model (HMM) techniques.

12.6.1.4 *Frameworks for Labeling Sequential Data*

The Hidden Markov model (HMM) is a common machine learning technique with published applications in sequential pattern recognition tasks. HMMs were successfully applied to related problems such as: IE, POS tagging and many more. Specifically, HMM was successfully applied to POS tagging of bio-medical texts. Similarly, we can utilize HMM POS taggers for solving the negation problem. Applying a HMM POS tagger to the negation detection problem is not a trivial task since there are many possible approaches for structuring the HMM. The hidden states are the POS tags (e.g. noun, verb, adjective, etc.) and the arrows represent the possible transitions between states.

Conditional random fields (CRFs) is a newer framework for labeling sequential data. CRFs define a conditional probability over label sequences given a certain observation sequence. This relaxes the unwarranted independence assumptions about the sequences which HMMs make. Like HMMs, CRFs have been successfully used for part-of-speech tagging. A comparative study showed that CRFs outperform HMMs in this application.

12.6.1.5 *Identifying Negative Context in Non-domain Specific Text (General NLP)*

Negation is an active linguistic research topic with roots dating back to Aristotle. Today this topic is still being widely studied. Negation is considered difficult in natural language processing due to the overwhelming complexity of the form and the function of sentences with negation. Negation is one of the constants of classical logic and has complex and systematic interaction with the other logical operators, especially quantifiers and modals.

In English grammar, negation is the process that turns a positive statement *("the patient has <diagnosis>")* into its opposite denial *("the patient does not have <diagnosis>")*. Nouns as well as verbs can be negated with a negative adjective *("There is no <diagnosis>")*; a negative pronoun (*no one, nobody, neither, none, nothing*); or a negative adverb (*"he never was <diagnosis>"*). It is easy to identify specific negation words such as: *not, neither*, and *never*, as well as for *Not*-negation, e.g., *not, n't*, and *No*-negation. However, in many cases, these specific words are not presented, e.g., *deny, fail*, and *lack*. Words in this second category are called inherent negatives, i.e., they have a negative meaning but a positive form. An additional morphological form of negation is the affixal negation. Prefix negations *un-* and *in-* , may create negation words *unhappy, unwise*, and *unfit* . Negations can also be created with suffixes such as *-less*, e.g., *lifeless*. Another complexity arise from double negation, e.g. the sentence *"it is not unlikely"*. The neg-raising phenomenon adds additional complexity, e.g. sentences such as: *"I don't believe he is ill"* or *"I don't think he is ill"*.

We could not locate any NLP research on identifying negated concepts in specific non-domain areas. However, some NLP techniques such as syntactic and semantic processing can be applied to a negation identification framework, especially part of speech tagging and shallow parsing. These features can be combined into a machine learning classification scheme for negation identification. The effectiveness of such NLP techniques very much depends on the quality of the text, particularly its compliance with grammatical rules. The language used in medical narratives, however, is often grammatically ill-formed. For example, the positive finding cough in the sentence *"the patient reported she was not feeling well due to mild cough"*. Thus NLP techniques that rely on grammatical sentences may not be sufficient for identification of negation in medical narratives.

12.6.1.6 *Identifying Negative Context in Medical Narratives*

Researchers in medical informatics have suggested methods for automatically extracting information contained in narrative reports for decision support, guideline implementation, and detection and management of epidemics. Some of the researches concentrate on methods for improving information retrieval from narrative reports. A number of investigators have tried to cope with the problem of a negative context. These works can be classified into two research domain categories, which are presented in the following two sections.

12.6.1.7 *Works Based on Knowledge Engineering*

The knowledge engineering approach is based on human expert writing rules or patterns. These rules and patterns are designed to capture syntactic and semantic features of the free text. The methods used are mostly from the NLP research field utilizing also deep parsing technologies and sometimes rule engines. These methods are complex and very expensive to develop and maintain, useful mostly when the target text is written according to proper language rules.

12.6.1.8 *Works based on Machine Learning*

Many of the recent works in the field of text classification are based on the machine learning approach. Machine learning has proven effective for text classification. The advantages are that such methods are much faster to develop than knowledge engineering. In addition they are more effective when the text is not written according to proper grammar rules.

12.6.2 *Using CREDT for Solving the Negation Problem*

We now show how the CREDT algorithm can be used to solve the negation problem. Section 5.6.1 below explains the complete process of training a regular expression based classifier from an input of training and test corpora. Sections 5.6.2-12.6.2.8 specifiy in detail each of the steps. Finally, Section 5.6.6 suggests the concept of cascading several classifiers for improving the performance.

12.6.2.1 *The Process Overview*

We suggest the following process of training a classifier to predict negation concepts using regular expressions patterns. The process includes four steps:

Corpus preparation A domain specific task designed to normalize, generalize and tag the free text so that it can be further processed.

Regular expression patterns learning The automatic creation of a regular expression patterns from the training set.

Patterns selection Applying heuristics and features selection techniques to select the best patterns for correct classification of the concept.

Classifier training Training a decision tree classifier.

The following sections describe each of the above steps.

12.6.2.2 *Step 1: Corpus Preparation*

The objective of the corpus preparation phase is to transform the input discharge summaries data into a usable corpus for the training and test phases. The following sections describe each sub-step.

12.6.2.3 *Step 1.1: Tagging*

In the first step we parse all the discharge summaries. All known medical terms are tagged using a tagging procedure presented in [Rokach *et al.* (2004),]. Consider for example the following text:

We use the UMLS metathesaurus, for tagging the sentence, i.e. replacing medical terms with their concept type. For example, when the parser reaches the term *coronary* it queries the UMLS for terms starting with *"coronary*"*. The result set includes several terms starting with *coronary*. The parser then uses a sliding window in order to match the longest possible UMLS term to the given sentence. The UMLS terms relevant for the above sentence are listed in Table 12.2.

Table 12.2 Tagging using the UMLS

ID	Term	Type	CUI (concept unique identifier)
1	coronary artery by-pass graft	Procedure	10010055
2	coronary artery disease	Diagnosis	10010054
3	hypertension	Diagnosis	10020538
4	diabetes mellitus	Diagnosis	10011849
5	kidney stones	Diagnosis	10022650

Since we are only interested in the generalized form of the sentence (the specific diagnosis or procedure does not matter), the output text following the tagging process takes the following form:

12.6.2.4 *Step 1.2: Sentence Boundaries*

Physicians are trained to convey the salient features of a case concisely and unambiguously as the cost of miscommunication can be very high. Thus it is assumed that negations in dictated medical narrative are unlikely to cross sentence boundaries, and are also likely to be simple in structure.

An additional processing step includes breaking discharge summaries documents into sentences using a sentence boundary identifier as suggested by [Averbuch *et al.* (2005)]. The sentence boundary is identified by searching for terminating signs such as { ".", "?", "!" }. This approach is not sufficient since periods and other signs are frequently appear inside sentences (for instance: *"Patient was discharged on Lopressor 25 milligrams p.o. b.i.d.*[1]". We detect such exceptions using regular expressions (an expression that describes a set of strings) to exclude expressions that might mistakenly be considered end of sentence (Table 12.3).

Table 12.3 Regular expressions to exclude sentence end

(b|t|q)\.i\.d\.?	p\.o\.?	\.([0-9]+)	cc\.
p\.r\.n	q\.d\.?	\.of	\.,and
q\.h\.s	mg\.	(Dr\.)(\s?)(\w+)	\sq\.

12.6.2.5 *Step 1.3: Manual Labeling*

This step refers to the creation of the training corpus. Physicians should review each document and label each medical term, indicating whether it appears in positive or negative context. Since most sentences include more than one diagnosis. it is necessary to tag each of them during the manual tagging process. Consider for instance the compound sentence: *"She denied shortness of breath, but did have fever"*. In this case *"shortness of breath"* is negative while *"fever"* is positive. Thus, this sentence will be represented in the dataset as two different instances – one for each diagnosis term. Since each instance has one label (positive or negative), each has exactly one anchor diagnosis term to which the label refers. This anchor term is tagged as "<DIAGNOSIS>" while any other diagnosis terms in the sentence will be denoted as "<DIAG>". Note that we will be able to obtain different patterns from the same sentence. For instance, in the example, the pattern ".* *denied <DIAGNOSIS> .*"* can be learned for identifying negative context, and the pattern ".* *denied <DIAG> but .* <DIAGNOSIS>"* can be learned for identifying positive context.

12.6.2.6 *Step 2: Patterns Creation*

For the reasons explained below, instead of using a single regular expression representation for the entire sentence, we use two regular expressions: one for the string that precedes the targeted medical term (the seed) and one for the string that follows it. This split may help to resolve some of the problems that arise in compound sentences that include both positive and negative contexts in the same sentence. Recall the example *"The patient states she had fever, but denies any chest pain or shortness of breath"*. In this case, the appearance of the verb *"denies"* after the term *"fever"*

---

[1] From Latin: oral administration two times daily

indicates that the term *"fever"* is left in positive context. The appropriate regular expression will be in this case as follows: *".{0,200}denies any.{0,200}<DIAGNOSIS>"*, where the distance 200 is arbitrary determined per the expected sentence length in the domain.

To learn regular expressions, we have adapted two different algorithms to our task and compared them . The first algorithm, LCS, is commonly used to compare characters in a word. The second algorithm, Teiresias, was designed for discovering motifs in biological sequences. We describe how we adapted these algorithms to the task of learning regular expressions for negation patterns below.

Learning regular expression patterns using longest common subsequence algorithm

The basis for discovering a regular expression is a method that compares two texts with the same context and incorporates the same concept types (i.e. diagnosis, medication, procedure, etc.). By employing the longest common subsequence (LCS) algorithm [Myers (1986)] on each part of the sentence (before the targeted term and after the targeted term) a regular expression that fits these two sentences is created. The LCS employs a brute force policy: given a sequence X, determine all possible subsequences of X, and check to see if each subsequence was a subsequence of Y, keeping track of the longest subsequence found. For instance, assume we are given the following two sentences:

```
The patient was therefore admitted to the hospital and
started on <MEDICINE> as treatments for <DIAGNOSIS>.
The patient was ruled in for <DIAG> and started <MEDICINE>
for <DIAGNOSIS>.
```

We execute the LCS algorithm on the two normalized sentences as presented in Table 12.4.

Note that the LCS algorithm was revised to compare tokens as opposed to comparing characters in its classical implementation. It should also be noted that whenever there was only insertion (or only deletion) we added a wild card string with a minimum length of 0 and a maximum length of the inserted string (including the leading and trailing spaces). On the other hand, whenever there was simultaneously insertion and deletion, we

Table 12.4   Longest Common Subsequence Generation for Medical Text

Sentence 1	Sentence 2	Pattern
The patient was	The patient was	The patient was
therefore admitted to the hospital		.{24,35}
	ruled in for <DIAG>	
and started	and started	and started
	on	.{0,4}
<MEDICINE>	<MEDICINE>	<MEDICINE>
as treatments		.{0,15}
for <DIAGNOSIS>	for <DIAGNOSIS>	for <DIAGNOSIS>

added a wild card string with the minimum length of the shortest string and maximum length of the largest string (without leading and trailing spaces because they are part of the common substring).

As a result of running the LCS algorithm we obtain the following pattern. This pattern can now be used to classify concept of type medication appearing in positive contexts.

```
The patient was .{24,35} and started .{0,4}<MEDICINE>.{0,15}
for <DIAGNOSIS>
```

Learning regular expression patterns using Teiresias algorithm

The Teiresias algorithm was designed to discover motifs in biological sequences, an important research problem [Rigoutsos and Floratos (1998)]. The method is combinatorial in nature and able to produce all patterns that appear in at least a (user-defined) minimum number of sequences, yet it manages to be very efficient by avoiding the enumeration of the entire pattern space. Furthermore, the reported patterns are maximal: any reported pattern cannot be made more specific and still keep on appearing at the exact same positions within the input sequences.

Teiresias searches for patterns which satisfy certain density constraints, limiting the number of wild-cards occurring in any stretch of pattern. More specifically, Teiresias looks for maximal <L,W> patterns with the support of at least K (i.e. in the corpus there are at least K distinct sequences of that match this pattern). A pattern P is called <L,W> pattern if every sub pattern of P with length of at least W words (combination of specific words and "." wild-cards) contains at least L specific words.

For example, given the following corpus of six negative sentences:

```
no further <diagnosis> was noted
no history of <diagnosis>
no intraoperative or immediate <diagnosis> were noted
no other <diagnosis>
past medical history no other <diagnosis>
patient had no further episodes of <diagnosis>
```

The Teiresias program (L=K=2, W=5) discovers six recurring patterns shown in the following file:

```
2 2 no other <diagnosis>
2 2 no further
2 2 of <diagnosis>
3 3 no .  <diagnosis>
2 2 <diagnosis> .  noted
2 2 no .  .  .  <diagnosis>
```

The first two columns represent the support of the pattern. The dot represents a missing word. Note that the program yields also patterns that do not include the <diagnosis> seed. These patterns are not useful for our purpose and are filtered out. Next we transform the Teiresias patterns to regular expression patterns by replacing each dot (missing word) with a regular expression such as .{*0,L*}, where L is calculated by counting the number of dots and multiplying by the average word length (8 characters as per our corpus).

The resulting regular expression patterns are presented in the following example:

```
no other <diagnosis>
of <diagnosis>
no .{0,8} <diagnosis>
<diagnosis> .{0,8} noted
no .  {0,24} <diagnosis>
```

12.6.2.7 *Step 3: Patterns Selection*

Obviously there are many patterns that can be created via the LCS (each pair of sentences with the same concept type and context). In fact, initially too many patterns are created and it is essential to keep a manageable number of patterns. For example, a training set of 140 negative sentences and 140 positive sentences yielded 2*(140*139/2)=19,460 patterns.

Many of the generated patterns differ only in the distance of important keywords from the seed concept. Grouping such patterns by smoothing distances eliminates many patterns. For example, the patterns "*had no.{12,27}<diagnosis>*" and "*had no.{17,32}<diagnosis>*" are generalized using the pattern "*had no.{10,40}<diagnosis>*". Trivial patterns such as "*a.{70,100} <diagnosis>*" are omitted. For example from the original 19,460 patterns, 17,235 were identified as redundant and trivial. After eliminating these patterns, only 2,225 patterns are remained.

Feature selection is the process of identifying relevant features in the dataset and discarding everything else as irrelevant and redundant. For this purpose each "regular expression" pattern represents a different feature.

We use a non-ranker filter feature selection algorithm. Filtering means that the selection is performed independently of any learning algorithm. Non-ranker means that the algorithm does not score each pattern but only indicates which pattern is relevant and which is not. The rows are training sentences (negative and positive); the first K columns are the regular expression patterns; and the last column is the target class (negative / positive). The cell value is 1 if the regular expression matches the sentence, otherwise it is 0. The matrix described above is the input to the features selection algorithm.

In this work we use the correlation-based feature subset selection (CFS) as a subset evaluator. CFS evaluates the worth of a subset of attributes by considering the individual predictive ability of each feature along with the degree of redundancy among them. Subsets of features that are highly correlated with the class while having low inter-correlation are preferred. This approach is suitable to this case, because there are many correlated patterns (for instance, when one pattern generalized another pattern). For example the 2,225 remaining patterns create a dataset of 280 instances with 2,225 input binary attributes (0 if the pattern does not match the sentence; 1 if pattern matches sentence) and target attribute that represent the concept classification ("Positive" or "Negative"). The filter further reduced the set into 35 'relevant' patterns.

12.6.2.8   *Step 4: Classifier Training*

The filtered matrix, together with the manual classification of each concept, is fed into a decision tree induction algorithm which creates a classification decision tree. An illustrative example of decision tree generated is presented in Figure 12.1. It describes a classification decision path where pattern ".{*0,200*}*have*.{*0,50*}<*diagnosis*>", learned from positive examples, indicates a positive context with probability P5 in case the sentence does not match the three (negative) patterns: ."{*0,200*}*without*.{*0,10*}<*diagnosis*>"; ".{*0,200*}*rule out*.{*0,10*}<*diagnosis*>"; ".{*0,200*}*had no*.{*0,10*}<*diagnosis*>" (with probabilities P1, P2, and P3 for negative) but matches the negative pattern ".{*0,200*}*no*.{*0,50*}<*diagnosis*>". Here we denote "negative pattern" as a pattern learned from negative context examples. This demonstrates the power of decision based on matching a sentence with multiple regular expressions.

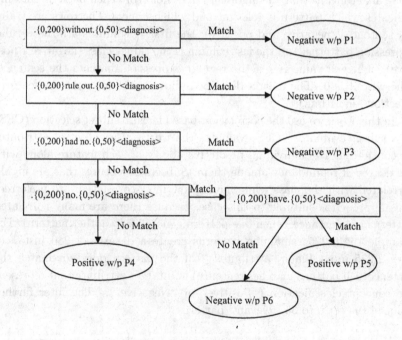

Fig. 12.1   Example decision tree.

12.6.2.9 *Cascade of Three Classifiers*

It is well known that the classification accuracy of a single decision tree can be significantly improved by growing an ensemble of trees and letting them vote for the most popular class. Analyzing the problem domain, we brought up the hypothesis that it is possible to create a more powerful ensemble structure than the structure obtained from such general purpose ensembles method as Adaboost. Specifically, we noticed that: (1) training set size is a limiting issue due to the computational complexity of the machine learning algorithms used; (2) in the corpus, there are simple sentences versus compound sentences or instructions; (3) Some of the patterns yield very high precision. This is obvious since for some of the negation terms attached (anchored) to the seed, mean that the seed is negated. For example, in a sentence such as, *". . . denied **nausea** . . . "* the nausea is negated with near 100% probability. Thus, it makes sense to train a simple classifier using only such (anchored) patterns, using it to identify the simple instances with very high precision. Then, only instances not classified as negative by the first cascade are used to train a second classifier.

These observations triggered the idea of constructing a cascade of classifiers. The idea is to build a cascade of classifiers. The selection of tree cascades is due to the problem characteristics: the first cascade consists of anchored patterns; the second cascade consists of negative patterns (learned from negative sentences) and the third cascade classifier also includes positive patterns.

The first cascade includes only anchored patterns, ensuring high precision (very few positive sentences will be classified as negative). Anchored patterns are patterns where the word is anchored (no separating words) to the seed. For example, the following anchored patterns form the first cascade classifier:

```
no <diagnosis>
denied <diagnosis>
denies <diagnosis>
not <diagnosis>
negative for <diagnosis>
without <diagnosis>
ruled out <diagnosis>
```

The training set of negated instances for the second cascade comprises negation patterns that failed to classify as negative by the first cascade *"Trained classifier 1"*. The training set of positive instances for the first cascade is used as is in the second cascade. In the third cascade we learn patterns from the negative and positive corpora, taking only negative instances which failed to classify as negative by the first and second cascades. The third cascade classifier includes also positive patterns (patterns learned from the positive corpus). In that sense, these patterns are different from the previous works that rely only on negation patterns.

Figure 12.2 demonstrates how the cascaded classifiers perform the classification of three unseen sentences. The first sentence *"the patient denied <diagnosis>"* is matched by an anchored pattern *"denied <diagnosis>"* and is classified negative by "Trained classifier 1". The second sentence *"the patient did not experience recent <diagnosis>"* does not match with any of the "Trained classifier 1" anchored patterns, therefore it is fed into "Trained classifier 2" for further classification as negative due to the patterns comprising "Trained classifier 2". The third sentence is classified as negative by the "Trained classifier 3". The last sentence is not classified as negative by all three cascades and is therefore classified as positive.

An experimental study that was performed provides strong evidence that in the negation problem, regular expressions are better than bag-of-words, in both accuracy and compactness (i.e. obtaining smaller models). In fact, regular expressions can be considered to be a generalization of the bag-of-words representation or any n-gram representation.

Using a decision tree as a base classifier in this case has several advantages. (1) The sentence is not classified according to a single regular expression, but is classified based on a set of regular expressions, i.e. this classifier can be used to indicate that a sentence is classified to the label "positive" only if it matched two regular expressions and does not match a third regular expression. This is more expressive than the classical approach in which the classification is based on a single regular expression. Moreover, in this way, instead of searching for complicated regular expressions, we can search for simple regular expressions and "rely" on the decision tree to combine them. In some cases, it is possible to express a tree path comprised of several simple regular expressions as a single complicated regular expression; (2) The hierarchical structure of a decision tree enforces an order (priority) in the usage of regular expressions, i.e. given a new sentence, not all regular expressions should be matched in advance but one regular expression at a time based on the specific branch traversing. In this way, the desired property of lexical analysis known as un-ambiguity (also known

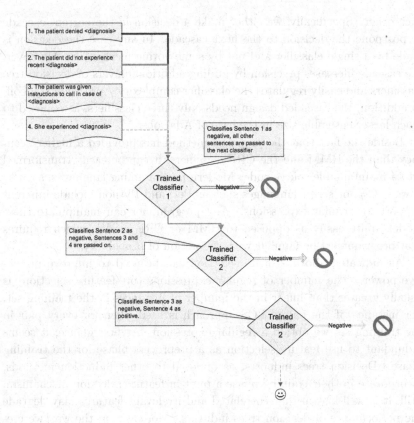

Fig. 12.2 Cascade classifier classification examples.

as conflict resolution in Expert Systems) which is usually resolved by the longest match and rule priority is inherently resolved here; (3) As opposed to other classifiers (such as neural networks) the decision tree is a white box model whose meaning can be easily explained.

The experimental study strengthens the well-known fact that it is possible to boost the predictive performance by combining several decision trees. Nevertheless, an important drawback of general-purpose ensemble methods, such as AdaBoost, is that they are difficult to understand. The resulting ensemble is considered to be less comprehensible since the user is required to capture several decision trees instead of a single decision tree. In addition, the ensemble members might even contradict one another. On the other hand, in the proposed cascaded design, the classifiers do not compete with each other and do not contradict one another, but they are complementing each other. Specifically, we either make a decision in the current cascade or postpone the decision to the next cascade. In any case the decision is made by a single classifier and not by some voting mechanism. Moreover, the cascade increases precision by adding additional layers of decision tree classifiers and easily regulates the classifier complexity / precision tradeoff. In addition, the cascaded design needs only three classifiers, as opposed to much larger ensemble size in the case of AdaBoost.

Beside the fact that the proposed method has provided a higher accuracy than the HMM and the CRF classifiers, it can be easily transformed into a maintainable source code. Modern programming languages, such as Java or C#, or script languages such as Perl and Python include inherent support for regular expressions. Any programmer can manipulate these models quite easily as opposed to HMM or CRF models which requires that programmers be familiar with the notion of probability.

As indicated above, feature selection can be used to improve predictive power. The number of regular expressions (pre-feature selection) is usually greater than linear in the number of instances in the training set. For instance, if the paired LCS approach is used, then for every pair in the training set we obtain a regular expression. At first glance, it seems redundant to use feature selection as a preprocess phase for the training phase. Decision trees inducers, as opposed to other induction methods, incorporate in their training phase a built-in feature selection mechanism. Still, it is well known that correlated and irrelevant features may degrade the performance of decision trees inducers. Moreover, in the way we create regular expressions, there are many features that are correlative. This phenomenon can be explained by the fact that feature selection in decision trees is performed on one attribute at a time and only at the root node over the entire decision space. In subsequent nodes, the training set is divided into several sub-sets and the features are selected according to their local predictive power. Geometrically, it means that the selection of features is done in orthogonal decision subspaces, which do not necessarily represent the distribution of the entire instance space. It has been shown that the predictive performance of decision trees could be improved with an appropriate feature pre-selection phase. Moreover using feature selection can reduce the number of nodes in the tree, making it more compact.

Another way to avoid the "curse of dimensionality" in this case, is to merge several expressions into one expression by generalizing them. However, this increases the risk of over generalization. This is the typical sensitivity-specificity problem. A criterion for merging regular expressions can be based on existing computational learning theoretical bounds (such as the VC dimension) that trade training accuracy with model complexity. Merging regular expressions reduces a model's complexity but at the same time it might also reduce training accuracy (due to generalization). The merging can be performed in any stage: pre-training, like feature selection, during the actual training of decision trees (as an extension to the splitting criterion), or post growing as an extension to the pruning phase.

Regular expressions seem quite useful for the examined task but they do have limitations. For instance, because they do not use syntax but only words and character length gaps, they can make mistakes due to, for example, a training set that only showed one adjective modifying a negated noun (e.g., no persistent cough) but a test set that has multiple adjectives intervening between the negation phrase and the negated concept. Moreover, in order that a negative modifier will be included in the model, it should be repeated at least twice in two different instances in the training set. This is because the regular expressions are created by comparing two strings and identifying the common substring. If the modifier appears only once, then it will never be included in any of the regular expressions.

Bibliography

Aha, D. W.; Kibler, D.; and Albert, M. K., Instancebased learning algorithms. Machine Learning 6(1):37-66, 1991.

A1-Sultan K. S., A tabu search approach to the clustering problem, Pattern Recognition, 28:1443-1451,1995.

Al-Sultan K. S. , Khan M. M. : Computational experience on four algorithms for the hard clustering problem. Pattern Recognition Letters 17(3): 295-308, 1996.

Ali K. M., Pazzani M. J., Error Reduction through Learning Multiple Descriptions, Machine Learning, 24: 3, 173-202, 1996.

Almuallim H., An Efficient Algorithm for Optimal Pruning of Decision Trees. Artificial Intelligence 83(2): 347-362, 1996.

Almuallim H,. and Dietterich T.G., Learning Boolean concepts in the presence of many irrelevant features. Artificial Intelligence, 69: 1-2, 279-306, 1994.

Alsabti K., Ranka S. and Singh V., CLOUDS: A Decision Tree Classifier for Large Datasets, Conference on Knowledge Discovery and Data Mining (KDD-98), August 1998.

An A. and Wang Y., "Comparisons of classification methods for screening potential compounds". In IEEE International Conference on Data Mining, 2001.

Anand R, Methrotra K, Mohan CK, Ranka S. Efficient classification for multiclass problems using modular neural networks. IEEE Trans Neural Networks, 6(1): 117-125, 1995.

Anderson, J.A. and Rosenfeld, E. Talking Nets: An Oral History of Neural Network Research. Cambridge, MA: MIT Press, 2000.

Ashenhurst, R. L., The decomposition of switching functions, Technical report, Bell Laboratories BL-1(11), pp. 541-602, 1952.

Athanasopoulos, D. (1991). Probabilistic Theory. Stamoulis, Piraeus.

Attneave F., Applications of Information Theory to Psychology. Holt, Rinehart and Winston, 1959.

Averbuch M., Maimon O., Rokach L., and Ezer E., Free-Text Information Retrieval System for a Rapid Enrollment of Patients into Clinical Trials, Clinical Pharmacology and Therapeutics, 77(2): 13-14, 2005.

Avnimelech R. and Intrator N., Boosted Mixture of Experts: an ensemble learning scheme, Neural Computations, 11(2):483-497, 1999.

Baker E., and Jain A. K., On feature ordering in practice and some finite sample effects. In Proceedings of the Third International Joint Conference on Pattern Recognition, pages 45-49, San Diego, CA, 1976.

Bala J., Huang J., Vafaie H., De Jong K., Wechsler H., Hybrid Learning Using Genetic Algorithms and Decision Trees for Pattern Classification, IJCAI conference, 1995.

R. Banfield, OpenDT, http://opendt.sourceforge.net/, 2005.

Robert E. Banfield, Lawrence O. Hall, Kevin W. Bowyer, W.P. Kegelmeyer, A Comparison of Decision Tree Ensemble Creation Techniques, IEEE Transactions on Pattern Analysis and Machine Intelligence, vol. 29, no. 1, pp. 173-180, Jan., 2007

Banfield J. D. and Raftery A. E. . Model-based Gaussian and non-Gaussian clustering. Biometrics, 49:803-821, 1993.

Bartlett P. and Shawe-Taylor J., Generalization Performance of Support Vector Machines and Other Pattern Classifiers, In "Advances in Kernel Methods, Support Vector Learning", Bernhard Scholkopf, Christopher J. C. Burges, and Alexander J. Smola (eds.), MIT Press, Cambridge, USA, 1998.

Basak J., Online adaptive decision trees, Neural Computations, 16(9):1959-1981, 2004.

Basak J., Online Adaptive Decision Trees: Pattern Classification and Function Approximation, Neural Computations, 18(9):2062-2101, 2006.

Bauer, E. and Kohavi, R., "An Empirical Comparison of Voting Classification Algorithms: Bagging, Boosting, and Variants". Machine Learning, 35: 1-38, 1999.

Baxt, W. G., Use of an artificial neural network for data analysis in clinical decision making: The diagnosis of acute coronary occlusion. Neural Computation, 2(4):480-489, 1990.

Bay, S., Nearest neighbor classification from multiple feature subsets. Intelligent Data Analysis, 3(3): 191-209, 1999.

Bellman, R., Adaptive Control Processes: A Guided Tour, Princeton University Press, 1961.

BenBassat M., Myopic policies in sequential classification. IEEE Trans. on Computing, 27(2):170-174, February 1978.

Kristin P. Bennett and Ayhan Demiriz and Richard Maclin, Exploiting unlabeled data in ensemble methods, Proceedings of the eighth ACM SIGKDD international conference on Knowledge discovery and data mining, pp. 289–296, ACM Press, New York, NY, USA, 2002.

Bennett X. and Mangasarian O.L., Multicategory discrimination via linear programming. Optimization Methods and Software, 3:29-39, 1994.

Bensusan H. and Kalousis A., Estimating the Predictive Accuracy of a Classifier, In Proc. Proceedings of the 12th European Conference on Machine Learning, pages 25-36, 2001.

Bentley J. L. and Friedman J. H., Fast algorithms for constructing minimal spanning trees in coordinate spaces. IEEE Transactions on Computers, C-

27(2):97-105, February 1978. 275

Bernard M.E., Decision trees and diagrams. Computing Surveys, 14(4):593-623, 1982.

Berry M., and Linoff G., Mastering Data Mining, John Wiley & Sons, 2000.

Bhargava H. K., Data Mining by Decomposition: Adaptive Search for Hypothesis Generation, INFORMS Journal on Computing Vol. 11, Iss. 3, pp. 239-47, 1999.

Biermann, A. W., Faireld, J., and Beres, T. (1982). Signature table systems and learning. IEEE Trans. Syst. Man Cybern., 12(5):635-648.

Black, M. and Hickey, R.J., Maintaining the Performance of a Learned Classifier under Concept Drift, Intelligent Data Analysis 3(1),pp. 453474, 1999.

Blum, A. L. and Langley, P., 1997, Selection of relevant features and examples in machine learning, Artificial Intelligence, 97, pp.245-271.

Blum A., and Mitchell T., Combining Labeled and Unlabeled Data with CoTraining. In Proc. of the 11th Annual Conference on Computational Learning Theory, pages 92-100, 1998.

Bonner, R., On Some Clustering Techniques. IBM journal of research and development, 8:22-32, 1964.

Booker L., Goldberg D. E., and Holland J. H., Classifier systems and genetic algorithms. Artificial Intelligence, 40(1-3):235-282, 1989.

Brachman, R. and Anand, T., 1994, The process of knowledge discovery in databases, in: Advances in Knowledge Discovery and Data Mining, AAAI/MIT Press, pp. 37-58.

Bratko I., and Bohanec M., Trading accuracy for simplicity in decision trees, Machine Learning 15: 223-250, 1994.

Brazdil P., Gama J., Henery R., Characterizing the Applicability of Classification Algorithms using Meta Level Learning, in Machine Learning: ECML-94, F.Bergadano e L. de Raedt (eds.), LNAI No. 784: pp. 83-102, Springer-Verlag, 1994.

Breiman L., Bagging predictors, Machine Learning, 24(2):123-140, 1996.

Breiman, L., Random forests. Machine Learn-ing, 45, 532, 2001.

Breiman L., Friedman J., Olshen R., and Stone C.. Classification and Regression Trees. Wadsworth Int. Group, 1984.

Br Brodley, C. E., Automatic selection of split criterion during tree growing based on node selection. In Proceedings of the Twelth International Conference on Machine Learning, 73-80 Taho City, Ca. Morgan Kaufmann, 1995.

Brodley C. E. and Utgoff. P. E., Multivariate decision trees. Machine Learning, 19:45-77, 1995.

Brown G., Wyatt J. L., Negative Correlation Learning and the Ambiguity Family of Ensemble Methods. Multiple Classifier Systems 2003: 266–275

Brown G., Wyatt J., Harris R., Yao X., Diversity creation methods: a survey and categorisation, Information Fusion, 6(1):5–20.

Bruzzone L., Cossu R., Vernazza G., Detection of land-cover transitions by combining multidate classifiers, Pattern Recognition Letters, 25(13): 1491–1500, 2004.

Buchanan, B.G. and Shortliffe, E.H., Rule Based Expert Systems, 272-292,

Addison-Wesley, 1984.

Buhlmann, P. and Yu, B., Boosting with L_2 loss: Regression and classification, Journal of the American Statistical Association, 98, 324338. 2003.

Buja, A. and Lee, Y.S., Data mining criteria for tree based regression and classification, Proceedings of the 7th International Conference on Knowledge Discovery and Data Mining, (pp 27-36), San Diego, USA, 2001.

Buntine, W., A Theory of Learning Classification Rules. Doctoral dissertation. School of Computing Science, University of Technology. Sydney. Australia, 1990.

Buntine, W. (1992), "Learning Classification Trees", Statistics and Computing, 2, 63–73.

Buntine, W., "Graphical Models for Discovering Knowledge", in U. Fayyad, G. Piatetsky-Shapiro, P. Smyth, and R. Uthurusamy, editors, Advances in Knowledge Discovery and Data Mining, pp 59-82. AAAI/MIT Press, 1996.

Buntine W., Niblett T., A Further Comparison of Splitting Rules for Decision-Tree Induction. Machine Learning, 8: 75-85, 1992.

Buczak A. L. and Ziarko W., "Neural and Rough Set Based Data Mining Methods in Engineering", Klosgen W. and Zytkow J. M. (Eds.), Handbook of Data Mining and Knowledge Discovery, pages 788-797. Oxford University Press, 2002.

Califf M.E. and Mooney R.J., Relational learning of pattern-match rules for information extraction. Proceedings of the Sixteenth National Conf. on Artificial Intelligence, page 328-334, 1999.

Can F. , Incremental clustering for dynamic information processing, in ACM Transactions on Information Systems, no. 11, pp 143-164, 1993.

Cantu-Paz E., Kamath C., Inducing oblique decision trees with evolutionary algorithms, IEEE Trans. on Evol. Computation 7(1), pp. 54-68, 2003.

Cardie, C. (1995). Using decision trees to improve cased- based learning. In *Proceedings of the First International Conference on Knowledge Discovery and Data Mining.* AAAI Press.

Caropreso M., Matwin S., and Sebastiani F., A learner-independent evaluation of the useful-ness of statistical phrases for automated text categorization, Text Databases and Document Management: Theory and Practice. Idea Group Publishing , page 78-102, 2001.

Caruana R., Niculescu-Mizil A. , Crew G. , Ksikes A., Ensemble selection from libraries of models, Twenty-first international conference on Machine learning, July 04-08, 2004, Banff, Alberta, Canada.

Carvalho D.R., Freitas A.A., A hybrid decision-tree - genetic algorithm method for data mining, Information Science 163, 13-35, 2004.

Catlett J., Mega induction: Machine Learning on Vary Large Databases, PhD, University of Sydney, 1991.

Chai B., Huang T., Zhuang X., Zhao Y., Sklansky J., Piecewise-linear classifiers using binary tree structure and genetic algorithm, Pattern Recognition 29(11), pp. 1905-1917, 1996.

Chan P. K. and Stolfo, S. J., Toward parallel and distributed learning by meta-learning, In AAAI Workshop in Knowledge Discovery in Databases, pp.

227-240, 1993.

Chan P.K. and Stolfo, S.J., A Comparative Evaluation of Voting and Meta-learning on Partitioned Data, Proc. 12th Intl. Conf. On Machine Learning ICML-95, 1995.

Chan P.K. and Stolfo S.J, On the Accuracy of Meta-learning for Scalable Data Mining, J. Intelligent Information Systems, 8:5-28, 1997.

Charnes, A., Cooper, W. W., and Rhodes, E., Measuring the efficiency of decision making units, European Journal of Operational Research, 2(6):429-444, 1978.

Chawla N. V., Moore T. E., Hall L. O., Bowyer K. W., Springer C., and Kegelmeyer W. P.. Distributed learning with bagging-like performance. Pattern Recognition Letters, 24(1-3):455-471, 2002.

Chawla N. V., Hall L. O., Bowyer K. W., Kegelmeyer W. P., Learning Ensembles from Bites: A Scalable and Accurate Approach, The Journal of Machine Learning Research archive, 5:421–451, 2004.

Chen K., Wang L. and Chi H., Methods of Combining Multiple Classifiers with Different Features and Their Applications to Text-Independent Speaker Identification, International Journal of Pattern Recognition and Artificial Intelligence, 11(3): 417-445, 1997.

Cheeseman P., Stutz J.: Bayesian Classification (AutoClass): Theory and Results. Advances in Knowledge Discovery and Data Mining 1996: 153-180

Cherkauer, K.J., Human Expert-Level Performance on a Scientific Image Analysis Task by a System Using Combined Artificial Neural Networks. In Working Notes, Integrating Multiple Learned Models for Improving and Scaling Machine Learning Algorithms Workshop, Thirteenth National Conference on Artificial Intelligence. Portland, OR: AAAI Press, 1996.

Cherkauer, K. J. and Shavlik, J. W., Growing simpler decision trees to facilitate knowledge discovery. In *Proceedings of the Second International Conference on Knowledge Discovery and Data Mining*. AAAI Press, 1996.

Chizi, B., Maimon, O. and Smilovici A. On Dimensionality Reduction of High Dimensional Data Sets, Frontiers in Artificial Intelligence and Applications, IOS press, pp. 230-236, 2002.

Christensen S. W. , Sinclair I., Reed P. A. S., Designing committees of models through deliberate weighting of data points, The Journal of Machine Learning Research, 4(1):39–66, 2004.

Cios K. J. and Sztandera L. M., Continuous ID3 algorithm with fuzzy entropy measures, Proc. IEEE Internat. Con/i on Fuzz)' Systems,1992, pp. 469-476.

Clark P., and Niblett T., The CN2 rule induction algorithm. Machine Learning, 3:261-284, 1989.

Clark, P. and Boswell, R., "Rule induction with CN2: Some recent improvements." In Proceedings of the European Working Session on Learning, pp. 151-163, Pitman, 1991.

Clearwater, S., T. Cheng, H. Hirsh, and B. Buchanan. Incremental batch learning. In Proceedings of the Sixth International Workshop on Machine Learning, San Mateo CA:, pp. 366-370. Morgan Kaufmann, 1989.

Clemen R., Combining forecasts: A review and annotated bibliography. International Journal of Forecasting, 5:559-583, 1989

S. Cohen, L. Rokach, O. Maimon, Decision Tree Instance Space Decomposition with Grouped Gain-Ratio, Information Science, Volume 177, Issue 17, pp. 3592-3612, 2007.

Coppock D. S., Data Modeling and Mining: Why Lift?, Published in DM Review online, June 2002.

Crawford S. L., Extensions to the CART algorithm. Int. J. of ManMachine Studies, 31(2):197-217, August 1989.

Cunningham P., and Carney J., Diversity Versus Quality in Classification Ensembles Based on Feature Selection, In: R. L. de Mntaras and E. Plaza (eds.), Proc. ECML 2000, 11th European Conf. On Machine Learning,Barcelona, Spain, LNCS 1810, Springer, 2000, pp. 109-116.

Curtis, H. A., A New Approach to the Design of Switching Functions, Van Nostrand, Princeton, 1962.

Dhillon I. and Modha D., Concept Decomposition for Large Sparse Text Data Using Clustering. Machine Learning. 42, pp.143-175. (2001).

Dempster A.P., Laird N.M., and Rubin D.B., Maximum likelihood from incomplete data using the EM algorithm. Journal of the Royal Statistical Society, 39(B), 1977.

Derbeko P. , El-Yaniv R. and Meir R., Variance optimized bagging, European Conference on Machine Learning, 2002.

Dietterich, T. G., "Approximate statistical tests for comparing supervised classification learning algorithms". Neural Computation, 10(7): 1895-1924, 1998.

Dietterich, T. G., An Experimental Comparison of Three Methods for Constructing Ensembles of Decision Trees: Bagging, Boosting and Randomization. 40(2):139-157, 2000.

Dietterich T., Ensemble methods in machine learning. In J. Kittler and F. Roll, editors, First International Workshop on Multiple Classifier Systems, Lecture Notes in Computer Science, pages 1-15. Springer-Verlag, 2000

Dietterich, T. G., and Ghulum Bakiri. Solving multiclass learning problems via error-correcting output codes. Journal of Artificial Intelligence Research, 2:263-286, 1995.

Dietterich, T. G., and Kong, E. B., Machine learning bias, statistical bias, and statistical variance of decision tree algorithms. Tech. rep., Oregon State University, 1995.

Dietterich, T. G., and Michalski, R. S., A comparative review of selected methods for learning from examples, Machine Learning, an Artificial Intelligence approach, 1: 41-81, 1983.

Dietterich, T. G., Kearns, M., and Mansour, Y., Applying the weak learning framework to understand and improve C4.5. Proceedings of the Thirteenth International Conference on Machine Learning, pp. 96-104, San Francisco: Morgan Kaufmann, 1996.

Dimitriadou E., Weingessel A., Hornik K., A cluster ensembles framework, Design and application of hybrid intelligent systems, IOS Press, Amsterdam, The Netherlands, 2003.

Domingos, P., Using Partitioning to Speed Up Specific-to-General Rule Induction.

In Proceedings of the AAAI-96 Workshop on Integrating Multiple Learned Models, pp. 29-34, AAAI Press, 1996.

Dominigos P. (1999): *MetaCost: A general method for making classifiers cost sensitive*. In proceedings of the Fifth International Conference on Knowledge Discovery and Data Mining, pp. 155-164. ACM Press.

Domingos, P. and Hulten, G., Mining Time-Changing Data Streams, Proc. of KDD-2001, ACM Press, 2001.

Domingos, P., & Pazzani, M., On the Optimality of the Naive Bayes Classifier under Zero-One Loss, Machine Learning, 29: 2, 103-130, 1997.

Dougherty, J., Kohavi, R, Sahami, M., Supervised and unsupervised discretization of continuous attributes. Machine Learning: Proceedings of the twelfth International Conference, Morgan Kaufman pp. 194-202, 1995.

Duda, R., and Hart, P., Pattern Classification and Scene Analysis, New-York, Wiley, 1973.

Duda, P. E. Hart and D. G. Stork, Pattern Classification, Wiley, New York, 2001.

Dunteman, G.H., Principal Components Analysis, Sage Publications, 1989.

Džeroski S., Ženko B., Is Combining Classifiers with Stacking Better than Selecting the Best One?, Machine Learning, 54(3): 255–273, 2004.

Elder I. and Pregibon, D., "A Statistical Perspective on Knowledge Discovery in Databases", In U. Fayyad, G. Piatetsky-Shapiro, P. Smyth, and R. Uthurusamy editors., Advances in Knowledge Discovery and Data Mining, pp. 83-113, AAAI/MIT Press, 1996.

Esmeir, S., and Markovitch, S. 2004. Lookahead-basedalgorithms for anytime induction of decision trees. InICML04, 257264.

Esposito F., Malerba D. and Semeraro G., A Comparative Analysis of Methods for Pruning Decision Trees. EEE Transactions on Pattern Analysis and Machine Intelligence, 19(5):476-492, 1997.

Ester M., Kriegel H.P., Sander S., and Xu X., A density-based algorithm for discovering clusters in large spatial databases with noise. In E. Simoudis, J. Han, and U. Fayyad, editors, Proceedings of the 2nd International Conference on Knowledge Discovery and Data Mining (KDD-96), pages 226-231, Menlo Park, CA, 1996. AAAI, AAAI Press.

Estivill-Castro, V. and Yang, J. A Fast and robust general purpose clustering algorithm. Pacific Rim International Conference on Artificial Intelligence, pp. 208-218, 2000.

Fraley C. and Raftery A.E., "How Many Clusters? Which Clustering Method? Answers Via Model-Based Cluster Analysis", Technical Report No. 329. Department of Statistics University of Washington, 1998.

Fayyad, U., Piatesky-Shapiro, G. & Smyth P., From Data Mining to Knowledge Discovery: An Overview. In U. Fayyad, G. Piatetsky-Shapiro, P. Smyth, & R. Uthurusamy (Eds), Advances in Knowledge Discovery and Data Mining, pp 1-30, AAAI/MIT Press, 1996.

Fayyad, U., Grinstein, G. and Wierse, A., Information Visualization in Data Mining and Knowledge Discovery, Morgan Kaufmann, 2001.

Fayyad U., and Irani K. B., The attribute selection problem in decision tree generation. In proceedings of Tenth National Conference on Artificial Intelligence, pp. 104–110, Cambridge, MA: AAAI Press/MIT Press, 1992.

Feigenbaum E. (1988): *Knowledge Processing – From File Servers to Knowledge Servers. In J.R. Queinlan ed., "Applications of Expert Systems". Vol. 2, Turing Institute Press, Chpater 1, pp. 3-11*

Ferri C., Flach P., and Hernández-Orallo J., Learning Decision Trees Using the Area Under the ROC Curve. In Claude Sammut and Achim Hoffmann, editors, Proceedings of the 19th International Conference on Machine Learning, pp. 139-146. Morgan Kaufmann, July 2002

Fifield D. J., Distributed Tree Construction From Large Datasets, Bachelor's Honor Thesis, Australian National University, 1992.

Fisher, D., 1987, Knowledge acquisition via incremental conceptual clustering, in machine learning 2, pp. 139-172.

Fischer, B., "Decomposition of Time Series - Comparing Different Methods in Theory and Practice", Eurostat Working Paper, 1995.

Fix, E., and Hodges, J.L., Discriminatory analysis. Nonparametric discrimination. Consistency properties. Technical Report 4, US Air Force School of Aviation Medicine. Randolph Field, TX, 1957.

Fortier, J.J. and Solomon, H. 1996. Clustering procedures. In proceedings of the Multivariate Analysis, '66, P.R. Krishnaiah (Ed.), pp. 493-506.

Fountain, T. Dietterich T., Sudyka B., "Mining IC Test Data to Optimize VLSI Testing", ACM SIGKDD Conference, 2000, pp. 18-25, 2000.

Frank E., Hall M., Holmes G., Kirkby R., Pfahringer B., WEKA - A Machine Learning Workbench for Data Mining, in O. Maimon, L. Rokach, editors The Data Mining and Knowledge Discovery Handbook, Springer, pp. 1305-1314, 2005.

Frawley W. J., Piatetsky-Shapiro G., and Matheus C. J., "Knowledge Discovery in Databases: An Overview," G. Piatetsky-Shapiro and W. J. Frawley, editors, Knowledge Discovery in Databases, 1-27, AAAI Press, Menlo Park, California, 1991.

Freitas A. (2005), "Evolutionary Algorithms for Data Mining", in O. Maimon and L. Rokach (Eds.), The Data Mining and Knowledge Discovery Handbook, Springer, pp. 435-467.

Freitas X., and Lavington S. H., Mining Very Large Databases With Parallel Processing, Kluwer Academic Publishers, 1998.

Freund Y. and Schapire R. E., Experiments with a new boosting algorithm. In Machine Learning: Proceedings of the Thirteenth International Conference, pages 325-332, 1996.

Friedman J. H., A recursive partitioning decision rule for nonparametric classifiers. IEEE Trans. on Comp., C26:404-408, 1977.

Friedman, J. H., "Multivariate Adaptive Regression Splines", The Annual Of Statistics, 19, 1-141, 1991.

Friedman, J.H. (1997a). Data Mining and Statistics: What is the connection? 1997.

Friedman, J.H. (1997b). On bias, variance, 0/1 - loss and the curse of dimensionality, Data Mining and Knowledge Discovery, 1: 1, 55-77, 1997.

Friedman, J.H. & Tukey, J.W., A Projection Pursuit Algorithm for Exploratory

Data Analysis, IEEE Transactions on Computers, 23: 9, 881-889, 1973.

Friedman N., Geiger D., and Goldszmidt M., Bayesian Network Classifiers, Machine Learning 29: 2-3, 131-163, 1997.

Friedman, J., Kohavi, R., Yun, Y. 1996. Lazy decision trees. Proceedings of the Thirteenth National Conference on Artificial Intelligence. (pp. 717-724). Cambridge, MA: AAAI Press/MIT Press.

Fukunaga, K., Introduction to Statistical Pattern Recognition. San Diego, CA: Academic, 1990.

Fürnkranz, J., More efficient windowing, In Proceeding of The 14th national Conference on Artificial Intelegence (AAAI-97), pp. 509-514, Providence, RI. AAAI Press, 1997.

Gallinari, P., Modular Neural Net Systems, Training of. In (Ed.) M.A. Arbib. The Handbook of Brain Theory and Neural Networks, Bradford Books/MIT Press, 1995.

Gama J., A Linear-Bayes Classifier. In C. Monard, editor, Advances on Artificial Intelligence – SBIA2000. LNAI 1952, pp 269-279, Springer Verlag, 2000

Gams, M., New Measurements Highlight the Importance of Redundant Knowledge. In European Working Session on Learning, Montpeiller, France, Pitman, 1989.

Gago, P. and Bentos, C. (1998). A metric for selection of the most promising rules. In *Proceedings of the 2nd European Conference on The Pronciples of Data Mining and Knowledge Discovery (PKDD'98)*.

Gardner M., Bieker, J., Data mining solves tough semiconductor manufacturing problems. KDD 2000: pp. 376-383, 2000.

Gehrke J., Ganti V., Ramakrishnan R., Loh W., BOAT-Optimistic Decision Tree Construction. SIGMOD Conference 1999: pp. 169-180, 1999.

Gehrke J., Ramakrishnan R., Ganti V., RainForest - A Framework for Fast Decision Tree Construction of Large Datasets,Data Mining and Knowledge Discovery, 4 (2/3) 127-162, 2000.

Gelfand S. B., Ravishankar C. S., and Delp E. J., An iterative growing and pruning algorithm for classification tree design. IEEE Transaction on Pattern Analysis and Machine Intelligence, 13(2):163-174, 1991.

Geman S., Bienenstock, E., and Doursat, R., Neural networks and the bias/variance dilemma. Neural Computation, 4:1-58, 1995.

George, E. and Foster, D. (2000),Calibration and empirical Bayes variable selection, Biometrika, 87(4):731-747.

Gilad-Bachrach, R., Navot, A. and Tisliby. (2004) N. Margin based feature selection - theory and algorithms. *Proceeding of the 21'st International Conferenc on Machine Learning*, 2004.

Gillo M. W., MAID: A Honeywell 600 program for an automatised survey analysis. Behavioral Science 17: 251-252, 1972.

Giraud–Carrier Ch., Vilalta R., Brazdil R., Introduction to the Special Issue of on Meta-Learning, Machine Learning, 54 (3), 197-194, 2004.

Gluck, M. and Corter, J. (1985). Information, uncertainty, and the utility of categories. Proceedings of the Seventh Annual Conference of the Cognitive Science Society (pp. 283-287). Irvine, California: Lawrence Erlbaum

Associates.

Grossman R., Kasif S., Moore R., Rocke D., and Ullman J., Data mining research: Opportunities and challenges. Report of three NSF workshops on mining large, massive, and distributed data, 1999.

Grumbach S., Milo T., Towards Tractable Algebras for Bags. Journal of Computer and System Sciences 52(3): 570-588, 1996.

Guo Y. and Sutiwaraphun J., Knowledge probing in distributed data mining, in Proc. 4h Iht. Conf. Knowledge Discovery Data Mining, pp 61-69, 1998.

Guha, S., Rastogi, R. and Shim, K. CURE: An efficient clustering algorithm for large databases. In Proceedings of ACM SIGMOD International Conference on Management of Data, pages 73-84, New York, 1998.

Gunter S., Bunke H. , Feature Selection Algorithms for the generation of multiple classifier systems, Pattern Recognition Letters, 25(11):1323–1336, 2004.

Guyon I. and Elisseeff A., "An introduction to variable and feature selection", Journal of Machine Learning Research 3, pp. 1157-1182, 2003.

Hall, M. Correlation- based Feature Selection for Machine Learning. University of Waikato, 1999.

Han, J. and Kamber, M. Data Mining: Concepts and Techniques. Morgan Kaufmann Publishers, 2001.

Hancock T. R., Jiang T., Li M., Tromp J., Lower Bounds on Learning Decision Lists and Trees. Information and Computation 126(2): 114-122, 1996.

Hand, D., Data Mining – reaching beyond statistics, Research in Official Stat. 1(2):5-17, 1998.

Hampshire, J. B., and Waibel, A. The meta-Pi network - building distributed knowledge representations for robust multisource pattern-recognition. Pattern Analyses and Machine Intelligence 14(7): 751-769, 1992.

Hansen J., Combining Predictors. Meta Machine Learning Methods and Bias/Variance & Ambiguity Decompositions. PhD dissertation. Aurhus University. 2000.

Hansen, L. K., and Salamon, P., Neural network ensembles. IEEE Transactions on Pattern Analysis and Machine Intelligence, 12(10), 993–1001, 1990.

Hartigan, J. A. Clustering algorithms. John Wiley and Sons., 1975.

Huang, Z., Extensions to the k-means algorithm for clustering large data sets with categorical values. Data Mining and Knowledge Discovery, 2(3), 1998.

He D. W., Strege B., Tolle H., and Kusiak A., Decomposition in Automatic Generation of Petri Nets for Manufacturing System Control and Scheduling, International Journal of Production Research, 38(6): 1437-1457, 2000.

Hilderman, R. and Hamilton, H. (1999). Knowledge discovery and interestingness measures: A survey. In *Technical Report CS 99-04*. Department of Computer Science, University of Regina.

Ho T. K., The Random Subspace Method for Constructing Decision Forests, IEEE Transactions on Pattern Analysis and Machine Intelligence, Vol. 20, No. 8, 1998, pp. 832-844.

Holmes, G. and Nevill-Manning, C. G. (1995) . Feature selection via the discovery of simple classification rules. In *Proceedings of the Symposium on Intelligent Data Analysis*, Baden- Baden, Germany.

Holmstrom, L., Koistinen, P., Laaksonen, J., and Oja, E., Neural and statistical classifiers - taxonomy and a case study. IEEE Trans. on Neural Networks, 8,:5–17, 1997.

Holte R. C., Very simple classification rules perform well on most commonly used datasets. Machine Learning, 11:63-90, 1993.

Holte, R. C.; Acker, L. E.; and Porter, B. W., Concept learning and the problem of small disjuncts. In Proceedings of the 11th International Joint Conference on Artificial Intelligence, pp. 813-818, 1989.

Hong S., Use of Contextual Information for Feature Ranking and Discretization, IEEE Transactions on Knowledge and Data Engineering, 9(5):718-730, 1997.

Hoppner F. , Klawonn F., Kruse R., Runkler T., Fuzzy Cluster Analysis, Wiley, 2000.

Hrycej T., Modular Learning in Neural Networks. New York: Wiley, 1992.

Hu, X., Using Rough Sets Theory and Database Operations to Construct a Good Ensemble of Classifiers for Data Mining Applications. ICDM01. pp 233-240, 2001.

Hubert, L. and Arabie, P. (1985) Comparing partitions. Journal of Classification, 5. 193-218.

Hunter L., Klein T. E., Finding Relevant Biomolecular Features. ISMB 1993, pp. 190-197, 1993.

Hwang J., Lay S., and Lippman A., Nonparametric multivariate density estimation: A comparative study, IEEE Transaction on Signal Processing, 42(10): 2795-2810, 1994.

Hyafil L. and Rivest R.L., Constructing optimal binary decision trees is NP-complete. Information Processing Letters, 5(1):15-17, 1976

Jacobs, R. A., Jordan, M. I., Nowlan, S. J., and Hinton, G. E. Adaptive mixtures of local experts. Neural Computation 3(1):79-87, 1991.

Jackson, J., *A User's Guide to Principal Components.* New York: John Wiley and Sons, 1991.

Jang J., "Structure determination in fuzzy modeling: A fuzzy CART approach," in Proc. IEEE Conf. Fuzzy Systems, 1994, pp. 480485.

Janikow, C.Z., Fuzzy Decision Trees: Issues and Methods, IEEE Transactions on Systems, Man, and Cybernetics, Vol. 28, Issue 1, pp. 1-14. 1998.

Jain, A.K. Murty, M.N. and Flynn, P.J. Data Clustering: A Survey. ACM Computing Surveys, Vol. 31, No. 3, September 1999.

Jain, A. and Zonker, D., Feature Selection: Evaluation, Application, and Small Sample Performance. IEEE Trans. on Pattern Analysis and Machine Intelligence, 19, 153-158, 1997.

Jenkins R. and Yuhas, B. P. A simplified neural network solution through problem decomposition: The case of Truck backer-upper, IEEE Transactions on Neural Networks 4(4):718-722, 1993.

Jimenez, L. O., & Landgrebe D. A., Supervised Classification in High- Dimensional Space: Geometrical, Statistical, and Asymptotical Properties of Multivariate Data. IEEE Transaction on Systems Man, and Cybernetics — Part C: Applications and Reviews, 28:39-54, 1998.

Johansen T. A. and Foss B. A., A narmax model representation for adaptive control based on local model -Modeling, Identification and Control, 13(1):25-39, 1992.

John G. H., Robust linear discriminant trees. In D. Fisher and H. Lenz, editors, Learning From Data: Artificial Intelligence and Statistics V, Lecture Notes in Statistics, Chapter 36, pp. 375-385. Springer-Verlag, New York, 1996.

John G. H., Kohavi R., and Pfleger P., Irrelevant features and the subset selection problem. In Machine Learning: Proceedings of the Eleventh International Conference. Morgan Kaufmann, 1994.

John G. H., and Langley P., Estimating Continuous Distributions in Bayesian Classifiers. Proceedings of the Eleventh Conference on Uncertainty in Artificial Intelligence. pp. 338-345. Morgan Kaufmann, San Mateo, 1995.

Jordan, M. I., and Jacobs, R. A., Hierarchical mixtures of experts and the EM algorithm. Neural Computation, 6, 181-214, 1994.

Jordan, M. I., and Jacobs, R. A. Hierarchies of adaptive experts. In Advances in Neural Information Processing Systems, J. E. Moody, S. J. Hanson, and R. P. Lippmann, Eds., vol. 4, Morgan Kaufmann Publishers, Inc., pp. 985-992, 1992.

Joshi, V. M., "On Evaluating Performance of Classifiers for Rare Classes", Second IEEE International Conference on Data Mining, IEEE Computer Society Press, pp. 641-644, 2002.

Kamath, C., and E. Cantu-Paz, Creating ensembles of decision trees through sampling, Proceedings, 33-rd Symposium on the Interface of Computing Science and Statistics, Costa Mesa, CA, June 2001.

Kamath, C., Cant-Paz, E. and Littau, D. (2002). Approximate splitting for ensembles of trees using histograms. In Second SIAM International Conference on Data Mining (SDM-2002).

Kanal, L. N., "Patterns in Pattern Recognition: 1968-1974". IEEE Transactions on Information Theory IT-20, 6: 697-722, 1974.

Kargupta, H. and Chan P., eds, Advances in Distributed and Parallel Knowledge Discovery , pp. 185-210, AAAI/MIT Press, 2000.

Kaufman, L. and Rousseeuw, P.J., 1987, Clustering by Means of Medoids, In Y. Dodge, editor, Statistical Data Analysis, based on the L1 Norm, pp. 405-416, Elsevier/North Holland, Amsterdam.

Kaufmann, L. and Rousseeuw, P.J. Finding groups in data. New-York: Wiley, 1990.

Kass G. V., An exploratory technique for investigating large quantities of categorical data. Applied Statistics, 29(2):119-127, 1980.

Kearns M. and Mansour Y., A fast, bottom-up decision tree pruning algorithm with near-optimal generalization, in J. Shavlik, ed., 'Machine Learning: Proceedings of the Fifteenth International Conference', Morgan Kaufmann Publishers, Inc., pp. 269-277, 1998.

Kearns M. and Mansour Y., On the boosting ability of top-down decision tree learning algorithms. Journal of Computer and Systems Sciences, 58(1): 109-128, 1999.

Kenney, J. F. and Keeping, E. S. "Moment-Generating and Characteristic Functions," "Some Examples of Moment-Generating Functions," and "Uniqueness Theorem for Characteristic Functions." §4.6-4.8 in Mathematics of Statistics, Pt. 2, 2nd ed. Princeton, NJ: Van Nostrand, pp. 72-77, 1951.

Kerber, R., 1992, ChiMerge: Descretization of numeric attributes, in AAAI-92, Proceedings Ninth National Conference on Artificial Intelligence, pp. 123-128, AAAI Press/MIT Press.

Kim J.O. & Mueller C.W., Factor Analysis: Statistical Methods and Practical Issues. Sage Publications, 1978.

Kim, D.J., Park, Y.W. and Park,. A novel validity index for determination of the optimal number of clusters. IEICE Trans. Inf., Vol. E84-D, no.2 (2001), 281-285.

King, B. Step-wise Clustering Procedures, J. Am. Stat. Assoc. 69, pp. 86-101, 1967.

Kira, K. and Rendell, L. A., A practical approach to feature selection. In *Machine Learning: Proceedings of the Ninth International Conference.*, 1992.

Klosgen W. and Zytkow J. M., "KDD: The Purpose, Necessity and Chalanges", Klosgen W. and Zytkow J. M. (Eds.), Handbook of Data Mining and Knowledge Discovery, pp. 1-9. Oxford University Press, 2002.

Kohavi, R., Bottom-up induction of oblivious read-once decision graphs, in F. Bergadano and L. De Raedt, editors, Proc. European Conference on Machine Learning, pp. 154-169, Springer-Verlag, 1994.

Kohavi R., Scaling up the accuracy of naive-bayes classifiers: a decision-tree hybrid. In Proceedings of the Second International Conference on Knowledge Discovery and Data Mining, pages 114–119, 1996.

Kohavi R., Becker B., and Sommerfield D., Improving simple Bayes. In Proceedings of the European Conference on Machine Learning, 1997.

Kohavi R. and John G., The Wrapper Approach, In Feature Extraction, Construction and Selection: A Data Mining Perspective, H. Liu and H. Motoda (eds.), Kluwer Academic Publishers, 1998.

Kohavi, R. and Kunz, C. (1997), Option decision trees with majority votes, in D. Fisher, ed., 'Machine Learning: Proceedings of the Fourteenth International Conference', Morgan Kaufmann Publishers, Inc., pp. 161–169.

Kohavi R., and Provost F., Glossary of Terms, Machine Learning 30(2/3): 271-274, 1998.

Kohavi R. and Quinlan J. R., Decision-tree discovery. In Klosgen W. and Zytkow J. M., editors, Handbook of Data Mining and Knowledge Discovery, chapter 16.1.3, pages 267-276. Oxford University Press, 2002.

Kohavi R. and Sommerfield D., Targeting business users with decision table classifiers, in R. Agrawal, P. Stolorz & G. Piatetsky-Shapiro, eds, 'Proceedings of the Fourth International Conference on Knowledge Discovery and Data Mining', AAAI Press, pp. 249-253, 1998.

Kohavi R. and Wolpert, D. H., Bias Plus Variance Decomposition for Zero-One Loss Functions, Machine Learning: Proceedings of the 13th International Conference. Morgan Kaufman, 1996.

Kolen, J. F., and Pollack, J. B., Back propagation is sesitive to initial conditions. In Advances in Neural Information Processing Systems, Vol. 3, pp. 860-867

San Francisco, CA. Morgan Kaufmann, 1991.

Kolcz, A. Chowdhury, and J. Alspector, Data duplication: An imbalance problem "In Workshop on Learning from Imbalanced Data Sets" (ICML), 2003.

Koller, D. and Sahami, M. (1996). Towards optimal feature selection. In *Machine Learning: Proceedings of the Thirteenth International Conference on machine Learning.* Morgan Kaufmann, 1996.

Kononenko, I., Comparison of inductive and Naive Bayes learning approaches to automatic knowledge acquisition. In B. Wielinga (Ed.), Current Trends in Knowledge Acquisition, Amsterdam, The Netherlands IOS Press, 1990.

Kononenko, I., SemiNaive Bayes classifier, Proceedings of the Sixth European Working Session on Learning, pp. 206-219, Porto, Portugal: SpringerVerlag, 1991.

Krtowski M., An evolutionary algorithm for oblique decision tree induction, Proc. of ICAISC'04, Springer, LNCS 3070, pp.432-437, 2004.

Krtowski M., Grze M., Global learning of decision trees by an evolutionary algorithm (Khalid Saeed and Jerzy Peja), Information Processing and Security Systems, Springer, pp. 401-410, 2005.

Krogh, A., and Vedelsby, J., Neural network ensembles, cross validation and active learning. In Advances in Neural Information Processing Systems 7, pp. 231-238 1995.

Kuhn H. W., The Hungarian method for the assignment problem. Naval Research Logistics Quarterly, 2:83–97, 1955.

Kuncheva L.I. Diversity in multiple classifier systems (Editorial), Information Fusion, 6 (1), 2005, 3-4.

Kuncheva, L., & Whitaker, C., Measures of diversity in classifier ensembles and their relationship with ensemble accuracy. Machine Learning, pp. 181–207, 2003.

Kusiak, A., Decomposition in Data Mining: An Industrial Case Study, IEEE Transactions on Electronics Packaging Manufacturing, Vol. 23, No. 4, pp. 345-353, 2000.

Kusiak, A., Rough Set Theory: A Data Mining Tool for Semiconductor Manufacturing, IEEE Transactions on Electronics Packaging Manufacturing, 24(1): 44-50, 2001A.

Kusiak, A., 2001, Feature Transformation Methods in Data Mining, IEEE Transactions on Elctronics Packaging Manufacturing, Vol. 24, No. 3, pp. 214–221, 2001B.

Kusiak A., Kurasek C., Data Mining of Printed-Circuit Board Defects, IEEE Transactions on Robotics and Automation, 17(2): 191-196, 2001.

Kusiak, E. Szczerbicki, and K. Park, A Novel Approach to Decomposition of Design Specifications and Search for Solutions, International Journal of Production Research, 29(7): 1391-1406, 1991.

Langdon W. B., Barrett S. J., Buxton B. F., Combining decision trees and neural networks for drug discovery, in: Genetic Programming, Proceedings of the 5th European Conference, EuroGP 2002, Kinsale, Ireland, 2002, pp. 60–70.

Langley, P., Selection of relevant features in machine learning, in Proceedings of the AAAI Fall Symposium on Relevance, pp. 140-144, AAAI Press, 1994.

Langley, P. and Sage, S., Oblivious decision trees and abstract cases. in Working Notes of the AAAI-94 Workshop on Case-Based Reasoning, pp. 113-117, Seattle, WA: AAAI Press, 1994.

Langley, P. and Sage, S., Induction of selective Bayesian classifiers. in Proceedings of the Tenth Conference on Uncertainty in Artificial Intelligence, pp. 399-406. Seattle, WA: Morgan Kaufmann, 1994.

Larsen, B. and Aone, C. 1999. Fast and effective text mining using linear-time document clustering. In Proceedings of the 5th ACM SIGKDD, 16-22, San Diego, CA.

Last, M., Online Classification of Nonstationary Data Streams, Intelligent Data Analysis 5, IDA83, pp. 119, 2001.

Last M., Kandel A., Data Mining for Process and Quality Control in the Semiconductor Industry, in Data Mining for Design and Manufacturing: Methods and Applications, D. Braha (ed.), Kluwer Academic Publishers, pp. 207-234, 2001.

Last M., Kandel A., Maimon O., Eberbach E., Anytime Algorithm for Feature Selection. Rough Sets and Current Trends in Computing 2000: 532-539

Last, M., Maimon, O. and Minkov, E., Improving Stability of Decision Trees, International Journal of Pattern Recognition and Artificial Intelligence, 16(2),145-159, 2002.

Lee, S., Noisy Replication in Skewed Binary Classification, Computational Statistics and Data Analysis, 34, 2000.

Leigh W., Purvis R., Ragusa J. M., Forecasting the NYSE composite index with technical analysis, pattern recognizer, neural networks, and genetic algorithm: a case study in romantic decision support, Decision Support Systems 32(4): 361-377, 2002.

Lewis D., and Catlett J., Heterogeneous uncertainty sampling for supervised learning. In Machine Learning: Proceedings of the Eleventh Annual Conference, pp. 148-156 , New Brunswick, New Jersey, Morgan Kaufmann, 1994.

Lewis, D., and Gale, W., Training text classifiers by uncertainty sampling, In seventeenth annual international ACM SIGIR conference on research and development in information retrieval, pp. 3-12, 1994.

Li X. and Dubes R. C., Tree classifier design with a Permutation statistic, Pattern Recognition 19:229-235, 1986.

Liao Y., and Moody J., Constructing Heterogeneous Committees via Input Feature Grouping, in Advances in Neural Information Processing Systems, Vol.12, S.A. Solla, T.K. Leen and K.-R. Muller (eds.),MIT Press, 2000.

Lim X., Loh W.Y., and Shih X., A comparison of prediction accuracy, complexity, and training time of thirty-three old and new classification algorithms . Machine Learning 40:203-228, 2000.

Lin Y. K. and Fu K., Automatic classification of cervical cells using a binary tree classifier. Pattern Recognition, 16(1):69-80, 1983.

Lindbergh D.A.B. and Humphreys B.L., The Unified Medical Language System. In: van Bemmel JH and McCray AT, 1993 Yearbook of Medical Informatics. IMIA, the Nether-lands, page 41-51, 1993.

Ling C. X., Sheng V. S., Yang Q., Test Strategies for Cost-Sensitive Decision Trees IEEE Transactions on Knowledge and Data Engineering,18(8):1055-1067, 2006.

Liu Y.: Generate Different Neural Networks by Negative Correlation Learning. ICNC (1) 2005: 149-156

Liu, H., Hsu, W., and Chen, S. (1997). Using general impressions to analyze discovered classification rules. In *Proceedings of the Third International Conference on Knowledge Discovery and Data Mining (KDD'97)*. Newport Beach, California.

Liu H., Mandvikar A., Mody J., An Empirical Study of Building Compact Ensembles. WAIM 2004: pp. 622-627.

Liu H. & Motoda H., Feature Selection for Knowledge Discovery and Data Mining, Kluwer Academic Publishers, 1998.

Liu, H. and Setiono, R. (1996) A probabilistic approach to feature selection: A filter solution. In Machine Learning: *Proceedings of the Thirteenth International Conference on Machine Learning*. Morgan Kaufmann.

Loh W.Y.,and Shih X., Split selection methods for classification trees. Statistica Sinica, 7: 815-840, 1997.

Loh W.Y. and Shih X., Families of splitting criteria for classification trees. Statistics and Computing 9:309-315, 1999.

Loh W.Y. and Vanichsetakul N., Tree-structured classification via generalized discriminant Analysis. Journal of the American Statistical Association, 83:715-728, 1988.

Long C., Bi-Decomposition of Function Sets Using Multi-Valued Logic, Eng.Doc. Dissertation, Technischen Universitat Bergakademie Freiberg 2003.

Lopez de Mantras R., A distance-based attribute selection measure for decision tree induction, Machine Learning 6:81-92, 1991.

Lu B.L., Ito M., Task Decomposition and Module Combination Based on Class Relations: A Modular Neural Network for Pattern Classification, IEEE Trans. on Neural Networks, 10(5):1244-1256, 1999.

Lu H., Setiono R., and Liu H., Effective Data Mining Using Neural Networks. IEEE Transactions on Knowledge and Data Engineering, 8 (6): 957-961, 1996.

Luba, T., Decomposition of multiple-valued functions, in Intl. Symposium on Multiple-Valued Logic', Bloomigton, Indiana, pp. 256-261, 1995.

Lubinsky D., Algorithmic speedups in growing classification trees by using an additive split criterion. Proc. AI&Statistics93, pp. 435-444, 1993.

Maher P. E. and Clair D. C, Uncertain reasoning in an ID3 machine learning framework, in Proc. 2nd IEEE Int. Conf. Fuzzy Systems, 1993, pp. 712.

Maimon O. and Last M., Knowledge Discovery and Data Mining: The Info-Fuzzy network (IFN) methodology, Kluwer Academic Publishers, 2000.

Maimon O., and Rokach, L. Data Mining by Attribute Decomposition with semiconductors manufacturing case study, in Data Mining for Design and Manufacturing: Methods and Applications, D. Braha (ed.), Kluwer Academic Publishers, pp. 311-336, 2001.

Maimon O. and Rokach L., "Improving supervised learning by feature decomposition", Proceedings of the Second International Symposium on Foundations of Information and Knowledge Systems, Lecture Notes in Computer Science, Springer, pp. 178-196, 2002.

Maimon O., Rokach L., Ensemble of Decision Trees for Mining Manufacturing Data Sets, Machine Engineering, vol. 4 No1-2, 2004.

Maimon O., Rokach L., Decomposition Methodology for Knowledge Discovery and Data Mining: Theory and Applications, World Scientific Publishing, 2005.

Mallows, C. L., Some comments on Cp . *Technometrics* 15, 661- 676, 1973.

Mangiameli P., West D., Rampal R., Model selection for medical diagnosis decision support systems, Decision Support Systems, 36(3): 247–259, 2004.

Mansour, Y. and McAllester, D., Generalization Bounds for Decision Trees, in Proceedings of the 13th Annual Conference on Computer Learning Theory, pp. 69-80, San Francisco, Morgan Kaufmann, 2000.

Marcotorchino, J.F. and Michaud, P. Optimisation en Analyse Ordinale des Donns. Masson, Paris.

Margineantu D. and Dietterich T., Pruning adaptive boosting. In Proc. Fourteenth Intl. Conf. Machine Learning, pages 211–218, 1997.

Margineantu, D. (2001). Methods for Cost-Sensitive Learning. Doctoral Dissertation, Oregon State University.

Martin J. K., An exact probability metric for decision tree splitting and stopping. An Exact Probability Metric for Decision Tree Splitting and Stopping, Machine Learning, 28 (2-3):257-291, 1997.

Mehta M., Rissanen J., Agrawal R., MDL-Based Decision Tree Pruning. KDD 1995: pp. 216-221, 1995.

Mehta M., Agrawal R. and Rissanen J., SLIQ: A fast scalable classifier for data mining: In Proc. If the fifth Int'l Conference on Extending Database Technology (EDBT), Avignon, France, March 1996.

Melville P., Mooney R. J., Constructing Diverse Classifier Ensembles using Artificial Training Examples. IJCAI 2003: 505-512

Meretakis, D. and Wthrich, B., Extending Nave Bayes Classifiers Using Long Itemsets, in Proceedings of the Fifth International Conference on Knowledge Discovery and Data Mining, pp. 165-174, San Diego, USA, 1999.

Merkwirth C., Mauser H., Schulz-Gasch T., Roche O., Stahl M., Lengauer T., Ensemble methods for classification in cheminformatics, Journal of Chemical Information and Modeling, 44(6):1971–1978, 2004.

Merz, C. J., Using Correspondence Analysis to Combine Classifier, Machine Learning, 36(1-2):33-58, 1999.

Merz, C. J. and Murphy. P.M., UCI Repository of machine learning databases. Irvine, CA: University of California, Department of Information and Computer Science, 1998.

Michalski R. S., A theory and methodology of inductive learning. Artificial Intelligence, 20:111- 161, 1983.

Michalski R. S., Understanding the nature of learning: issues and research directions, in R. Michalski, J. Carbonnel and T. Mitchell,eds, Machine Learning: An Artificial Intelligence Approach, Kaufmann, Paolo Alto, CA, pp. 3–25,

1986.

Michalski R. S., and Tecuci G.. Machine Learning, A Multistrategy Approach, Vol. J. Morgan Kaufmann, 1994.

Michie, D., Problem decomposition and the learning of skills, in Proceedings of the European Conference on Machine Learning, pp. 17-31, Springer-Verlag, 1995.

Michie D., Spiegelhalter D.J., Taylor C .C., Machine Learning, Neural and Statistical Classification, Prentice Hall, 1994.

Mingers J., An empirical comparison of pruning methods for decision tree induction. Machine Learning, 4(2):227-243, 1989.

Minsky M., Logical vs. Analogical or Symbolic vs. Connectionist or Neat vs. Scruffy, in Artificial Intelligence at MIT., Expanding Frontiers, Patrick H. Winston (Ed.), Vol 1, MIT Press, 1990. Reprinted in AI Magazine, 1991.

Mishra, S. K. and Raghavan, V. V., An empirical study of the performance of heuristic methods for clustering. In Pattern Recognition in Practice, E. S. Gelsema and L. N. Kanal, Eds. 425436, 1994.

Mitchell, T., Machine Learning, McGraw-Hill, 1997.

Mitchell, T., The need for biases in learning generalizations. Technical Report CBM-TR-117, Rutgers University, Department of Computer Science, New Brunswick, NJ, 1980.

Moody, J. and Darken, C., Fast learning in networks of locally tuned units. Neural Computations, 1(2):281-294, 1989.

Morgan J. N. and Messenger R. C., THAID: a sequential search program for the analysis of nominal scale dependent variables. Technical report, Institute for Social Research, Univ. of Michigan, Ann Arbor, MI, 1973.

Muller W., and Wysotzki F., Automatic construction of decision trees for classification. Annals of Operations Research, 52:231-247, 1994.

Murphy, O. J., and McCraw, R. L. 1991. Designing storage efficient decision trees. IEEE-TC 40(3):315320.

Murtagh, F. A survey of recent advances in hierarchical clustering algorithms which use cluster centers. Comput. J. 26 354-359, 1984.

Murthy S. K., Automatic Construction of Decision Trees from Data: A Multi-Disciplinary Survey. Data Mining and Knowledge Discovery, 2(4):345-389, 1998.

Murthy S. K., Kasif S., and Salzberg S.. A system for induction of oblique decision trees. Journal of Artificial Intelligence Research, 2:1-33, August 1994.

Murthy, S. and Salzberg, S. (1995), Lookahead and pathology in decision tree induction, in C. S. Mellish, ed., 'Proceedings of the 14th International Joint Con- ference on Articial Intelligence', Morgan Kaufmann, pp. 1025-1031.

Myers E.W., An O(ND) Difference Algorithm and Its Variations, Algorithmica, 1(1): page 251-266, 1986.

Naumov G.E., NP-completeness of problems of construction of optimal decision trees. Soviet Physics: Doklady, 36(4):270-271, 1991.

Neal R., Probabilistic inference using Markov Chain Monte Carlo methods. Tech. Rep. CRG-TR-93-1, Department of Computer Science, University of Toronto, Toronto, CA, 1993.

Ng, R. and Han, J. 1994. Very large data bases. In Proceedings of the 20th International Conference on Very Large Data Bases (VLDB94, Santiago, Chile, Sept.), VLDB Endowment, Berkeley, CA, 144155.

Niblett T., Constructing decision trees in noisy domains. In Proceedings of the Second European Working Session on Learning, pages 67-78, 1987.

Niblett T. and Bratko I., Learning Decision Rules in Noisy Domains, Proc. Expert Systems 86, Cambridge: Cambridge University Press, 1986.

Nowlan S. J., and Hinton G. E. Evaluation of adaptive mixtures of competing experts. In Advances in Neural Information Processing Systems, R. P. Lippmann, J. E. Moody, and D. S. Touretzky, Eds., vol. 3, pp. 774-780, Morgan Kaufmann Publishers Inc., 1991.

Nunez, M. (1988): *Economic induction: A case study*. In D. Sleeman (Ed.), Proceeding of the Third European Working Session on Learning. London: Pitman Publishing

Nunez, M. (1991): *The use of Background Knowledge in Decision Tree Induction*. Machine Learning, 6(1), pp. 231-250.

Oates, T., Jensen D., 1998, Large Datasets Lead to Overly Complex Models: An Explanation and a Solution, KDD 1998, pp. 294-298.

Ohno-Machado, L., and Musen, M. A. Modular neural networks for medical prognosis: Quantifying the benefits of combining neural networks for survival prediction. Connection Science 9, 1 (1997), 71-86.

Olaru C., Wehenkel L., A complete fuzzy decision tree technique, Fuzzy Sets and Systems, 138(2):221–254, 2003.

Oliveira L.S., Sabourin R., Bortolozzi F., and Suen C. Y. (2003) A Methodology for Feature Selection using Multi-Objective Genetic Algorithms for Handwritten Digit String Recognition, *International Journal of Pattern Recognition and Artificial Intelligence*, 17(6):903-930.

Opitz, D., Feature Selection for Ensembles, In: Proc. 16th National Conf. on Artificial Intelligence, AAAI,1999, pp. 379-384.

Opitz, D. and Maclin, R., Popular Ensemble Methods: An Empirical Study, Journal of Artificial Research, 11: 169-198, 1999.

Opitz D. and Shavlik J., Generating accurate and diverse members of a neural-network ensemble. In David S. Touretzky, Michael C. Mozer, and Michael E. Hasselmo, editors, Advances in Neural Information Processing Systems, volume 8, pages 535–541. The MIT Press, 1996.

Pagallo, G. and Huassler, D., Boolean feature discovery in empirical learning, Machine Learning, 5(1): 71-99, 1990.

S. Pang, D. Kim, S. Y. Bang, Membership authentication in the dynamic group by face classification using SVM ensemble. Pattern Recognition Letters, 24: 215–225, 2003.

Park C., Cho S., Evolutionary Computation for Optimal Ensemble Classifier in Lymphoma Cancer Classification. 521-530. Ning Zhong, Zbigniew W. Ras, Shusaku Tsumoto, Einoshin Suzuki (Eds.): Foundations of Intelligent Systems, 14th International Symposium, ISMIS 2003, Maebashi City, Japan, October 28-31, 2003, Proceedings. Lecture Notes in Computer Science, pp. 521-530, 2003.

Parmanto, B., Munro, P. W., and Doyle, H. R., Improving committee diagnosis with resampling techinques. In Touretzky, D. S., Mozer, M. C., and Hesselmo, M. E. (Eds). Advances in Neural Information Processing Systems, Vol. 8, pp. 882-888 Cambridge, MA. MIT Press, 1996.

Pazzani M., Merz C., Murphy P., Ali K., Hume T., and Brunk C. (1994): *Reducing Misclassification costs*. In Proc. 11th International conference on Machine Learning, 217-25. Morgan Kaufmann.

Pearl, J., Probabilistic Reasoning in Intelligent Systems: Networks of Plausible Inference. Morgan-Kaufmann, 1988.

Peng, F. and Jacobs R. A., and Tanner M. A., Bayesian Inference in Mixtures-of-Experts and Hierarchical Mixtures-of-Experts Models With an Application to Speech Recognition, Journal of the American Statistical Association 91, 953-960, 1996.

Peng Y., Intelligent condition monitoring using fuzzy inductive learning, Journal of Intelligent Manufacturing, 15 (3): 373-380, June 2004.

Perkowski, M. A., A survey of literature on function decomposition, Technical report, GSRP Wright Laboratories, Ohio OH, 1995.

Perkowski, M.A., Luba, T., Grygiel, S., Kolsteren, M., Lisanke, R., Iliev, N., Burkey, P., Burns, M., Malvi, R., Stanley, C., Wang, Z., Wu, H., Yang, F., Zhou, S. and Zhang, J. S., Unified approach to functional decompositions of switching functions, Technical report, Warsaw University of Technology and Eindhoven University of Technology, 1995.

Perkowski, M., Jozwiak, L. and Mohamed, S., New approach to learning noisy Boolean functions, Proceedings of the Second International Conference on Computational Intelligence and Multimedia Applications, pp. 693–706, World Scientific, Australia, 1998.

Perner P., Improving the Accuracy of Decision Tree Induction by Feature Pre-Selection, Applied Artificial Intelligence 2001, vol. 15, No. 8, p. 747-760.

Pfahringer, B., Controlling constructive induction in CiPF, In Bergadano, F. and De Raedt, L. (Eds.), Proceedings of the seventh European Conference on Machine Learning, pp. 242-256, Springer-Verlag, 1994.

Pfahringer, B., Compression- based feature subset selection. In *Proceeding of the IJCAI- 95 Workshop on Data Engineering for Inductive Learning*, pp. 109-119, 1995.

Pfahringer, B., Bensusan H., and Giraud-Carrier C., Tell Me Who Can Learn You and I Can Tell You Who You are: Landmarking Various Learning Algorithms, In Proc. of the Seventeenth International Conference on Machine Learning (ICML2000), pages 743-750, 2000.

Piatetsky-Shapiro, G. (1991). *Discovery analysis and presentation of strong rules*. Knowledge Discovery in Databases, AAAI/MIT Press.

Poggio T., Girosi, F., Networks for Approximation and Learning, Proc. IEER, Vol 78(9): 1481-1496, Sept. 1990.

Pratt, L. Y., Mostow, J., and Kamm C. A., Direct Transfer of Learned Information Among Neural Networks, in: Proceedings of the Ninth National Conference on Artificial Intelligence, Anaheim, CA, 584-589, 1991.

Prodromidis, A. L., Stolfo, S. J. and Chan, P. K., Effective and efficient pruning of metaclassifiers in a distributed data mining system. Technical report CUCS-017-99, Columbia Univ., 1999.

Provan, G. M. and Singh, M. (1996). Learning Bayesian networks using feature selection. In D. Fisher and H. Lenz, (Eds.), *Learning from Data, Lecture Notes in Statistics*, pages 291– 300. Springer- Verlag, New York.

Provost, F. (1994): *Goal-Directed Inductive learning: Trading off accuracy for reduced error cost*. AAAI Spring Symposium on Goal-Driven Learning.

Provost F. and Fawcett T. (1997): *Analysis and visualization of Classifier Performance Comparison under Imprecise Class and Cost Distribution*. In Proceedings of KDD-97, pages 43-48. AAAI Press.

Provost F. and Fawcett T. (1998): *The case against accuracy estimation for comparing induction algorithms*. Proc. 15th Intl. Conf. On Machine Learning, pp. 445-453, Madison, WI.

Provost, F. and Fawcett, T. (2001), Robust {C}lassification for {I}mprecise {E}nvironments, Machine Learning, 42/3:203-231.

Provost, F.J. and Kolluri, V., A Survey of Methods for Scaling Up Inductive Learning Algorithms, Proc. 3rd International Conference on Knowledge Discovery and Data Mining, 1997.

Provost, F., Jensen, D. and Oates, T., 1999, Efficient Progressive Sampling, In Proceedings of the Fifth International Conference on Knowledge Discovery and Data Mining, pp.23-32.

Quinlan, J.R. *Learning efficient classification procedures and their application to chess endgames*. R. Michalski, J. Carbonell, T. Mitchel. Machine learning: an AI approach. Los Altos, CA. Morgan Kaufman , 1983.

Quinlan, J.R., Induction of decision trees, Machine Learning 1, 81-106, 1986.

Quinlan, J.R., Simplifying decision trees, International Journal of Man-Machine Studies, 27, 221-234, 1987.

Quinlan, J.R., Decision Trees and Multivalued Attributes, J. Richards, ed., Machine Intelligence, V. 11, Oxford, England, Oxford Univ. Press, pp. 305-318, 1988.

Quinlan, J. R., Unknown attribute values in induction. In Segre, A. (Ed.), Proceedings of the Sixth International Machine Learning Workshop Cornell, New York. Morgan Kaufmann, 1989.

Quinlan, J. R., Unknown attribute values in induction. In Segre, A. (Ed.), Proceedings of the Sixth International Machine Learning Workshop Cornell, New York. Morgan Kaufmann, 1989.

Quinlan, J. R., C4.5: Programs for Machine Learning, Morgan Kaufmann, Los Altos, 1993.

Quinlan, J. R., Bagging, Boosting, and C4.5. In Proceedings of the Thirteenth National Conference on Artificial Intelligence, pages 725-730, 1996.

Quinlan, J. R. and Rivest, R. L., Inferring Decision Trees Using The Minimum Description Length Principle. Information and Computation, 80:227-248, 1989.

Ragavan, H. and Rendell, L., Look ahead feature construction for learning hard concepts. In Proceedings of the Tenth International Machine Learning Conference: pp. 252-259, Morgan Kaufman, 1993.

Rahman, A. F. R., and Fairhurst, M. C. A new hybrid approach in combining multiple experts to recognize handwritten numerals. Pattern Recognition Letters, 18: 781-790,1997.

Ramamurti, V., and Ghosh, J., Structurally Adaptive Modular Networks for Non-Stationary Environments, IEEE Transactions on Neural Networks, 10 (1):152-160, 1999.

Rand, W. M., Objective criteria for the evaluation of clustering methods. Journal of the American Statistical Association, 66: 846–850, 1971.

Rao, R., Gordon, D., and Spears, W., For every generalization action, is there really an equal or opposite reaction? Analysis of conservation law. In Proc. of the Twelveth International Conference on Machine Learning, pp. 471-479. Morgan Kaufmann, 1995.

Rastogi, R., and Shim, K., PUBLIC: A Decision Tree Classifier that Integrates Building and Pruning,Data Mining and Knowledge Discovery, 4(4):315-344, 2000.

Ratsch G., Onoda T., and Muller K. R., Soft Margins for Adaboost, Machine Learning 42(3):287-320, 2001.

Ray, S., and Turi, R.H. Determination of Number of Clusters in K-Means Clustering and Application in Color Image Segmentation. Monash university, 1999.

R'enyi A., Probability Theory, North-Holland, Amsterdam, 1970

Buczak A. L. and Ziarko W., "Stages of The Discovery Process", Klosgen W. and Zytkow J. M. (Eds.), Handbook of Data Mining and Knowledge Discovery, pages 185-192. Oxford University Press, 2002.

Ridgeway, G., Madigan, D., Richardson, T. and O'Kane, J. (1998), "Interpretable Boosted Naive Bayes Classification", Proceedings of the Fourth International Conference on Knowledge Discovery and Data Mining, pp 101-104.

Rigoutsos I. and Floratos A., Combinatorial pattern discovery in biological sequences: The TEIRESIAS algorithm., Bioinformatics, 14(2): page 229, 1998.

Rissanen, J., Stochastic complexity and statistical inquiry. World Scientific, 1989.

Rokach L., Averbuch M. and Maimon O., Information Retrieval System for Medical Narra-tive Reports, Lecture Notes in Artificial intelligence 3055, page 217-228 Springer-Verlag, 2004.

Rokach L., Chizi B., Maimon O., A Methodology for Improving the Performance of Non-ranker Feature Selection Filters, International Journal of Pattern Recognition and Artificial Intelligence, 21(5): 809-830, 2007.

Rokach L. and Maimon O., "Theory and Application of Attribute Decomposition", Proceedings of the First IEEE International Conference on Data Mining, IEEE Computer Society Press, pp. 473-480, 2001

Rokach L. and Maimon O., Top Down Induction of Decision Trees Classifiers: A Survey, IEEE SMC Transactions Part C. Volume 35, Number 3, 2005a.

Rokach L. and Maimon O., Feature Set Decomposition for Decision Trees, Journal of Intelligent Data Analysis, Volume 9, Number 2, 2005b, pp 131-158.

Ronco, E., Gollee, H., and Gawthrop, P. J., Modular neural network and self-decomposition. CSC Research Report CSC-96012, Centre for Systems and

Control, University of Glasgow, 1996.

Rosen B. E., Ensemble Learning Using Decorrelated Neural Networks. Connect. Sci. 8(3): 373-384 (1996)

Rounds, E., A combined non-parametric approach to feature selection and binary decision tree design, Pattern Recognition 12, 313-317, 1980.

Rudin C., Daubechies I., and Schapire R. E., The Dynamics of Adaboost: Cyclic behavior and convergence of margins, Journal of Machine Learning Research Vol. 5, 1557-1595, 2004.

Rumelhart, D., G. Hinton and R. Williams, Learning internal representations through error propagation. In Parallel Distributed Processing: Explorations in the Microstructure of Cognition, Volume 1: Foundations, D. Rumelhart and J. McClelland (eds.) Cambridge, MA: MIT Press., pp 2540, 1986.

Saaty, X., The analytic hierarchy process: A 1993 overview. Central European Journal for Operations Research and Economics, Vol. 2, No. 2, p. 119-137, 1993.

Safavin S. R. and Landgrebe, D., A survey of decision tree classifier methodology. IEEE Trans. on Systems, Man and Cybernetics, 21(3):660-674, 1991.

Sakar A., Mammone R.J., Growing and pruning neural tree networks, IEEE Trans. on Computers 42, 291-299, 1993.

Salzberg. S. L., On Comparing Classifiers: Pitfalls to Avoid and a Recommended Approach. Data Mining and Knowledge Discovery, 1: 312-327, Kluwer Academic Publishers, Bosto, 1997.

Samuel, A., Some studies in machine learning using the game of checkers II: Recent progress. IBM J. Res. Develop., 11:601-617, 1967.

Schaffer, C., When does overfitting decrease prediction accuracy in induced decision trees and rule sets? In Proceedings of the European Working Session on Learning (EWSL-91), pp. 192-205, Berlin, 1991.

Schaffer, C., Selecting a classification method by cross-validation. Machine Learning 13(1):135-143, 1993.

Schaffer J., A Conservation Law for Generalization Performance. In Proceedings of the 11th International Conference on Machine Learning: pp. 259-265, 1993.

Schapire, R.E., *The strength of week learnability*. In Machine learning 5(2), 197-227, 1990.

Schmitt , M., On the complexity of computing and learning with multiplicative neural networks, Neural Computation 14: 2, 241-301, 2002.

Schlimmer, J. C. , Efficiently inducing determinations: A complete and systematic search algorithm that uses optimal pruning. In Proceedings of the 1993 International Conference on Machine Learning: pp 284-290, San Mateo, CA, Morgan Kaufmann, 1993.

Seewald, A.K. and Fürnkranz, J., Grading classifiers, Austrian research institute for Artificial intelligence, 2001.

Selim, S.Z., and Ismail, M.A. K-means-type algorithms: a generalized convergence theorem and characterization of local optimality. In IEEE transactions on pattern analysis and machine learning, vol. PAMI-6, no. 1, January, 1984.

Selim, S. Z. AND Al-Sultan, K. 1991. A simulated annealing algorithm for the clustering problem. Pattern Recogn. 24, 10 (1991), 10031008.

Selfridge, O. G. Pandemonium: a paradigm for learning. In Mechanization of Thought Processes: Proceedings of a Symposium Held at the National Physical Laboratory, November, 1958, 513-526. London: H.M.S.O., 1958.

Servedio, R., On Learning Monotone DNF under Product Distributions. Information and Computation 193, pp. 57-74, 2004.

Sethi, K., and Yoo, J. H., Design of multicategory, multifeature split decision trees using perceptron learning. Pattern Recognition, 27(7):939-947, 1994.

Shapiro, A. D. and Niblett, T., Automatic induction of classification rules for a chess endgame, in M. R. B. Clarke, ed., Advances in Computer Chess 3, Pergamon, Oxford, pp. 73-92, 1982.

Shapiro, A. D., Structured induction in expert systems, Turing Institute Press in association with Addison-Wesley Publishing Company, 1987.

Sharkey, A., On combining artificial neural nets, Connection Science, Vol. 8, pp.299-313, 1996.

Sharkey, A., Multi-Net Iystems, In Sharkey A. (Ed.) Combining Artificial Neural Networks: Ensemble and Modular Multi-Net Systems. pp. 1-30, Springer-Verlag, 1999.

Shafer, J. C., Agrawal, R. and Mehta, M. , SPRINT: A Scalable Parallel Classifier for Data Mining, Proc. 22nd Int. Conf. Very Large Databases, T. M. Vijayaraman and Alejandro P. Buchmann and C. Mohan and Nandlal L. Sarda (eds), 544-555, Morgan Kaufmann, 1996.

Shilen, S., Multiple binary tree classifiers. Pattern Recognition 23(7): 757-763, 1990.

Shilen, S., Nonparametric classification using matched binary decision trees. Pattern Recognition Letters 13: 83-87, 1992.

Sklansky, J. and Wassel, G. N., Pattern classifiers and trainable machines. SpringerVerlag, New York, 1981.

Skurichina M. and Duin R.P.W., Bagging, boosting and the random subspace method for linear classifiers. Pattern Analysis and Applications, 5(2):121–135, 2002

Smyth, P. and Goodman, R. (1991). *Rule induction using information theory.* Knowledge Discovery in Databases, AAAI/MIT Press.

Sneath, P., and Sokal, R. Numerical Taxonomy. W.H. Freeman Co., San Francisco, CA, 1973.

Snedecor, G. and Cochran, W. (1989). *Statistical Methods.* owa State University Press, Ames, IA, 8th Edition.

Sohn S. Y., Choi, H., Ensemble based on Data Envelopment Analysis, ECML Meta Learning workshop, Sep. 4, 2001.

van Someren M.,Torres C. and Verdenius F. (1997): *A systematic Description of Greedy Optimisation Algorithms for Cost Sensitive Generalization.* X. Liu, P.Cohen, M. Berthold (Eds.): "Advance in Intelligent Data Analysis" (IDA-97) LNCS 1280, pp. 247-257.

Sonquist, J. A., Baker E. L., and Morgan, J. N., Searching for Structure. Institute for Social Research, Univ. of Michigan, Ann Arbor, MI, 1971.

Spirtes, P., Glymour C., and Scheines, R., Causation, Prediction, and Search. Springer Verlag, 1993.

Steuer R.E.,Multiple Criteria Optimization: Theory, Computation and Application. John Wiley, New York, 1986.

Strehl A. and Ghosh J., Clustering Guidance and Quality Evaluation Using Relationship-based Visualization, Proceedings of Intelligent Engineering Systems Through Artificial Neural Networks, 5-8 November 2000, St. Louis, Missouri, USA, pp 483-488.

Strehl, A., Ghosh, J., Mooney, R.: Impact of similarity measures on web-page clustering. In Proc. AAAI Workshop on AI for Web Search, pp 58–64, 2000.

Tadepalli, P. and Russell, S., Learning from examples and membership queries with structured determinations, Machine Learning, 32(3), pp. 245-295, 1998.

Tan A. C., Gilbert D., Deville Y., Multi-class Protein Fold Classification using a New Ensemble Machine Learning Approach. Genome Informatics, 14:206–217, 2003.

Tani T. and Sakoda M., Fuzzy modeling by ID3 algorithm and its application to prediction of heater outlet temperature, Proc. IEEE Internat. Conf. on Fuzzy Systems, March 1992, pp. 923-930.

Taylor P. C., and Silverman, B. W., Block diagrams and splitting criteria for classification trees. Statistics and Computing, 3(4):147-161, 1993.

Tibshirani, R., Walther, G. and Hastie, T. (2000). Estimating the number of clusters in a dataset via the gap statistic. Tech. Rep. 208, Dept. of Statistics, Stanford University.

Towell, G. Shavlik, J., Knowledge-based artificial neural networks, Artificial Intelligence, 70: 119-165, 1994.

Tresp, V. and Taniguchi, M. Combining estimators using non-constant weighting functions. In Tesauro, G., Touretzky, D., & Leen, T. (Eds.), Advances in Neural Information Processing Systems, volume 7: pp. 419-426, The MIT Press, 1995.

Tsallis C., Possible Generalization of Boltzmann-Gibbs Statistics, J. Stat.Phys., 52, 479-487, 1988.

Tsymbal A., and Puuronen S., Ensemble Feature Selection with the Simple Bayesian Classification in Medical Diagnostics, In: Proc. 15thIEEE Symp. on Computer-Based Medical Systems CBMS2002, Maribor, Slovenia,IEEE CS Press, 2002, pp. 225-230.

Tsymbal A., and Puuronen S., and D. Patterson, Feature Selection for Ensembles of Simple Bayesian Classifiers,In: Foundations of Intelligent Systems: ISMIS2002, LNAI, Vol. 2366, Springer, 2002, pp. 592-600

Tsymbal A., Pechenizkiy M., Cunningham P., Diversity in search strategies for ensemble feature selection. Information Fusion 6(1): 83-98, 2005.

Tukey J.W., Exploratory data analysis, Addison-Wesley, Reading, Mass, 1977.

Tumer, K. and Ghosh J., Error Correlation and Error Reduction in Ensemble Classifiers, Connection Science, Special issue on combining artificial neural networks: ensemble approaches, 8 (3-4): 385-404, 1996.

Tumer, K., and Ghosh J., Linear and Order Statistics Combiners for Pattern

Classification, in Combining Articial Neural Nets, A. Sharkey (Ed.), pp. 127-162, Springer-Verlag, 1999.

Tumer, K., and Ghosh J., Robust Order Statistics based Ensembles for Distributed Data Mining. In Kargupta, H. and Chan P., eds, Advances in Distributed and Parallel Knowledge Discovery , pp. 185-210, AAAI/MIT Press, 2000.

Turney P. (1995): *Cost-Sensitive Classification: Empirical Evaluation of Hybrid Genetic Decision Tree Induction Algorithm.* Journal of Artificial Intelligence Research 2, pp. 369-409.

Turney P. (2000): *Types of Cost in Inductive Concept Learning.* Workshop on Cost Sensitive Learning at the 17th ICML, Stanford, CA.

Tuv, E. and Torkkola, K., Feature filtering with ensembles using artificial contrasts. In *Proceedings of the SIAM 2005 Int. Workshop on Feature Selection for Data Mining*, Newport Beach, CA, 69-71, 2005.

Tyron R. C. and Bailey D.E. Cluster Analysis. McGraw-Hill, 1970.

Urquhart, R. Graph-theoretical clustering, based on limited neighborhood sets. Pattern recognition, vol. 15, pp. 173-187, 1982.

Utgoff, P. E., Perceptron trees: A case study in hybrid concept representations. Connection Science, 1(4):377-391, 1989.

Utgoff, P. E., Incremental induction of decision trees. Machine Learning, 4:161-186, 1989.

Utgoff, P. E., Decision tree induction based on efficient tree restructuring, Machine Learning 29 (1):5-44, 1997.

Utgoff, P. E., and Clouse, J. A., A Kolmogorov-Smirnoff Metric for Decision Tree Induction, Technical Report 96-3, University of Massachusetts, Department of Computer Science, Amherst, MA, 1996.

Vafaie, H. and De Jong, K. (1995). Genetic algorithms as a tool for restructuring feature space representations. In *Proceedings of the International Conference on Tools with A. I.* IEEE Computer Society Press.

Valiant, L. G. (1984). A theory of the learnable. Communications of the ACM 1984, pp. 1134-1142.

Van Rijsbergen, C. J., Information Retrieval. Butterworth, ISBN 0-408-70929-4, 1979.

Van Zant, P., Microchip fabrication: a practical guide to semiconductor processing, New York: McGraw-Hill, 1997.

Vapnik, V.N., The Nature of Statistical Learning Theory. Springer-Verlag, New York, 1995.

Veyssieres, M.P. and Plant, R.E. Identification of vegetation state-and-transition domains in California's hardwood rangelands. University of California, 1998.

Wallace, C. S., MML Inference of Predictive Trees, Graphs and Nets. In A. Gammerman (ed), Computational Learning and Probabilistic Reasoning, pp 43-66, Wiley, 1996.

Wallace, C. S., and Patrick J., Coding decision trees, Machine Learning 11: 7-22, 1993.

Wallace C. S. and Dowe D. L., Intrinsic classification by mml – the snob program. In Proceedings of the 7th Australian Joint Conference on Artificial Intelligence, pages 37-44, 1994.

Walsh P., Cunningham P., Rothenberg S., O'Doherty S., Hoey H., Healy R., An artificial neural network ensemble to predict disposition and length of stay in children presenting with bronchiolitis. European Journal of Emergency Medicine. 11(5):259-264, 2004.

Wan, W. and Perkowski, M. A., A new approach to the decomposition of incompletely specified functions based on graph-coloring and local transformations and its application to FPGAmapping, In Proc. of the IEEE EURO-DAC '92, pp. 230-235, 1992.

Wang W., Jones P., Partridge D., Diversity between neural networks and decision trees for building multiple classifier systems, in: Proc. Int. Workshop on Multiple Classifier Systems (LNCS 1857), Springer, Calgiari, Italy, 2000, pp. 240–249.

Wang, X. and Yu, Q. Estimate the number of clusters in web documents via gap statistic. May 2001.

Ward, J. H. Hierarchical grouping to optimize an objective function. Journal of the American Statistical Association, 58:236-244, 1963.

Warshall S., A theorem on Boolean matrices, Journal of the ACM 9, 1112, 1962.

Widmer, G. and Kubat, M., 1996, Learning in the Presence of Concept Drift and Hidden Contexts, Machine Learning 23(1), pp. 69101.

Webb G., MultiBoosting: A technique for combining boosting and wagging. Machine Learning, 40(2): 159-196, 2000.

Webb G., and Zheng Z., Multistrategy Ensemble Learning: Reducing Error by Combining Ensemble Learning Techniques. IEEE Transactions on Knowledge and Data Engineering, 16 No. 8:980-991, 2004.

Weigend, A. S., Mangeas, M., and Srivastava, A. N. Nonlinear gated experts for time-series - discovering regimes and avoiding overfitting. International Journal of Neural Systems 6(5):373-399, 1995.

Wolf L., Shashua A., Feature Selection for Unsupervised and Supervised Inference: The Emergence of Sparsity in a Weight-Based Approach, Journal of Machine Learning Research, Vol 6, pp. 1855-1887, 2005.

Wolpert, D.H., Stacked Generalization, Neural Networks, Vol. 5, pp. 241-259, Pergamon Press, 1992.

Wolpert, D. H., The relationship between PAC, the statistical physics framework, the Bayesian framework, and the VC framework. In D. H. Wolpert, editor, The Mathematics of Generalization, The SFI Studies in the Sciences of Complexity, pages 117-214. AddisonWesley, 1995.

Wolpert, D. H., "The lack of a priori distinctions between learning algorithms," Neural Computation 8: 1341–1390, 1996.

Woods K., Kegelmeyer W., Bowyer K., Combination of multiple classifiers using local accuracy estimates, IEEE Transactions on Pattern Analysis and Machine Intelligence 19:405–410, 1997.

Wyse, N., Dubes, R. and Jain, A.K., A critical evaluation of intrinsic dimensionality algorithms, Pattern Recognition in Practice, E.S. Gelsema and L.N. Kanal (eds.), North-Holland, pp. 415–425, 1980.

Yuan Y., Shaw M., Induction of fuzzy decision trees, Fuzzy Sets and Systems 69(1995):125-139.

Zahn, C. T., Graph-theoretical methods for detecting and describing gestalt clusters. IEEE trans. Comput. C-20 (Apr.), 68-86, 1971.

Zaki, M. J., Ho C. T., and Agrawal, R., Scalable parallel classification for data mining on shared- memory multiprocessors, in Proc. IEEE Int. Conf. Data Eng., Sydney, Australia, WKDD99, pp. 198– 205, 1999.

Zaki, M. J., Ho C. T., Eds., Large- Scale Parallel Data Mining. New York: Springer- Verlag, 2000.

Zantema, H., and Bodlaender H. L., Finding Small Equivalent Decision Trees is Hard, International Journal of Foundations of Computer Science, 11(2):343-354, 2000.

Zadrozny B. and Elkan C. (2001): *Learning and Making Decisions When Costs and Probabilities are Both Unknown.* In Proceedings of the Seventh International Conference on Knowledge Discovery and Data Mining (KDD'01).

Zeira, G., Maimon, O., Last, M. and Rokach, L,; Change detection in classification models of data mining, Data Mining in Time Series Databases. World Scientific Publishing, 2003.

Zenobi, G., and Cunningham, P. Using diversity in preparing ensembles of classifiers based on different feature subsets to minimize generalization error. In Proceedings of the European Conference on Machine Learning, 2001.

Zhou Z., Chen C., Hybrid decision tree, Knowledge-Based Systems 15, 515-528, 2002.

Zhou Z., Jiang Y., NeC4.5: Neural Ensemble Based C4.5, IEEE Transactions on Knowledge and Data Engineering, vol. 16, no. 6, pp. 770-773, Jun., 2004.

Zhou Z. H., and Tang, W., Selective Ensemble of Decision Trees, in Guoyin Wang, Qing Liu, Yiyu Yao, Andrzej Skowron (Eds.): Rough Sets, Fuzzy Sets, Data Mining, and Granular Computing, 9th International Conference, RSFDGrC, Chongqing, China, Proceedings. Lecture Notes in Computer Science 2639, pp.476-483, 2003.

Zhou, Z. H., Wu J., Tang W., Ensembling neural networks: many could be better than all. Artificial Intelligence 137: 239-263, 2002.

Zimmermann H. J., Fuzzy Set Theory and its Applications, Springer, 4th edition, 2005.

Zupan, B., Bohanec, M., Demsar J., and Bratko, I., Feature transformation by function decomposition, IEEE intelligent systems & their applications, 13: 38-43, 1998.

Zupan, B., Bratko, I., Bohanec, M. and Demsar, J., 2000, Induction of concept hierarchies from noisy data, in Proceedings of the Seventeenth International Conference on Machine Learning (ICML-2000), San Francisco, CA, pp. 1199-1206.

Index